MAKING THE JOURNEY

BEING AND BECOMING A TEACHER OF ENGLISH LANGUAGE ARTS

LEILA CHRISTENBURY

Boynton/Cook Publishers
HEINEMANN
Portsmouth, New Hampshire

Boynton/Cook Publishers, Inc.
A subsidiary of Reed Elsevier Inc.
361 Hanover Street
Portsmouth, NH 03801-3912
Offices and agents throughout the world

© 1994 by Leila Christenbury

Acquisitions editor: Dawn Boyer
Production editor: Alan Huisman
Copy editor: Robin Hogan
Book and cover design: Jenny Jensen Greenleaf
Illustrations: Ann Glover

Credits for previously published material are on page viii.

We gratefully acknowledge the people who have given their permission to include in this book material written for classes they attended while students at Virginia Commonwealth University. Every effort has been made to contact copyright holders for permission to reprint borrowed material where necessary, but if any oversights have occurred, we would be happy to rectify them in future printings of this work.

Library of Congress Cataloging-in-Publication Data
Christenbury, Leila.
    Making the journey : being and becoming a teacher of English
  language arts   /   Leila Christenbury.
        p.   cm.
    Includes bibliographical references.
    ISBN 0-86709-333-1
    1. Language arts (Secondary)—United States.   2. Teaching.
  3. English teachers—Vocational guidance—United States.   4. English
  language—Study and teaching—United States.   5. Classroom
  management—United States.   I. Title.
  LB1631.C4486   1994
  428'.0071'2—dc20   93-36061
                                                                          CIP

Printed in the United States of America on acid-free paper
98   97   96   95   EB   2   3   4   5   6   7   8   9

to Paul and Leila,
my first teachers

If it is dark
when this is given to you,
have care for its content
when the moon shines.

—**Robert Creeley**
"A Form of Women" (*For Love*)

CONTENTS

5. TEACHING LITERATURE: PRACTICAL MATTERS   115

6. TEACHING LANGUAGE   153

7. TEACHING WRITING   177

ACKNOWLEDGMENTS

In this book I tell stories from my own years of high school and middle school teaching. In some cases it has been appropriate not to use my students' actual names; therefore, when a student's first name only is cited, it is a pseudonym. Many of the stories, however, do not call for anonymity, and when first *and* last names are mentioned they are real names of students who, at one time, were in my classroom. For whatever errors of memory or detail in these stories, I take full responsibility.

Throughout this book I also quote from the papers, journals, and notes of my students at Virginia Commonwealth University, all of whom I have taught in English Education and most of whom either are in their first years in an English language arts classroom or are preparing now to enter the classroom. For their permission to use their words and insights, I am very grateful: I think their voices are the strength of this book. I thank Jan Butterworth, Melissa Campbell, Carol Smith Catron, Melissa Chai, Connie Chantelau, Werner Doerwaldt, Jane Dowrick, Patty Duffy, Paul Fanney, Susanna Field, Ronnie Fleming, Jenni Gallo, Brenda Gates, Sheryl Gibson, Faye Girardi, Larry Goldman, Sandra Greer, Beth Hagy, Ralph B. Holmes, Jr., Jane Hunter, Donna Johnson, Jeffrey Landon, Julie Lepard, Debbie Martin, Laurie Messer, Sheryl Miller, Elizabeth Milne, Johnathan Morris, Julie Morrison, Holly O'Donnell, M. Kevin O'farrell, Mitra Palmer, Barbara Pope, Esther Raycroft, Lori Shacreaw, Ellen Sigler, David Small, Patti Smith, Katherine Sullivan, Heather Talley, Wendy Taylor, Anne Trippeer, and Jill Williamson.

In Chapter 3 I cite the work of my friend and teaching colleague Nancy Rosenbaum of Patrick Henry High School, Roanoke (Virginia) City Schools; I am grateful, as I have been for many years, for her practical and useful ideas.

Chapter 4 details a research study; to the gifted teachers who allowed my tape recorder into their classrooms—Ellen Seay Young, of Midlothian High School, Chesterfield County (Virginia) Schools, and Mil Norman-Risch, of The Collegiate Schools, Richmond, Virginia—I say thank you; and I thank their students as well.

The artist whose illustrations are on these pages is my longtime friend Ann Glover, who now paints in Los Angeles. Her work hangs in almost every room of my house, and I am appreciative that she has also lent her talents to this book.

For their thoughtful comments on this book in its varying stages, I thank my intelligent and perceptive editor, Dawn Boyer of Heinemann, who also has a wicked sense of humor and made me laugh a lot; my friend and first reader, Alan McLeod, School of Education, Virginia Commonwealth University; my writing project co-director Elizabeth Hodges, English Department, Virginia Commonwealth University, who gave a great deal of insight and care to her reading; my writing project assistant director Bonnie Griffith, John Rolfe Middle School, Henrico County (Virginia) Schools; my colleagues John Seyfarth, School of Education, Virginia Commonwealth University and Eileen Ford, Providence Middle School, Chesterfield County (Virginia) Schools; and Ruth Hubbard, Lewis and Clark College (Portland, Oregon), who thoughtfully reviewed this manuscript at the very beginning and at the end.

The making of a book is a complicated process. I also thank Alan Huisman and Robin Hogan for their careful work.

Friends mean a lot in this writing business. I thank EO and TC for listening and being there, as always, on the journey.

All through this book are stories about my students and what they taught me. It would be hard to overstate my indebtedness to the thousands of people with whom I have shared the classroom through the years. Again, I thank my students, each and every one of them, and gratefully acknowledge their powerful influence on my life.

USING THIS BOOK

In many ways, *Making the Journey* is a very personal book, and your reactions and comments are important as you read. The **Journal** suggestions throughout the chapters may help you codify your own response to the activities and ideas presented here; I urge you to buy a journal and to use it with this book. The habit of journal writing is a valuable one, and what you write may surprise you. In addition, a journal is a good place for you to consider issues about you, your ideas, and why and how you are making this journey of being and becoming a teacher.

The **References** at the end of each chapter are just that, bibliographic citations pertaining to the text. The **Resources**, however, are something you may want to do more than skim. There is a wealth of material on English language arts teaching, and in the resources sections I have tried to select books and articles and periodicals that you may find very useful.

CHAPTER 1

THE TEACHER, THE STUDENT, THE SCHOOL

We Americans have a sublime faith in education. Faced with any difficult problem of life we set our minds at rest sooner or later by the appeal to the school. We are convinced that education is the one unfailing remedy for every ill to which man is subject, whether it be vice, crime, war, poverty, riches, injustice, racketeering, race hatred, class conflict, or just plain original sin. We even speak glibly and often about the general reconstruction of society through the school . . . [but] our schools, instead of directing the course of change, are themselves driven by the very forces that are transforming the rest of the social order.

—**George S. Counts, *Dare the School Build a New Social Order?***

Beginnings

My story: how I became a teacher

I never planned to be a middle school or high school English teacher. It was very much a second choice. What I really wanted to be, a college professor specializing in medieval literature, got lost in the now almost legendary English teacher glut of the 1970s and a complete lack of funds. There were few jobs, and I, who had been on scholarship, faced the inescapable fact that time *is* money. I had completed my undergraduate degree in three and a half years and my master's in a record nine months; at the end of this dubious achievement I couldn't afford any more education—financially or psychologically.

So I filled out about two dozen applications, interviewed at every commutable school system, and, after this grueling job search, gratefully accepted my first job as an English teacher, grades eight through twelve, in a tiny high school.

But because teaching high school had not been in my plans, I was not prepared. I had had no student teaching and had taken no courses that gave me the slightest indication of what I was getting ready to do. I came to the high school classroom with a Phi Beta

Kappa key, a bachelor's and a master's in English, an appreciation for fourteenth-century alliterative poetry and the origins of English biography—and not a clue as to how to connect what I knew to the 120 teenagers I would be teaching. Fortunately, as any teacher will tell you, my students taught me. During my first semester they endured my unscoreable exams, my lame directions, my changes of curriculum, my indecipherable comments on their essays, my wavering concept of discipline. Directly and indirectly, sometimes tactfully, sometimes sharply, they gave me advice about what I could do to improve over those first few months; when they found me fairly receptive, our relationship stabilized.

And, for my part, I was too overwhelmed at first to feel awfully upset about teaching "just" high school. In fact, it quickly became my guilty secret: I found my students interesting—no, that's not accurate—I found them consuming. I found myself talking a great deal about them and what they said and what I said, often to the exasperation of friends and family. My classroom blunders became fuel for thought, and I began to plot and plan each day, each period, with a new sense of adventure. I began to watch my students' reactions and body language and expressions, convinced that actually the key to what to do was right there in the class, right in front of me—if only I could clear my eyes and just *see* it. I was experiencing something very intense, and I was struggling to make sense of it.

And then, as in a scene from a bad movie, I had my epiphany. One wintry morning somebody in the back row—somebody whose name I no longer remember and, tellingly, from whom I *do* remember I hadn't expected that much—made an observation about the short story we were reading. I heard his comment. And then I really *heard* it. The comment was so original, so insightful, so fraught with possibilities, that I was stunned. It was the proverbial standing still of time; if it *had* been a movie, the heavens would have opened, a shaft of sunlight would have flooded the classroom, and music would have swelled. But real life is usually nothing at all like the movies. My recollection is that I halted and, for a moment at least, just froze. The comment was one that with all my knowledge and education and insight—and class preparation—I had not anticipated. Further, the observation blew the top off our—the class's and my—assumptions about that particular short story.

My next reaction was one of almost overwhelming excitement, an excitement that was infectious as the class began to discuss this wonderful possibility about this story. Well, what about that? Is it true? Why do you think so? If that's right, what else can we assume? I was excited, exhilarated, and the students were too. I know now that I saw that day what could happen in a class and how, if I was lucky, I could spend my life. It was a central and almost searing experience: I turned, really saw that student, that classroom, really heard that comment, and, essentially, in that class, on that day, fell in love with teaching. It was, for me, the experience that Rainer Maria Rilke describes in "Archaïscher Torso Apollos" ("Archaic Torso of Apollo") when, after viewing a powerful piece of sculpture, he is overwhelmed and realizes, simply, awfully, "You must change your life" (181). After that experience I had, actually, to change my life. And I did.

My vision of being a medievalist yielded, replaced by the reality and guts and fascination of the classroom and my students. I had found my home, almost by accident, and my blood seemed to run quicker than it ever had in the library looking up the etymology of words in the *Oxford English Dictionary* or while studying alliterative devices in the fourteenth-century poem *Pearl*.

I would never recommend that anyone come into teaching as I did; it was unnecessarily hard on me and, more to the point, it was demonstrably not fair to my students for me to learn at their expense. Certainly, after my first fairly isolated semester, I began to seek—and find—other sources of help; I talked with other teachers, took courses, and began reading professional journals and books. Fellow and sister teachers gave advice and shared techniques; organizations such as the National Council of Teachers of English (NCTE) and my own state English-teaching organization published journals and held conferences. I tried to catch up as quickly as I could and become a teaching professional. It was, however, an uneven learning process, some of which had to do with the inevitable difficulty of learning to teach and a great deal of which had to do with my complete lack of professional preparation.

Hit-and-miss is a difficult and dangerous way to enter this business, and I was often highly self-conscious about my shortcomings. Even in the midst of progress, I almost aborted my teaching career after one crisis too many; and, truth be told, I have always suspected that if some of my instructional stumbling and lurching had been regularly observed by those in charge, I might have, charitably, been invited to leave.

But, as is the case in many school settings, I was largely left alone, and because I was self-conscious about my teaching, I was glad to be left alone. I hung in, made what I felt were some breathtaking mistakes, and learned some vivid and painful lessons. During my biggest crisis, when I had left the security of a small school for a larger and more challenging one and was finding the transition overwhelming, I felt I was taking my personality apart and putting it back together so that I could succeed in the classroom. It was a daunting task, and I do not encourage anyone to follow my example.

My interest in helping others become teachers is therefore part of my own experience as a far less prepared beginner than most. There is knowledge and theoretical basis in our field, and you can come into the classroom with a far more comprehensive view than I had.

I also trust you will find what I found: that teaching can be a marriage of soul and mind, that the classroom can be a place of discovery, passion, and very real joy. While not every class is wonderful every day—for there is occasional bitterness and pain and disappointment in this business—teaching is, for me, a consuming and deeply satisfying profession. Once I emerged on the other side and realized that I was a teacher, had *become* a teacher, I realized that I had also found, in essence, my calling, my life's work.

Your story: becoming a teacher

You are, right now, writing your own story of becoming a teacher, and one emphasis of this book, besides imparting technical and professional information, is to encourage you to look at yourself and your experiences. While it is dangerous to generalize from yourself to each and every one of your students, it is also terribly shortsighted not to use your own insights and discoveries when you think about teaching and being and becoming a teacher. Being self-conscious and self-aware can be a powerful tool as you begin this great adventure. My belief in that power is the major reason I start this book with my own unflattering story of how I became a teacher.

Throughout this book I tell more of my stories and let some of my students—who, like you, are embarking on their first years as English language arts teachers—tell theirs. Their words, coming as they do from the journal entries and papers of "experts" at this being and becoming, may help you puzzle out some of the great issues facing middle and secondary language arts teachers.

Finally, this book outlines existing research and knowledge about classrooms and students and teachers, patterns and techniques and concepts.

The limitation of any one person's point of view

I am, as are many in this business of teaching, conscious of the limitations of one person's perspective. I can tell you that I have been a teacher for over fifteen years, that I have two degrees in English and one in education, that I have publications and editorships and have been elected to professional offices. I can tell you I have taught in private and public schools; have taught remedial classes and classes for the gifted; have taught experimental courses, summer enrichment programs, and even classes for adults in a city jail. Yet I also need to remind you that I come from a background, a culture, and that I bring with me a specific perspective and a point of view. While to a certain extent I have earned the right to talk to you in this book, to function as an expert, my experiences are not universal, and everything I feel about teaching and learning may not echo the feelings of others, may not, in fact, echo yours.

The books and articles I cite are ones I like and have read. The activities and games and procedures I propose are ones I used as a high school teacher and suggest my students use in their own English classes. I do not want to imply that I have read everything in the field or that I have experienced every conceivable teaching approach. I offer what I know with the acknowledgment that it is—as is all knowledge—undeniably partial.

Finally, I am terribly aware of the many people—pioneers in this business of English teaching, great thinkers, gifted theorists—who have written and practiced at levels I can only dream of. I do not assume that I am one of them. I take heart, however, from a section of *The Four Quartets* and add my slice of teaching experience, largely because, as T. S. Eliot reminds us:

> There is only the fight to recover what has been lost
> And found and lost again and again: and now, under conditions
> That seem unpropitious. But perhaps neither gain nor loss.
> For us, there is only the trying. The rest is not our business.
> ("East Coker," 128)

Making the journey

So what about this *trying* that Eliot talks about? Actually, it goes to the heart of teaching and is the reason for the title of this book. Regardless of how prepared or (like me) unprepared for English teaching you may be, you are from day one a teacher making a journey. But the paradox is that from day one you will continue to become, evolve, and change as a teacher. It is, oddly enough, happily enough, a simultaneous process of both *being* a teacher and *becoming* a teacher. The two events are not separable and, actually, are not mutually exclusive.

Right now you are probably a lot more interested in arriving at your destination than in making the journey. You are more concerned about *being* a teacher: looking like the real thing, acting like a person who can take charge of a class, negotiating a school day gracefully. But as you will see or have perhaps already glimpsed, *becoming,* the ongoing process of changing and shifting and redefining, is also part of this business of teaching.

And that is what makes teaching so exciting: it is never the same. Not only, of course, are the students different each year, each class, but, necessarily, so are you. Unless you lose your curiosity and passion and interest, teaching will continue to evolve and change, *become* more and more, as you continue in the profession.

Teaching today

These are tough times in which to be a teacher. Issues of curricular control, of teacher salary and status, of student behavior, school funding, test scores, community involvement, swirl everywhere and threaten to overwhelm even the most dedicated. For English language arts teachers the constant battles over what subject areas are of most value, how much writing we can squeeze into a crowded schedule, and how we balance the teaching of skills with the excitement of reading and talking about literature complicate the picture. Despite these issues, you have decided to make the journey, to *be* (and to continue to *become*) an English language arts teacher. For that decision, you have my respect, and all of us in the classroom welcome you into the profession. It is exhausting and exhilarating and important work, work that is as enduring as it is difficult.

Teaching is the central defining truth of my life, the core and heart of my identity. For you, too, teaching may become that important and that sustaining. Not for the complacent nor for the fainthearted, making the journey toward being and becoming a teacher is an adventure of the first order.

For Your Journal

Journals are a good way to keep track of your thoughts and ideas. Many times, after reading a section of this book, you will be invited to write a response to the issues and ideas raised. If you wonder how those responses should "look," you might pay close attention to the passages I quote from my students who, like you, are entering teaching and who, in my classes, use a journal to record ideas and questions and responses.

Journals are usually handwritten, and an entry should be two or three pages long; they are informal and should be concerned more with ideas and content than with correctness or spelling or even neatness. The point is to address a subject or issue and to write your way into ideas and answers.

So, in this first journal entry, think of how people get started in a profession and how that may or may not relate to your choosing to be a teacher. One way to start might be to do some quick field research on how people choose professions: interview two or three people about how they entered their job field, informally poll relatives, friends, or co-workers.

Use the following questions as idea starters; you don't have to answer all of them, but they may help you focus this journal entry about people and choosing professions.

Questions to consider for your interviews: How did you choose your profession? What attracted you to that type of work? How long did you stay/have you stayed in the field? Why did you/didn't you leave? What do you consider to be the greatest rewards of your profession? the greatest drawbacks?

Now, think about you. Very briefly, in a paragraph or two, write about what has attracted you to English teaching. Was it an actual experience with a teacher? a film or a book about teaching? some other "trigger" (such as reading—and being moved by—a literary work)? Are your feelings about teaching similar to or different from the feelings of those you interviewed about their careers? How?

Teacher, Student, School: The Dance of the Three

The quotation at the beginning of this chapter, written by George S. Counts in 1932, is true today. And what he thundered about the schools and a new social order is electrifying stuff. The irony is, however, that most of us beginning language arts teaching give scant attention to context—that is, to the schools as part of the social vision Counts describes or as part of any wider vision. Instead, many of us center our thoughts on something closer to home when we begin teaching. We think of ourselves, the instructor, and what *we* are going to instruct—that novel we loved so much, that poem that changed our lives, that insight about language that seems to stay in our mind. While we know there will be students—some bright, some quiet, some not so bright, some motivated, some unhappy to be there—students are students, right? We are going into the classroom to bring to the students and to share with them what we have learned and learned to love. While we're not exactly missionaries, it's somewhere in the territory.

And, of course, as a beginning teacher, we know that we will be teaching in a setting, a physical classroom, a school with a mailing address and a janitor and other teachers and a principal. And we know that there will be bells and schedules and corridors. But school is a place in which we teach, right? It is, essentially, a neutral setting that will allow us to exercise our craft and, for some of us, operate as a "safe harbor" to continue our delight in our content, the written word.

Most experienced teachers know very well it's not that way at all. In fact these two visions of students and school are well-meaning—but seriously naive—concepts that are not only shared by the majority of beginning teachers but that also can engender misunderstanding, difficulty, and failure in beginning teachers.

Three truths about teaching

What is the truth about this business of teaching English language arts? Among others, there are three:

1. Teaching is far more than sharing what we learned to love as students in our own English classes.
2. Students and who they are shape what and how we instruct.
3. School as an institution is as real a factor in teaching as any other. Far from being a neutral setting, it limits and influences what we can and cannot do in our classrooms.

Whether we come prepared for it or not, we as teachers are only one part of a triad that also features a bewildering array of students, all of whom have fierce needs and aspirations and brilliance and weaknesses and problems and cultural expectations, and a setting, an institutional context, which we soon find can more often than not keep us from teaching and keep our students from learning.

It's a difficult dance, with the three partners moving and shifting and leading and taking turns. Although we might want to, we don't (can't) teach in the relative isolation or even protection of ourselves and our ideas about William Shakespeare's *Macbeth* or Virginia Woolf's *The Waves* or Richard Wright's *Native Son* or William Wordsworth's "Tintern Abbey." Because we are teachers, we must move among all those loud and messy and frequently challenging and restless people, our students, and we must move through a linoleum-tiled, bell-ringing, rule-driven place, school.

And, if this is true, does it change how we think about ourselves as English language arts teachers and what we can do in a classroom?

Yes.

And no.

So just how much can one teacher do?

Most teachers are not pessimists. During (and because of) their years of teaching they are necessary optimists, workers with lights in their eyes. But what has informed and even protected those teachers is the knowledge of what they are up against. It also took them a while to learn it.

So while I as a teacher can't give you 101 nifty activities that work with any group of students in any school setting—I can't, because I know they won't work with all students all the time—I want you to know about students, generally and specifically, and to recognize your formidable and sometimes difficult partner in this business—the school. Knowledge of these two elements will help you as you begin to teach. And then you can look more critically at activities and resources and techniques that you can adapt to your own teaching life.

It is worth it? Absolutely. Teaching is some of the most important work in the world; it transcends the concept of job or even career or profession into the sphere of *vocation*—as that word is used in a sense of being called, being chosen for a life role. Shamelessly put, it is also a chance at a bit of immortality. The science teacher Christa McAuliffe, who with others died tragically in the 1986 *Challenger* disaster, has been widely quoted in a statement that now borders on cliché. Although it may seem sappy, McAuliffe's "I touch the future. I teach" is actually to the heart of the matter for many of us who remain in the classroom. This is serious stuff, and while no one will insist that it be true for you or for all teachers, it's true for many teachers; it's why we stay in this business, and it's why we want you to be aware of what we know. Knowledge is not only empowering, it will keep you in the classroom and tell you what is going on in that incredibly demanding—but terribly exciting—place: school.

But now let's turn to you, the becoming teacher.

FOR YOUR JOURNAL

Let's assume you accept that teaching is a combination of teacher, student, and school, all in one big pie chart as it were. It's your task to divide up the pie. Questions to consider: At this point in your career, how would you assign a proportion to each segment? In other words, who or what is more important? less important? What, realistically, is the percentage of each of the three factors? What, ideally, *should* be the percentage of each of the factors? Why? If you take the quick compromise, one-third equally to each, can you see how one segment could feel shortchanged? Why? Why not?

The Teacher/Learner

Why do you want to be an English teacher?

While most people at the elementary level go into teaching because they like children and can see themselves working with the very young for a living, most of us who become middle or secondary school language arts teachers do so because we love our subject, especially literature. It is rare to want to teach language arts because of the lure of writing or linguistics; most of us were drawn to it by a piece of literature. Every one of us has a story to tell: the first novel that seemed to be written just about us and our lives; that night we stayed up reading until dawn; the poem—some of whose lines we can still recite—that changed our lives. These students would agree:

> When I was twelve I literally vanished from the real world into the world of literature. My older brother handed me *The Hobbit,* and suddenly everything else in my world was thrown aside.
>
> —Werner Doerwaldt

> In a single, pristine moment of understanding, *The Catcher in the Rye* made me realize that books weren't just escapism. They weren't just entertainments—thrills. It made me see that books could have a real effect on people's lives as it had done on mine.
>
> The book put me in a stupor for days. Holden Caulfield *was* me. His words were mine. Every attitude, every action we shared—or so it seemed. After reading *The Catcher in the Rye,* somehow I didn't feel so retarded—not quite so ugly. Holden had come down from the mountain carrying their sacred tablets and had shattered them at my feet. I was free to unashamedly be myself. I didn't have to go along—I could be different—an individual.
>
> —M. Kevin O'Farrell

> My teachers . . . used literature as a means of communicating "deeper lessons" about ourselves. I pondered the American Dream through Jay Gatsby, uncovered the harsh realities of murder and guilt through Lady Macbeth, and found strength of human spirit in Hester Prynne. Nearly every piece of literature held an important message about [my] life.
>
> —Jane Hunter

> [In English class] we studied the classics, of course; I remember reading *Silas Marner* . . . [but] the . . . book that stands out in my memory is *Gone with the Wind* . . . a great story with no objectionable language. It is a well written, exciting book with wonderful characters. I stayed home from school for two days to finish it, and it remains one of my all time favorites.
>
> —Esther Raycroft

Another student, Holly O'Donnell, wrote just before her practice teaching that "literature is personal, not just art for art's sake" and she wanted to use that power in the English classroom. Holly is right; literature is the power that propelled most of us into teaching in the first place.

Teachers we loved

And while literature propelled most of us into this field, a person may have also had a strong effect. Perhaps it was a teacher whose praise or encouragement led us to believe we could understand literature or even write it ourselves. One such student, Paul Fanney, remembers a teacher who was so powerful that in her class "sometimes I even forgot to feel so self-conscious about being a teenager, which is hard to do in high school." English class allowed Paul to come "to a closer awareness of the powerful rush in articulating what it's like to be a part of the human experience."

Here, also, are a few recollections from students about to begin their practice teaching:

> I remember being excited about eighth grade English and the writing assignments given to me. To help the class understand the concept of interpreting poetry, our teacher had us

write about the songs of [a popular rock group]. We listened to [an album], discussed several songs and then wrote our personal responses and interpretations of each. We then moved on to the poetry of William Carlos Williams and e.e. cummings. The teacher was successful in tapping into the enthusiasm and imagination of the students by tying what they valued into what he was trying to teach. Because the lyrics of the rock album and the poetry of Williams and Cummings were given equal validity, the students were better able to accept and understand the skills and techniques of critical interpretation.

—Barbara Pope

My 11th grade English teacher was . . . a Penn State man. He was cool. He was funny. He let us get away with murder. However, I do remember one day as we began our "poetry section," we examined just what made poetry poetry. We soon discarded rhyme, since free verse obviously broke that rule. And later were forced to discard length, as the *Odyssey* and the *Iliad* (among others) similarly trashed that idea. At the end of the period about the only thing we could agree on what made poetry poetry was the way it was written down. I hold that view to this day.   —Ralph B. Holmes, Jr.

Senior year was a very interesting year in English for me. . . . The first day of class [the teacher] brought in a Kitaro (new-age music) tape, and he told us to free write. I wrote several short stories, including one about a sheik and a British Lady having a romance in America. He loved my writing, found ways to help me improve individually, and boosted my confidence in general. He also had us do a multimedia project connecting words, music, pictures, and ideas to create a philosophical statement of some belief we held (it could be deep, humorous, or fluff as long as it was well done). . . . [He] allowed us to be ourselves, ask questions, discuss things with other students, and do a lot of work independently—which motivated most of us to do our best. He also took the time and energy to help us by doing some individualized instruction, and he's one of the main reasons I chose to teach high school English.   —Elizabeth Milne

It was in [my English teacher's] class that I discovered the joys of writing. We kept journals and wrote everyday. We listened to music, visited art galleries, and read books and magazines, all the while responding to these experiences in our journals. We had to complete one independent writing project either in prose or poetry. Our teacher . . . became our friend and mentor, always encouraging us to write, write, write. My project was poetry and by the end of the year my journal was full of poems expressive of my life. The year, 1968, times being what they were, was a mind opening one, made more so by a teacher who took us beyond the traditional classroom.   —Katherine Sullivan

Coach, the Minister of Doom, the Grand Enunciator, these all were the names of my eleventh grade English instructor. He was a slender man with a wit for words, always energetic and articulate. As we walked into his class at the blurry hour of 7:45 a.m. his words could be heard filling the class, "My little lemmings, prepare yourselves to enter into a vast panorama of pleasure as we immerse ourselves into the world of Stephen Crane." Words became musical notes and stories became songs, and *Red Badge of Courage* wanted me to keep reading on.   —David Small

The activities [in English class] were probably my favorite—we did group bulletin boards, mini-plays, and "Jeopardy" type game shows. The beauty of these activities was that we had fun while we were learning about Romeo and Juliet's plight, the many characters in *The Canterbury Tales,* and the symbolism rampant in "The Waste Land." The bulletin boards allowed us to show off our creativity, "Jeopardy" helped us remember character and plot, and mini-plays saturated us in the language of Shakespeare.   —Anne Trippeer

[My English teacher] looked like a koala bear, hence his nickname, Mr. K. Mr. K. was a short, stocky man who was gentle natured and smiled all of the time. He seemed to love all of the students including the trouble makers. I believe that is why all the students loved him. He had a way of never actually answering a question. Instead, he would turn things around and make you answer your own question. It was an art that he had refined so well that the technique rubbed off on his students. We would stop asking questions and evaluate the situation or problem in our own mind and come up with a solution. Independent thinking was Mr. K's motto. No thought was ever wrong, it was always correct as long as there was some basis for the thought.

[My other English teacher] was a throw back from the 60's. He wore raggedy pants and his hair was always messed up. He looked like he just rolled out of bed. But he had a great mind and he treated all the students with the respect that he wanted. He . . . had a way to open discussions up and to make everyone feel special. We wrote all the time and some of the stories that the "bad" kids wrote were incredible. These are the same kids that [the other teachers] had thrown out of class for bad behavior.   —Melissa Campbell

One of my best memories of [my English teacher's] class was when we were doing some seat work, reading in groups or something, and she hung up a large white sheet of paper in front of the class. Casually, she told us if we liked we could come up and write or draw our ideas about "Life" on this sheet with the colorful markers she provided. Throughout the class period, students meandered to the front, wrote poems, drew rainbows or angry faces, made a statement. I wrote "Whoops." Near the end of class, she scanned the filled sheet smiling at a few things, nodding her head.

Then she stopped, turned around and said, "Who wrote 'Whoops'?"

I raised my hand.

"What did you mean?" she asked.

"You know, like slipping on a banana peel," I said.

She laughed and nodded at me. . . . That smile and nod she gave me meant more to me than any grade I ever received. It was her way of saying that what I thought was important, even clever, that I had something to contribute. She is what high school English should be.   —Larry Goldman

Whatever the specific impetus, for most of us it was not so much a love of *who* we would be teaching but *what* we would teach (the literature) or *how* we would teach and emulate our model of a great teacher.

For me, it was finding *me* in an unlikely place—in a 1900s North Carolina town in Thomas Wolfe's *Look Homeward, Angel*. It was seventh grade in Linkhorn Park Elementary School, and I *could not* put the book down: I was so taken with it I brought it to and from school for three days. I read at home; I read in class. Wolfe spoke of passion and loss and the difficulty of knowing the world—and one another. He sang of longing and sadness and all the things I could not articulate (but so keenly felt) at thirteen. I concealed the novel on my lap and read it, virtually straight through, during work time in Mrs. Thompson's room. I am certain Mrs. Thompson saw me reading during class and— to her credit—left me alone. While the novel has no more charms for me—looking at it now, I find it dated and long-winded and self-indulgent—it was my introduction to the power of literature. And I have loved Mrs. Thompson ever since.

The teacher who inspired me was Larry Duncan, who in eleventh-grade English at Norfolk Catholic High School was both exotic and demanding. He put Ezra Pound's "In a Station of the Metro" on the board and asked us what we thought. He showed how close analysis of the opening lines of Shakespeare's *Richard III* could reveal level upon level of meaning, and then he asked us to try. He told us about the Harlem Renaissance and asked us to consider what "explode" really meant, then in 1967, in Langston Hughes's "Harlem." He chose pieces for the spring play like Eugene O'Neill's *The Hairy Ape* and actually expected us not only to learn but to understand the lines. In general, Mr. Duncan treated his students like intellectual peers. He asked us real questions as if he was interested in our giving him real answers. We didn't always respond, and often our class "discussions" consisted of a lot of puzzled silence on our part and a lot of frustration on his. We thought he was weird (and I still think that assessment was not only accurate but complimentary), but Mr. Duncan set an example and a tone you had to hear if not accept.

You have a story, too, and a reason for wanting to do this business of English teaching. That reason, that passion, will be part of your strength as a teacher and, further, conveying that story to your students may be appropriate at some time. It's valid; it's part of why you're here, and its power will carry you through the very dailyness and the occasional discouragement of teaching English.

But your love of your subject or a very good experience in English class is only part of the story.

Not everyone loved literature, their English teachers, or even school

Not all of our students like English, love English, will willingly take English classes if they further their education, or will continue to read literature or write poetry or essays after they leave—or escape—us. Many of our students have had very bad experiences with English (the subject and those who teach it) and feel that they and their language are not good enough, are not correct, are not acceptable. Many of our students are terrified of writing, feel they don't have anything to say, or, if they did, probably couldn't say it right anyway. Many of our students don't read frequently or fluently or with a whole lot of understanding. Many of them have encountered few books that seem to have any connection to their lives. For many students, English language arts is the primo arena of the majority—white, Anglo, Western, and male—and they do not see themselves reflected there. Many of our students in English language arts classes are asked questions that seem hardly worth answering about people and life choices and issues that seem to exist solely in books and solely for English teachers' tests. Listen to a few of these stories, written by people who are planning on entering the classroom:

> I know I had an English teacher in every grade from eighth to twelfth. I know that each year someone attempted to teach me high school English because that is what English teachers were instructed to do by the school board. The school board asked teachers to teach literature, reading and grammar. However, the school board failed to make it a rule that English teachers make high school English interesting, enlightening and entertaining enough that students be able to recall classroom experiences and teachers' names.
>
> —Jan Butterworth

> In the history of the English language course that I had my senior year, the entire class consisted of reading and doing exercises in a workbook. That was it. What should the class have been? Certainly it should have included some outside reading, and the opportunity to do some writing in conjunction with the required workbook. Even a subject as dry as the history of the English language could have been made interesting had this teacher [tried].
>
> —Wendy Taylor

Freshman English was conducted by [my teacher], a kindly aging spinster. I say *conducted,* but in actuality she was both the conductor and the chorus. The classroom was her stage, and any interruption by a student was a wrong note. We were there for her audience as she read to us some of the great works of literature. She read *The Merchant of Venice* from beginning to end, and a very effective Shylock she was, I might add!

— KATHERINE SULLIVAN

I got the impression that [my eleventh-grade English teacher] didn't know that much about literature; I'm not quite sure what gave me that impression. But, I remember she tried to teach us American Literature, and set out to accomplish her mission by having us read a paragraph each from *The Crucible, Moby Dick, Walden, Our Town,* and *The Scarlet Letter.* I think I may have read some of her assignments because they were short enough that I didn't have to sacrifice watching *Knots Landing* or talking to my boyfriend on the phone for two hours. She expected us to read *The Lottery* too, but I didn't bother since she showed us the film.

— PATTY DUFFY

[My eleventh-grade teacher] sat in her desk at the front of the evenly aligned rows of gleaming metal, orange desks. She rested the textbook on her chest which rested on top of the desk and drilled us. She was very predictable. She asked the questions from the back of the book. Her eyes saw everything. There was no talking, laughing, or writing. Of course she didn't react to you sleeping in class as long as it was quiet. Most of the time we had to do busy work, worksheets, crossword puzzles. . . . She would give us any assignment as long as it kept us quiet, so that she had time to read the book on top of her heaving chest and to rub hand lotion on her hands.

— MELISSA CAMPBELL

I was so afraid that if I expressed an opinion or asked a question both the students and the teacher would think I was "stupid" . . . if I could look those teachers in the face at this moment I would seriously consider spitting on them.

— SANDRA GREER

I once had a friend tell me, "English class ruined every good book I ever read."

— RALPH B. HOLMES, JR.

But since this, by and large, is not the experience of every person who takes English, why dwell on it? We dwell on it, we linger over it, because if we are to improve education, if we are to make the classroom an alive, languaging kind of place, events such as those described above must become even rarer in our classrooms.

If you have talked to anyone recently about being or planning to be an English teacher, have you noticed their reaction? More than likely you hear them tell you, "Uh oh, I'd better watch my grammar," or "English was not my best subject." Rarely do you meet someone whose eyes will light up at the prospect of talking with you, an English teacher — for many people English teachers represent something negative and almost fearful.

Why is this? I wonder at times if it is because a number of individuals have had bad experiences with English teachers and in English classes. Those bad experiences, I hope, will stop with you. And while I can write with energy and pride about Mrs. Thompson and Mr. Duncan, there is also my nameless eighth-grade English teacher at Blair Junior High School. Red pen in hand, she took the poem I had written about mountains (a poem that meant so much to me I not only showed it privately to her after class but had also painstakingly recopied in peacock ink on my best paper), read it, and first circled the spelling errors and then marked the punctuation with "UNNECESSARY" in large letters.

I was fourteen and about as morbidly sensitive as they come. I nearly stopped writing poetry, and I never showed that teacher anything that meant anything to me ever again.

For some students, there will be little chance they will show a teacher their poetry. Some of our students are fearful about their abilities, feel they have no place, no voice, in our classrooms, and come by compulsion, with no illusions about learning or even having a relatively pleasant experience. For these students, unsatisfactory incidents in English class will be far more serious than one marked-up poem.

What you are planning to do would not be such a challenge if the students with whom you worked saw immediately the reasons for the literature on the agenda Wednesday afternoon and if they fell with zest and comprehension to whatever tasks you assign. The bulk of our job, however, is not to ratify understanding and gracefully preside over the honing and polishing of skills. It is to do what our title dictates—teach. And sometimes that is terribly difficult to do.

We, as an education association bumper sticker proclaims, teach the children. We teach the Anglo, Latino, Native American, Asian American, African American; the learning disabled, the emotionally disturbed; male and female. Our preparation for the classroom may not give us a deep background with all these learners, but make no mistake about it: they are, once they walk into our classrooms, ours. Ours to teach.

Teacher ego: having it/losing it

And thus we come to the subject of ego.

You've got to have a special confidence even to think of being a teacher, of being in charge of and accountable for a class, of organizing what 150 or so people will be doing five hours a day five days a week in school. You have to be able to see yourself helping large groups negotiate subjects and facts and concepts. Somewhere along the line you have decided you can be the equal or superior of the teachers—good and not so good—you had in your own background. In short, you have a healthy ego if you can seriously contemplate being a teacher.

But one of the things you may not realize is that very early on, especially if you want to be successful in this teaching business—in other words, if you want your students to learn—you will need to lose a lot of that ego. You will, rapid-fire, need to:

1. Put into perspective what appears to be the occasional indifference or insensitivity of your students.
2. Care more about your students' learning than about your dominance.
3. Talk less and listen more.
4. Answer less and question more.

You will, actually, have to become the quintessential, archetypal adult, one who sublimates personal needs for others, who steps aside so that others can step in, who is silent so that others can learn to speak. If you are used to being the smartest kid in the class, now, as a teacher, you will have to modify if not totally relinquish that role. Can you do it? Maybe not immediately, maybe not even in the first couple of years, but sooner or later the ego will have to soften. And in the space that is left, your students will flourish.

Some of my students who are preparing to teach English already understand this, understand it long before I ever did. Jane Dowrick writes that she realizes the importance of making "oneself empty in order to be ready to receive—that in our efforts to be smart, and ready, and on top of things, we cannot hear what we need to hear" in the classroom.

For Jane, the whole process of getting ready to teach is a round of "filling myself up with information, advice, and now I need to make some room" for the emptiness and silence that can be necessary for an effective teacher.

As Sheryl Gibson, a teacher in the early stage of her career, notes:

> I now realize that it is not impossible to be a teacher who does not indoctrinate. Kids need to think on their own and develop their own interpretations. . . . Once I realized that teaching is not being the knowledge factory but the knowledge filter, my desire to teach was rekindled.

Sandra Greer sums it up well (and if all teachers were more like Sandra, the future would be in good hands):

> I know that when it is *me* standing in front of those high school students I want to put on a smiling face because I feel that way, and let those kids "express" to their hearts' content and write till doomsday if that's what they want to do. I don't want to change the world, I just want to encourage them to do what they're capable of and hopefully open up their minds to the exciting and wonderful (I won't get out the thesaurus for any more synonyms!) world of Literature. Yeah! I know . . . it sounds kind of sickening doesn't it. I guess it does sound like I want to change the world. Maybe I do. Maybe I do like to think that because of my effort I'll really help out some kid. But, you see, I want to. I really want to. Even if it's only one student, that's better than none at all. I want to be a good teacher. People ask me all the time, "What do you want to be a teacher for? You won't make much money." You know what I say? Who gives a *?!! about money, these kids need an education because that's about the only thing going for them these days. They are our future. And I'd hate to see our future go to waste.

FOR YOUR JOURNAL

Choose one or two of the following. Make a list of three things you would like to do as a teacher. Write about a memorable teacher who was great. Write about a memorable teacher who was awful. Write about one of the first "English" successes you had: in class; tutoring you did with another student; a book or poem you read that impressed you.

The Student/Learner

What is this thing called adolescence?

It's amazing how once we pass our own adolescence, we tend to forget what it was really like. With the best of intentions, but certainly inaccurately, we often romanticize those years—they were great and we were so carefree—and we cloak adolescence with veils of what it should have been, not what it was. It is tough being young. It was tough years ago, and it hasn't changed.

Adults, even fairly young adults, tend to become nostalgic or just amnesiac; as teachers, we really can't indulge ourselves so. In order to be successful, we need to look at the wily, fascinating, exhausting, exhilarating adolescent and who he or she is. We also need to make some distinctions about age groups.

Intellectual changes   At this point in your career you have had some developmental psychology and you are aware of learning stages and cycles. You know about the work of

Swiss psychologist Jean Piaget and his division of cognitive development into four stages: sensorimotor thought, preoperational thought, concrete operational thought, and formal operational thought. These last two stages particularly concern us. To briefly review: Piaget defined the stage of **concrete operations** as taking place from about ages seven to eleven. This is followed by a **transitional formal operations** stage from about eleven to fourteen and a **permanent formal operations** stage from about age fourteen on. Broadly speaking, concrete operations involve real, observable situations; formal operations deal with abstract, speculative thought.

The work of Piaget is a landmark in education, but you also need to know that it has not gone unchallenged. For many educators Piaget's belief that the concrete and formal operations stages are truly definable by age is misleading; further, many young people do not enter a permanent formal operations stage until much later than fourteen years of age. Researcher Margaret Donaldson, for instance, maintains that Piaget's developmental stages are not truly accurate when describing development of thought processes in young people (183ff). At any rate, the movement of your students from one stage to another is a very real phenomenon but is often not readily perceivable to you, the teacher. While it is helpful for you to know that some of your students will be struggling with a change in thinking abilities and patterns, this knowledge will not, unfortunately, give you a precise guide for dealing with the questions you may have about your students and their response to language arts tasks. While you can accept with some surety that some of your students will be moving through the stages, it is a fallacy to believe that the stages will be exact or readily demonstrable.

Psychological changes   The mythic "crisis" of adolescence may also be just a myth. It is not common to every culture that all adolescents go through the *sturm und drang* (storm and stress) of alienation and rebellion. You may not have experienced such huge upheavals nor may many of your friends. On the other hand, you may know of others in your own life and see young people in your class for whom growing up is painful and difficult. For sure, three factors are relatively unique challenges of adolescence (Furhmann, 173): rapid, uneven physical growth; a new self-consciousness; and a tremendous cognitive awareness.

Adolescence: early and beyond   The middle school concept was born out of a concern for what is termed the early adolescent, aged roughly ten to fourteen. About thirty years ago there was a renewed and widespread interest not so much to segregate those students as to try to make their educational experience more appropriate for their development. The idea of a middle school is to offer a more distinctive education than the literal "junior" high school, which had been in place since the 1920s as the educational setting after elementary school and a training ground of sorts for secondary school (Muth and Alvermann, 2–4). While the middle school concept has a very wide variance in this country, it is based on the fact that early adolescence is a special time and requires a different sort of educational setting.

What are some of the factors of early adolescence, of the middle schooler?

First, the years before puberty are characterized by more profound physical change than any other time of life—with the exception, of course, of infancy. Second, early adolescence is when cognitive development changes, in Piagetian terms, from concrete operations to formal operations. As sketched above, the latter is when students begin to think in the abstract, not in the purely observable, and that expanded capability in thinking has serious implications for what we do in our classrooms. Indeed, a "wide range of cognitive ability" is probably most demonstrable at the early adolescent stage (Muth and Alvermann, 29). Third, in the area of reading, early adolescents can encounter serious difficulties moving to a higher level of comprehension and, indeed, the sheer amount of reading often falls off alarmingly at this age (Flood et al., 312). Fourth, in the area of writing, early adolescents may have serious difficulty moving to higher order issues (Flood et al., 318) in the way they write and how they think about what they want to write.

What about middle and later adolescents?

In middle and later adolescence, students will show more social awareness, more orientation toward peer and away from parent, and will begin to master skills or fall more seriously behind in writing and reading tasks. They will also (some more gracefully than others) continue to master the tasks of maturation.

So what do adolescents want?

More than anything, young people want a part of the action, a piece of the control. As one of my students laments about her English classes in high school:

> Being a prospective educator myself I know exactly what was lacking in my own high school education. I should have been given the chance to question anything that I was learning; I should have been able to feel comfortable saying I didn't understand something. I should have been challenged to come up with my own ideas instead of my mind remaining dormant. I should have been in an environment where the student's word was equally important as the teacher's. I should have been given not only the opportunity but the instruction . . . to express myself in written work.
>
> —SANDRA GREER

A number of educational researchers have looked at what they call "locus of control" and have found that passive students who exhibit "learned helplessness" just don't learn efficiently (Furhmann, 167). Such passive students are also, as you can readily observe, relatively unhappy in their classrooms. Unfortunately, however, it is often in the school's interest to keep students largely passive.

And another story

Listen to this student's description of herself as a teenager in English class; she is representative of the large number of young people who aren't challenged in our classrooms. This young person, who, by the way, is now in her first years of English teaching, was neither gifted nor remedial; she is, however, a voice for the majority of students, and we may learn something from her story:

> I majored in English in college because in high school I thought that I was naturally and amazingly gifted in the subject. For instance, in [my] ninth-grade English class, we had a test, and one of the questions was, "Why did Sherlock Holmes beat the sidewalk with his walking stick before entering the building?" I had no clue. As usual, I hadn't even bothered to read the story, let alone study for the test. But I must have been pretty clever, because I took a wild guess and replied, "To see whether or not the ground was hollow—whether or not there was a room beneath." I was right! I got an A! I couldn't tell you what the name of the story was now; I've never even read a story by Sir Arthur Conan Doyle. I just know how to get through high school English without cheating or studying.
>
> I think [my English teacher] used to get frustrated with me and some of my friends, because she was usually pretty crabby when we were around. As hard as she tried, she

couldn't nail us for our disrespect. She would stand at the front of the class talking about gerunds or Sherlock Holmes while we carried on our own conversations. Eventually, she would glare in our direction and ask one of us to read aloud. We either had no idea what page she was on or we couldn't control our laughing well enough to oblige her. To add insult to her injury, no matter how disrespectful we were in class, we always did well on her tests. I don't really know exactly how the others got around her, but my secret was that I knew grammar rules intuitively, and I paid just enough attention in class to know what was in the reading that I was supposed to do but rarely did. She was serious about teaching English, but she just didn't challenge me enough for me to show her any respect. Getting away with murder became a sick little game to make fourth period go by more quickly.

[In other English classes with other teachers] I repeated her gerund exercises. . . . Bewilderingly enough to me, the mathematically inclined kids struggled with gerunds. . . . I, on the other hand, completed the exercises in a matter of minutes, which was nice because that left me with plenty of time to talk and pass notes. Thus I added another year of unearned As in English to my high school transcript.

High school English; what a pathetic experience! I get a little angry now when I think of how much I could have learned but didn't. Maybe it was my fault. I could have read the assignments and behaved better in class. But, why bother? I was doing well as I was. I was secretly quite interested in learning—especially reading and writing—but it wasn't cool to admit it then, and I had no reason to embarrass myself.

I always secretly felt a little sorry for [my English teacher] because, deep-down inside, I always got the feeling that she was trying to teach me something—that she wanted to challenge me more than harass me. I'm not sure why she failed. Why did she make her tests so easy? Perhaps she was too confined by the curriculum. Maybe her teaching abilities were stifled . . . I often wonder what she would think if she knew that I want to be an English teacher. Would she curse me? "Some day, I hope you have students who are just like you were." Or would she secretly feel sorry for me?   —PATTY DUFFY

Patty Duffy expresses well the sort of mind-numbing contact some students and teachers can engage in in our schools. No one is a particularly bad actor here, no great dramatic events occur, but learning is not the outcome. Further, for both teacher and student, contact is a trial. Patty, as an adult, now understands what her English teacher was doing, but at the time the two did not connect. Why is that?

Some of it is because teachers fail to take into account the adolescent and why he or she really comes to school and sits in our class. Some of it is because our students, in their development cycle, are often difficult to entice into the intellectual life— particularly as it is represented by school. Much of it, of course, is no one's direct fault at all, but we must make the best effort possible with the classes we have and with all the students in them.

A few observations about your students and their behavior

Students don't, by and large, want to be in school for the reasons teachers want them to be there. The action, the heart, is often outside the class in the halls and in the faces and lives of their classmates, not in their teachers. Many of them have already internalized what the society judges them to be and are trying to mirror that expectation. Many feel that the game is biased from the start, and they see you, the teacher, as another of the game masters.

The point is that our students are different from us as adults. Holly O'Donnell, a student teacher, trying to make sense of adolescents and her own perceptions, wrote in her journal:

I'm not surprised by the kids—well, I was at first. But I wasn't surprised about what they talk about—it's *how* they talk about stuff. Maybe I've just got good ears, but I hear more swearing! And I was initially surprised at how "belligerent" they were. I'm not really so sure as it's belligerence, now, as it is adolescence. They are so vocal, so verbal—at first it's scary because adults aren't like this. Adults get up every morning w/o asking why (or w/o asking it very loudly) and do what the capitalistic, bi-partisan democracy expects; kids get up and they want to know why—and they're not scared to ask, why? and, who died and left you boss? I mean, they *look* like us, but then they open their mouths and "everything's changed!"

The following observations regarding young people, teens, and preteens may give more specific insight:

- Adolescents can feel misunderstood and often misjudged. They suspect adults don't listen to them. Many times they are quite correct. When, as one student quoted here recalls, teachers only expect students "to accept and agree," we are contributing to their sense that no one listens.

- Emotions run high in these years; an hour can be an eternity, and a trivial incident can be a major disaster. Just because an adult's perspective "proves" this to be untrue, the young person's feelings to the contrary are not trivial or discountable.

- The culture of the young person and the culture of the adult are often at odds. It's often the adults, however, who try to impose their culture on the teens, not vice versa.

- Teens look at adults in a highly critical way. At no other time in life is the detection of what teenage Holden Caulfield (in J. D. Salinger's *The Catcher in the Rye*) called the "bullshit factor" more acute. Unfortunately, however, as most adults are well aware, that detection of bullshit is usually other-centered.

- It's all new for adolescents, which is not always that exciting or reassuring. Uncharted territory is scary—as the ancient map of the "edge" of the world indicated, "beyond this place here lie monsters."

- A great many males, especially Caucasian males, begin to find strength in these years; a male-defined culture is ready to receive them. A great many females begin to suspect—and become depressed by—the outline of their future lives and their place in the world. We spend a lot of time on the behavior of our males; young women rarely receive similar guidance. Young women suspect that their lives are changing profoundly: being smart and outspoken in tenth grade carries different implications than it did in sixth grade.

- Students who are a racial or ethnic minority in school feel even more keenly the alienation of adolescence. Being different, being one of the few in a group, can be uncomfortable and limiting, and often teachers and other students do not reach out.

- Adolescents don't come to school to see you or to go to class; they come to experience the real action: one another. In some ways you and your class are merely the backdrop of the play.

- In English class, students want to read something that speaks to them and their experience; they want to write about what they know; they want to talk about issues of importance. This does not mean that they can't or won't read about different cultures and different ages, but it must, somehow, relate to now. If you can't give this to them or don't think this is important, you may have problems in your classroom. Patti Smith tells us:

Teenagers want to be treated as adults, which they deserve; however, they are rarely given a forum in which to discuss the adult issues playing a huge part in their lives. Debate is a skill that can't be learned at home while students are still dependent on their parents; yet it is an essential skill for adult life. What better place to hone it than in the classroom?

- Our young students are not children; they usually know more and have experienced more than we give them credit for. Patronize them, let them know that they're just kids, and they'll dislike you for it. First, it's demeaning, and second, it's just not true. One student remembers that "I had always believed that adults didn't expect adolescents to have any worthwhile ideas." It's not what we want to be known for.

- Most of your students are participating to some extent in sexual activities, and many are using or experimenting with drugs, both hard and soft, and alcohol. Some of this is growing up and learning; some of it is highly dangerous. But scare tactics or a shallow approach to moralizing doesn't help here: some of it is what you and your friends did, too, and just saying no doesn't make the problem—or even the complexity of the issues—go away.

- Many of your students will have jobs outside of school, which, frankly, mean more to them than your class because, unlike your class, those jobs pay them money. Given a chance, some students will tell you this, too.

- Despite how untouched they may appear, your students want you to care about them and to be concerned about them. They do not, however, want you to invade their personal lives or their privacy. It's a fine line they ask you—that they expect you—to walk.

- Despite how indifferent they may appear, your students want to respect you as a teacher and as a person. In fact, despite all disclaimers to the contrary, they look to you for some sort of clue as to how they should live their lives and what choices they should make.

- Despite how broad-minded or sophisticated they may appear, adolescents do not want you to do drugs with them, drink with them, or use risque language or obscenities around them.

- Despite how infatuated they may become with you—or you with them—adolescents do not want you as a boyfriend or a girlfriend or as a sexual partner. You are an adult, a teacher, in a trusted role, and intimate contact is a flat violation of that trust. Fall in love with someone your own age; put your students' feelings of affection or just experiments with flirtation in perspective. In this area, you have limited rights; you are a teacher first and foremost. To violate that trust is a profound betrayal.

- Remember always that youth is a territory all its own: adults may visit but are guests only on temporary visa.

- Remember also that youth is necessarily, inescapably, self centered: young people really don't think your life or your problems are anywhere near as important as theirs and, anyway, it's your job to be there because you're the teacher. Furthermore, you get paid for this stuff.

- Remember, finally, that adolescents are the toughest audience in the world—and one of the most rewarding. They may never tell you thanks or write or phone or come back to school to let you know how they are doing, but don't worry; if you did your job, they'll remember, and they just might be better people for it. And you, necessarily, are much the better for having known them. Many of your students will, in fact, stay in your mind and your heart for the rest of your life. And that's a job benefit few professions can offer you.

FOR YOUR JOURNAL

Try to remember who you were during adolescence. *Questions to consider:* What is one thing you loved? hated? Who were your best friends? What was the major challenge you had during this time? What do you recall about your relationship with your parents? with your teachers? If you worked during the year or during the summer, what did you do? What did you read?

If none of the above questions seem appealing, find a young person between the age of thirteen and eighteen and informally interview him or her. Possible questions for the interview: What does the person think are the biggest hurdles to being that age? The deepest satisfactions? If there was one thing he or she would like teachers to understand, what would it be? What about for parents? for adults in general? What does the person think being an adult will be like?

Finally, if you hate the above questions and the interview, think about another avenue. One of the characters in young adult writer Richard Peck's *Unfinished Portrait of Jessica* remarks, "There were only three ages: *now, high school,* and *grown up.* All adults were the same age" (63–64). If this is true, if this is what most young people really assume, what is your responsibility, obligation, problem as a teacher? What, essentially, are the implications of such a statement?

The School

A little bit of selected history

Arthur N. Applebee wrote the book, literally, on the history of our profession. *Tradition and Reform in the Teaching of English* is the most comprehensive text to date, and if you are interested in the various movements and trends, it's worth your time. And, in a very self-serving way, it is to your advantage to know your educational history, if for no other reason than to appreciate that the latest outcry and call for change has probably been made, with just as much energy and intelligence, sometime in the past. Many of the issues in language arts teaching are perennial, and much of what American education debated at the turn of the nineteenth century is with us now at the turn of the twentieth.

There are, nevertheless, a few historical landmarks and a few issues worth reviewing, a number of which are sketched below.

Education for life versus education for college   So just what is a school for? Should it be geared to prepare a student for the world—that is, work—or for college?

Does this question sound familiar? It was a raging debate in 1892 when the National Education Association sponsored what came to be known as the Report of the Committee of Ten. The group was concerned that high school courses were taught differently depending on whether the students were going to college or not. The Committee of Ten also found that English language arts courses were not being geared to two basic needs: developing communication skills and cultivating a taste for reading. A few years later, in 1918, the significantly more influential *Cardinal Principles* report said much the same as the Committee of Ten, but it also added that English should include "studies of direct value" and that theory and student experience should be related.

The student's interest as the basis for all learning　The *Cardinal Principles* was influential, and the interest in preparing students for life became a major tenet of an encompassing concept called the Progressive Movement. The movement's most influential proponent was the legendary writer and educational theorist John Dewey, and the movement started formally in 1919 with the founding of the Progressive Education Association and didn't really fade until the 1950s.

For the Progressive Movement, the real needs of students were of great import, and in language arts, the 1935 publication of *An Experience Curriculum in English* tried to meet student interests in a realistic course of studies. The curriculum seemed successful, and research involving 240 schools and 3,600 students, called the Eight-Year Study, confirmed the fact. According to the Eight-Year Study's results, students prepared around problems and issues that concerned them did as well in college as their more traditionally educated counterparts.

The academic model and the romantic revolt　Carried to its extreme, the Progressive Movement, especially through an early 1950s manifestation called "life adjustment education," lost the faith of the American public. Meeting the real needs of students was carried to the extreme, actually went over the edge, and when units in English class on housing the family, choosing a mate, and even how to answer the telephone were brought to public attention—and ridicule—the bloom was off the Progressive rose. Especially with the fears of international competition, embodied by the former Soviet Union's bold launching in 1957 of the first orbiting space capsule, Sputnik, the English language arts curriculum drew back into what Arthur Applebee terms the "academic model."

It was the early 1960s, and rigor and the concept of English as a discipline was enforced. Drawing on the influential writing of Jerome Bruner in the seminal *The Process of Education* and rejecting the "soft" idea of student interest as being the basis of education, the English curriculum in particular became serious, structured, and rigorously tested. While some gains may have been made, the result was an alienation of certain students and teachers although, admittedly, many thrived in the classroom. English language arts in the early 1960s was not about adjusting to society. Instead, there was the academic formalism of studying structural linguistics and the close analysis of the New Criticism.

Nothing, of course, stays in place, and the academic orientation of the previous years was transformed in the mid-sixties. Education was not untouched by the upheavals of the age: the civil rights movement, the women's movement, and a general call for societal change. In the schools, a number of educators demanded that the English classroom open up and be more for all students of all persuasions; its intellectual rigor was seen as an impediment to learning, not an enhancement, especially for racial minorities and those not admitted into the prestigious, exclusive, and CEEB-sponsored Advanced Placement classes.

In the mid and late 1960s, it was a time of educational experiment. Students were invited to choose their courses in elective programs, schedule their classes in variable time slots, take courses pass/fail, and take classes with people younger and older than themselves and in spaces without walls or without rows or sometimes without desks. As Neil Postman and Charles Weingartner happily wrote in 1969, teaching could be viewed as a "subversive" activity. According to many 1960s reformers, the classroom could, appropriately, undermine and challenge the omnipresent and scorned "establishment."

Accountability: let's go back to the basics   Well of course it didn't last. By the mid 1970s the public temperature indicated that it was time to worry that standards were slipping, that teachers slap-happy with freedom and students talking much too expressively were taking over the English classes and not doing or learning a darned thing. A fear emerged that was somewhat akin to that of the late 1950s: where were the testable skills? Where was the practice development? So the wind shifted to going "back" to the basics of English and testing, testing, testing, under the umbrella term *accountability*. Competency tests were in vogue, and the idea of making materials or texts "teacher-proof" resurged.

Today, some years later, we are still dealing with some of these issues, and we can add to them a few others. There is, in general, a continual concern about standardized test scores and about the teaching of the "classics" in English; perhaps more positively, there is an interest in the writing process (not just product) and in the incorporation of computer technology in the classroom; and there is a renewed awareness of multiculturalism and the power of cooperative learning.

But all is not well in school. In 1983 the United States Department of Education issued *A Nation at Risk* and concluded that education just might drown "in a sea of mediocrity." While that report was written some years ago, it is the feeling of many today that it is a true description of the American public school.

School as repository of hopes and dreams—and traditions

There is ongoing discussion—as always—of the institution of school and how it is not serving education or young people. More specifically, we hear today that American business is not receiving qualified workers and that the national economy is falling and our country is in second—or third—place because of the failure of school, especially as it is now structured. There is barely repressed amazement that of all the American institutions with which we are familiar, school is the one—virtually the only one other than some organized religions—where someone deep-frozen in the nineteenth century could return to our age and be comfortable and feel a sense of familiarity. In high schools particularly, the same curriculum patterns, much of the same subject matter (including the very same pieces of literature taught in English classes), the same organization of the school day, have survived from early-twentieth-century American public education. And, ironically, the calls we hear now for school reform are many of the same calls that have been issued across this century, and some of the "new" proposals for flexible/modular scheduling days, for year-round school, and for school on ten-month patterns that do not automatically include a summer (maybe a winter?) vacation are ideas we have heard for the last thirty years. The perennial concern about school being preparation for college or preparation for life is a debate from the turn of the century.

America changed its eating habits from home to restaurant to fast-food establishment in less than a decade, shifted car sizes and most popular country of manufacture in the same time, adjusted to the word processor and the computer in about twenty years, and absorbed massive social change regarding women and minorities in a decade and a half. So why the foot-dragging with school?

As a teaching friend of mine notes, "school keeps." We may face tremendous changes around us, but school, with its familiar structure and content, is a reassuring touchstone of sorts for many Americans. It's also, maddeningly enough, a repository for many of our hopes and dreams about our future and what our youth, our young people, represent to us. It may seem to be just a graduation speech cliché, but for many Americans youth is indeed the future, and school is where many of us hope that youth will be formed and shaped.

School is where we try to transmit, carry on, and it's a sensitive issue for the majority of taxpaying, child-rearing adults. When it looks like what we experienced, many of us feel comforted. School is the "universal environment" for adolescents, a "vast, standardized, relatively homogeneous experience" that all students in this country share (Furhmann, 144). When we hear of practices we did not experience—such as the "new" math—there is often dislocation and confusion.

And, as George Counts wrote over sixty years ago, school is more driven by social change than it is the driver of it. That makes it often a controversial and touchy place to teach and to learn, especially when a society feels that its sense of order and values is threatened by any combination of social shifting. For example, debates over the place of grammar in the curriculum, which piece of literature to study, or how to teach English to those for whom it is a second language are often a product of politics in the very broad sense of the term and not just questions that well-meaning English departments can rationally solve in some sort of vacuum or isolation. School can be a political mine field, and it is certainly an accurate reflection of the anxieties of the culture.

It is important for you to know about school, the institution, how it is organized and how that affects you and your classes. There may, in the coming few years, be real changes in the shape of schools—those reforms often talked about may really come to pass—but in the meantime you will experience, at least for the first part of your teaching life, a high school or middle school structured not very differently from the way it was organized when your grandparents walked the halls.

And while that continuity may be comforting on one level, it also is not serving young people efficiently. As one educator grimly notes:

> The comprehensive high school, designed to meet the needs of everyone, is criticized for having become an assembly-line system that denies adolescents access to adults, breeds frustration, creates failure, and is concerned only with conformity and order rather than intellectual curiosity and love of learning. (Furhmann, 148–49)

Further, and this is a reality of the business, the structure of school often gets in the way of teaching and learning. You will find yourself in your classroom wondering if there isn't a better way to set up this contract among learners, and your speculation will be appropriate. Unfortunately, however—and this has been true of educational history in this country for a century—you, as the teacher, will probably be one of the last people seriously consulted about institutional change. It will be up to you at times to make the best of what can be a difficult situation, at times to make changes as you can in your own school community, and possibly at times to really get a piece of the teacher empowerment that is often touted. But that's another story. Let's look at what the issues are.

Five aspects of school that may not serve you or your students

The compulsory nature of school and your English class   First, you need to remember that your wonderful students, your clientele as it were, even in private or independent school, are there by compulsion. School is required, it is not optional, and by the time you get ready to meet your English classes, your students have been doing this compulsory stuff for many years. They may, by fourteen or seventeen, even be a little jaded. They often come, as Richard Hawley remarks in his article "Teaching as Failing," like an audience with little anticipation of being pleased. You may, indeed, pleasantly surprise them, but do not expect huzzahs as you enter the classroom. While you may know you are different, to many of your students you look a lot like every other teacher they have ever had. And that, by the way, is not necessarily a compliment.

As a result, you may be rather surprised at the absentee rate in your school and the practical effects of that rate on your classroom. Student teacher Debbie Martin wrote in her journal:

> These kids never come to school or, when they do, they come late or leave early. I had one student out of 120 who didn't miss a day last semester. By the same token there were 19 students who missed a total of 750 days out of the teaching days of the semester, and 212 students who were tardy over a total of 1,100 times in the same period of time. Trying to keep track of late work is an administrative nightmare.

Second, you need to recall that English is also not optional. School itself is compulsory, as is the one other subject that everyone has to take (with very few exceptions) every year: English.

Get the picture? You are not the instructional purveyor of the exotic, like Latin III or German I; what you offer in the classroom is not associated with excessive brilliance or arcane knowledge, like physics or calculus; you will not preside over classes where folks can learn about sex or can sweat and yell and play a game, like health and physical education. You don't help people make things they can eat or put in their bedrooms or hang on their walls like home ec or wood working or art. It's the most common, most broadly required, most repeated game in town: it's English language arts, and you're the teacher.

Grouping students into grade levels   It seems ridiculous to think that the one-room schoolhouse was actually a great educational idea. But, as we'll see, we could do worse than to go back to some of its principles. But that's getting ahead of the story—a little history first.

In the nineteenth century in this country, the one-room schoolhouse was rather grudgingly supported by the community through taxes and levies. It was predominately rural, undersupplied, and badly heated, ventilated, and lit. It was in session in direct relation to the local crops and economy and to the weather. There was often no continuity of instruction—the turnover in teachers and students was startlingly high. The one-room schoolhouse was presided over by one very young, unmarried, and undereducated teacher (most in the nineteenth century had not the equivalent of a high school diploma), usually female, for whom the job meant low pay, severe community scrutiny, and a great deal of work. That teacher taught and supervised as many young people as the single room could hold, and students often ranged from six years old to fourteen or fifteen.

Just for a minute imagine the distance intellectually between a six-year-old and, say, a thirteen-year-old, between first graders and seventh graders. What they can read and comprehend is wildly different, and when you go back in your mind and imagine our nineteenth-century school teacher trying, day after day, to structure learning experiences for such a widely disparate group, you can understand why educators thought it would be a great advance to group students by age, to put all of the six-year-olds together and all of the fourteen-year-olds together somewhere else. It was seen as an advance and a sensible way to deal with the differences between young people at varying stages of development.

What happened over the years, however, is that many of us in education lost sight of how nebulous and changeable some of those age differentials are. In fact, there will be more variation intellectually *among* your students in your third-period, ninth-grade English class than *between all of the ninth graders and all of the tenth graders* in your entire school. The segregation by age also seems to imply a few things that we need to examine carefully. Let's imagine we're talking about those tenth graders. If we accept grade levels by age, it tells us:

1. There is something all tenth graders should either be ready to learn or should already know, based on their chronological age.
2. All tenth graders should be taught pretty much alike because they are at the same stage of development.
3. Tenth graders will not benefit from intellectual contact with students either older or younger than themselves.

None of these three propositions are true. While we know something about how and when people learn, we don't know enough to be able to say with any certainty what a single year of school should offer intellectually. Further, the kind of crossover that occurred in the one-room schoolhouse—despite its many other manifest drawbacks—is something we could do well to return to. *Each one teach one, collaborative learning,* and *cooperative learning* are all current phrases for the same idea: we benefit when we can teach someone else, and we not only help that person, but, by helping them, we solidify our own skills.

So, when our overworked nineteenth-century school teacher had to give a geography lesson to the older students, she would, possibly, ask one of the older students to listen to and help two or three of the very young students with their reading. It was a cross-age endeavor. Further, this older student was probably more adept in reading than were those older kids getting the geography lesson; that student would not be kept in a group level but would be allowed to proceed at his or her own pace.

When you begin to teach, or when you teach this week, you may be puzzled at the disparity *among* your eleventh graders. Curricula plans that feature nongrouping—in other words, putting tenth and eleventh and twelfth graders together in a given class— militate against this sort of "Now you're fifteen; that means _____" kind of mentality.

Tracking Again, it seems a good idea at first glance; put the adept kids together, let them go on, and put the less adept kids together so they can receive extra attention and help. It sounds sensible, but it is based on a few things that we're not sure actually operate in the schools. For tracking to be *successful,* it must be based on the following principles:

1. **Neither teachers nor students should indulge in a "self-fulfilling prophecy" type of behavior;** that is, the kids tracked in the higher brackets cannot always be assumed to be smarter, and the kids tracked in the lower brackets cannot always be assumed to be slower. Lower-tracked students will often assume they aren't smart and therefore won't try. Higher-tracked students may just fail to exert the effort. Also, teachers often internalize these attitudes and deal differently with students in different tracks. And, by the way, disguising tracking designations is virtually impossible. Students and teachers *know*.

2. **Students must be mobile between the tracks;** once in a lower track, they must be allowed to achieve their way to a higher track and vice versa.

3. **The placement of students into tracks must be based on real evidence,** not on:

    - Ability gauged by single-measure tests or even standardized tests.
    - Race or economic background.
    - Personal characteristics ("such as speech patterns, dress, and ways of interacting with adults" Flood et al., 446).
    - Adherence to the school rules.

The sad fact is that these three conditions are rarely met in schools; kids are placed into tracks for reasons other than out-and-out ability and intelligence (Oakes, 9–14); kids, once placed, are rarely moved between tracks; and "smart" kids know they are in that track and can act accordingly, as do those designated less able. There is no strong research evidence that tracking is doing what we want it to do, especially for those students who are not at the top of the academic spectrum. (For a thorough look at the subject, see Jeannie Oakes's *Keeping Track*.) And, to compound the problem, we know that students in higher tracks, simply put, receive a better education (Furhmann, 158). Helen Featherstone discusses a recent study of 108 eighth- and ninth-grade classrooms, where researchers found that

> teachers in high-track classes ask more "authentic" questions, ones which have no predetermined answers, "but instead call for student opinions or for information the student must uncover independently of the teacher." They all follow up on student responses more often. . . . All this makes it sound as though schools conspire against low-track students, but that isn't true. . . . Almost all high school teachers would agree with researchers that students in low-track classes are less engaged than those in high-track classes, but things get more complex when we begin to speculate about the reasons for that disengagement. . . . Placed together in one classroom, without the leaven of more enthusiastic and academically successful classmates, disengaged adolescents create a culture unfriendly to effort. Teachers respond with teaching that asks less of students, perhaps reinforcing the students' disengagement. Before long neither teacher nor students have much heart for academic work. (7)

In addition, there is some evidence that lower-level students benefit strongly from the influence of other, more adept students. The cognitive psychologist Lev Vygotsky found that what students "can do with the assistance of others might be in some sense even more indicative of their mental development than what they can do alone" (85). Vygotsky called this a "zone of proximal development," and clearly students stronger in language arts skills can benefit those less strong. What we want to avoid is well described by Jane Dowrick, who writes:

> It seems that many of us [in my high school] had been written off as average students. Perhaps the tracking of students was to blame for the plodding methods I observed [in my English class]. It was as if these teachers expected little from their students, and therefore offered little in return. Heterogeneous classes, combining students with differing abilities and interests, might have succeeded in bringing the subject of English alive for me in more of my classes. I know that a higher level of vitality might have been possible. In my Junior year I was assigned to a "mixed" history class. The honors-level teacher, and the sprinkling of honors students challenged me and sparked my interest so much that I participated in an extracurricular cultural exchange project.

Jane Hunter also notes:

> For many years, I thought that all of the various "tracks" were taught the same things, in the same manner, and that they just varied in pace from one another. I couldn't have been farther from the truth! During my first semester of my senior year, I ran face-to-face into this prejudice after signing up for an advanced poetry class. The first sign that I was out of my territory came from a fellow student on the first day of class. "Andrew," one of the school's most promising students, walked over to my desk that morning and snarled, "Jane, what are you doing in this class?" I responded with a few choice words and wrote him off as being a stuck-up geek. As time went on, however, I began to realize where these kids' attitudes were coming from—the instructors! Students in these advanced English sections were handed a multitude of privileges by the instructors and the administration. These AP classes were run totally different from the "average" tracks—they all sat in a circle and held open discussions/debates amongst each other and with the instructor. They were also permitted to publish a class journal each month that was then distributed school wide. And worst of all, they were given first dibs in the computer room!

Finally, as Paul Fanney, a recent student of mine, writes, it can be a depressing experience to be placed in the "wrong" track:

> In tenth grade I discovered firsthand the horror of being placed [not in an honors class but] in a "regular" level class. Tenth-grade English had to be one of the most boring, irritating, and desultory experiences I have ever had. The teacher I remember did her best to keep it boring, too. The reason I got into trouble so much with her was because of how she taught and what she taught; like math classes I constantly asked myself "What's the point?" or "So what?" I got the impression that somehow we weren't to be trusted with books, *novels* I mean, based on the "probability" that we wouldn't know what to do with them once we got them. I actually remember feeling as if I was being intellectually insulted, if you know what I mean. I never forgave my advisor for putting me in that class, or the teacher for making me so restless. Instead of an interesting learning environment, we got worksheets; instead of stimulating talks on relevant and meaningful issues good English classes raise, we were given homework in monotone.

What does this mean to you? It means that you will encounter students who, at fifteen, know that it is too late; the school has judged them "slower" or "less able" or, as Paul writes, not to be trusted with books. That's a heavy burden for an adult—it's insupportable when you're a kid.

You will also have classes where the "smart" kids are on the fast track and no longer feel the need to work. They have, by the system's designation, succeeded, so why break a sweat? They have a perennial case of "senioritis" as sophomores or juniors. Finally, you will see a ghettoization of the student body: "smarties" over here, "dummies" over there, "averagies" in the middle. It just doesn't do a thing for real teaching and real learning.

A final reason tracking doesn't enhance teaching or learning is that despite your effort to be open-minded, once you enter a classroom you know has been designated as a certain track, your expectations will be subtly and not so subtly affected. You will have assumptions about the low-level class that are hard to shake. Paul's teacher, for example, did not see him as a misplaced bright person. You will also become accustomed to hearing other teachers discuss students and classes solely in relation to their tracking designation. In this game of tracking, then, the students have roles and designations that they are not allowed to change. And you, as their teacher, will also be affected.

Fifty-minute periods   When T. S. Eliot's character J. Alfred Prufrock complained about measuring his life out in coffee spoons ("The Love Song of J. Alfred Prufrock"), he might have been discussing the life of a middle school or high school teacher. Again, with best intentions, with the idea of organizing the school day intelligently, educators divided the seven or so hours into forty-five- to fifty-five-minute periods of instructional time. In English language arts particularly, that's a tight block of time to manage every day, every week, every month. Discussions can last longer, reading a piece of literature and then reacting to it often fails to fit into such a slice of the clock, and beginning a piece of writing can proceed in fits and starts much broader than forty-five minutes. For high school and middle school students, the class period can be difficult to negotiate.

Holly O'Donnell writes in her journal during the first few weeks of student teaching:

> I don't believe 45 min. a day is the best way or enough time to TEACH people much. Learning is a slow, arduous task many times & 45 min. is not even a drop in the bucket. Once in a while it is, but more often than not it is that myth about pushing a stone up a hill & never moving and occasionally going backwards & starting all over again. Like Sansom's "The Long Sheet" where the prisoners must wring out a long sheet & every night it is doused w/water. Don't misunderstand me, I don't "hate" the educ. system (otherwise I wouldn't be here) I just don't think the way we do things now is *the* best way.

In the meantime, understand that both you and your students are responsible to the clock. No matter how dull or how exhilarating the class, it comes to an end in forty-five or fifty-five minutes every day, every week, every month of the teaching year. It limits what you can do, and it is a recipe, of and by itself, for routine. You will need to fight that routine so that it becomes not the boredom of utter predictability but the comfort or outline of order. And, unlike the other "constraints" mentioned so far in this section, there are a few things you can do to improve the situation.

How do you do that? You mix it up and shake it up; you keep track of how many days in a row the students had a discussion, worked in small groups, did silent work at their desk, made presentations, or served on panels. You make sure that each week features a variety of large-group, small-group, and individual work, and that class time is alternated appropriately with films, silent reading, and talk. You do not want to have a class where students really don't know what to expect every day—that can get scary after a while. But we flourish, all of us, on variety, and one way to beat the fifty-minute boredom trap is to build variety into your class.

Finally, remember that school business may give you much less than forty-five to fifty-five minutes a day. Announcements, school pictures, field trips, and tardy slips will cut into that block of time. In addition, you may have school-scheduled events suspend your class during the week. After all, how do you think the whole school gets to see the play during the day or hear the special speech imported for their edification? It may be, and with little notice to you, that your Tuesday, fourth-period class doesn't meet, nor does your Wednesday, first-period class. You are responsible for adjusting and planning appropriately. And sometimes, I repeat, it's on short notice. So you remain flexible as you try to teach in this place called school.

Grades and quantification   We are a nation of competitors, who's in, who's out, the ten best, the twenty worst, a list and ranking society. We want to know the average, the top, the worst, the mean, the median, and most of us measure ourselves pitilessly against the standard, however we define it. Our students, and our schools, are no different. While we are concentrating on leading an exploration of the power of Martin Luther King's prose, the students—not unexpectedly—want to know whether it will be on the test. We are so pleased with the beginnings of a revision of a student's essay; she wants to know what her grade will be if she keeps on revising.

It's the serpent in the garden, but we can't duck it. We are in the business of teaching, for credit and grade, which in turn lead to an official recognition of achievement—a diploma. What we do is required by law, and we are paid for it. Not only are we expected to keep good records, we are also expected to know, for almost every assignment we give, what we are expecting students to learn (objectives), how we will tell if they learned it (evaluation), and how we will rank students' learning (grading).

That's a stiff assignment for us as English teachers, especially when so much of what we do is, frankly, difficult to quantify. Factual tests clearly don't fit into this category nor do some pieces of writing; but how, for example, do you assign a letter grade to each of the twenty-seven students who for two solid days discussed the meaning of Nathaniel Hawthorne's "Young Goodman Brown"? What constitutes an A or a C in that situation—or do you just give up and give everyone who participated a reasonably good grade? Do you ignore letter grades entirely and move to pass/fail or to check, check-plus, check-minus? If you decline to evaluate individually each student on an activity such as two days of class discussion, aren't you avoiding accountability? How do you justify such an activity if you can't grade it?

Well, the point is you *can* justify such discussion; you can give students credit—and response—for that discussion, but you can't, unlike other areas of academic endeavor, truly grade everything you do in English language arts. Nor should you.

Much of what we do is cumulative and builds on long periods of time. We are rarely given to know if a student's facility with language or a highly complex idea makes a grade-level change in our classroom. We evaluate what we can, and we simply leave the rest to a few instruments: tests, writing assignments, notations of participation and completion. Patti Smith, writing about preparing our students for the future, presents two aspects of literature, only one of which can be easily graded:

> Everyone agrees that education is supposed to prepare one for the future. The best way to do this is to prepare [students] intellectually, not with the ability to supply the names of the main characters of *Hamlet,* but with the ability to make the connection between *Hamlet* and modern problems. Critical thinking, that's what kids should learn in English class.

And while, certainly, one can grade aspects of a student's critical thinking about *Hamlet* (there has to be some external evidence that a student has connected the play with modern problems), it is a lot easier to grade his or her knowledge of the play's main characters and plot.

Our job, ladies and gentlemen, is not an easy one.

We also want to avoid the scene described below (even though we may admire the teacher's temporary solution and even though in this case the students responded positively):

> There was one incident that occurred in [my English teacher's] class that stands out in my mind and describes him and his philosophy of teaching perfectly. Since I was in an Advanced Placement class, the class was small (15 students). Most of my classmates were ambitious, competitive, goal-oriented kids. This is good . . . to a point. All they cared about were grades. They wanted to know at all times what was needed for a grade, and essays and subjective tests drove them crazy. The teacher hated this attitude. He wanted to have discussions and to make these kids think for themselves, not memorize for a grade.
>
> One day the grade-oriented students were really anxious. They kept asking how they were going to be graded on some assignments. They were wasting a great deal of time and we could not get back to the topic being discussed. Something triggered him; he went off! One of the students told him that he had to know how he was going to be graded because of college entrance requirements. Then the student went on to say he wanted to be taught what he needed to know for college and what he needed to know to score high on the SAT's. [The teacher] looked at us and said that he wasn't training us for a few crummy classes in college. . . . The next day he came in and tore up the grade book and said that from here on out it would be pass or fail. The only requirements for an A would be real discussions and participation. . . . After that day, class was great. The pressure was gone, and we could really discuss topics.
>
> —MELISSA CAMPBELL

Yet, as a student in the middle of her student teaching writes, the pressure to give and get grades is powerful:

> [Teaching] is frustrating because I want so much for all of my kids to do well. I have had to veer away from taking their success (or failure) as my success (or failure). To a certain extent, I must look at the whole class and evaluate if my teaching is soaking in. This can be gathered from looking at them, listening to them, and checking performance. But I realize now that not everyone is going to get an "A." It took me a long time to accept this.
>
> —JULIE LEPARD

And it may take you some time to sort out your feelings about grades and their pressures and realities. Regardless, they are a feature of school and the teaching life, and until things change markedly in public education, you will need to make your own compromise with grades and quantification, a subject that will run through almost all the chapters of this book.

Teacher, student, school. The three intertwine perhaps more intimately than you had first imagined. Our job is to find a balanced configuration that truly serves learning and teaching and that does not kill the mind and extinguish the spirit. It is an ongoing issue, an ongoing struggle of school, and no teacher, veteran or novice, has a quick or even permanent answer as to the exact dimensions of the balance. It is, actually, a daily endeavor, depending upon context and myriad other factors, and it is one of the most important jobs facing a teacher.

FOR YOUR JOURNAL

Look back at the five "constraints" you will face in the public school setting (pages 24–30). Choose any two of them and make *your* list of options/alternatives/practices that *you* think could lessen the impact of these potentially negative forces.

Think about your own schooling or what you have observed in school visits; what constraints do you remember experiencing or seeing?

Imagine an ideal school: How would it avoid the problems discussed above? What would the teachers be like? What attitudes/expectations would students have? How would an ideal community support an ideal school?

REFERENCES

Aikin, Wilford M. *The Story of the Eight-Year Study.* New York: Harper & Brothers, 1942.

Applebee, Arthur N. *Tradition and Reform in the Teaching of English.* Urbana, IL: NCTE, 1974.

Bruner, Jerome S. *The Process of Education.* New York: Random House, 1963.

Commission on the Reorganization of Secondary Education of the NEA. *Cardinal Principles of Secondary Education.* Washington, DC: GPO, 1918.

Counts, George S. *Dare the School Build a New Social Order?* New York: Arno Press, 1969.

Creely, Robert. "A Form of Women." In *Contemporary American Poetry,* edited by A. Poulin, Jr., 57. Boston: Houghton Mifflin, 1971.

Dewey, John. *Democracy and Education.* New York: Macmillan, [1916] 1961.

Donaldson, Margaret. *A Study of Children's Thinking.* London: Tavistock, 1963.

Eliot, T. S. *The Complete Poems and Plays 1909–1950.* New York: Harcourt Brace & World, 1952.

An Experience Curriculum in English. A Report of the Curriculum Committee of the National Council of Teachers of English (Wilbur W. Hatfield, Chairman). New York: D. Appleton-Century Company, 1935.

Featherstone, Helen. "Making Diversity Educational: Alternatives to Ability Grouping." *Changing Minds.* Michigan Educational Extension Service, Bulletin 4 (Fall). East Lansing, MI: 1991.

Flood, James, Julie M. Jensen, Dianne Lapp, James R. Squire, eds. *Handbook of Research on Teaching the English Language Arts.* New York: Macmillan, 1991.

Furhmann, Barbara Schneider. *Adolescence, Adolescents.* 2d ed. Glenview, IL: Scott Foresman/Little Brown, 1990.

Hawley, Richard A. "Teaching as Failing." *Phi Delta Kappan* 60 (April 1979): 597–600.

Hawthorne, Nathaniel. "Young Goodman Brown." In *Hawthorne: Selected Tales and Sketches.* 3d ed. San Francisco: Rinehart Press, 1970

Hughes, Langston. "Harlem." In *Selected Poems of Langston Hughes,* 268. New York: Vintage, 1959.

Muth, K. Denise and Donna E. Alvermann. *Teaching and Learning in the Middle Grades.* Lexington, MA: Allyn & Bacon, 1992.

Oakes, Jeannie. *Keeping Track: How Schools Structure Inequality.* New Haven, CT: Yale University Press, 1985.

O'Neill, Eugene. *Selections: The Emperor Jones. Anna Christie. The Hairy Ape.* New York: Vintage, 1972.

Oxford English Dictionary. New York: Oxford University Press, 1971.

Pearl. Edited by E. V. Gordon. New York: Oxford University Press, 1966.

Peck, Richard. *Unfinished Portrait of Jessica.* New York: Delacorte, 1991.

Piaget, Jean. *The Language and Thought of the Child.* 3d ed. London: Routledge & Kegan Paul, 1959.

Postman, Neil and Charles Weingartner. *Teaching as a Subversive Activity.* New York: Delacorte, 1969.

Pound, Ezra. "In a Station of the Metro." In *Lustra of Ezra Pound,* 45. New York: Haskell House, 1973.

Rilke, Rainer Maria. "Archaic Torso of Apollo." In *Translations from the Poetry of Rainer Maria Rilke,* 181. Translated by M. D. Herter Norton. New York: Norton, 1962.

Salinger, J. D. *The Catcher in the Rye.* Boston: Little, Brown, 1991.

Shakespeare, William. *Complete Plays and Poems of William Shakespeare.* Edited by William Allan Neilson and Charles Jarvis Hill. Boston: Houghton Mifflin, 1942.

United States Department of Education. *A Nation at Risk.* Washington, DC: GPO, 1983.

Vygotsky, Lev. *Mind in Society: The Development of Higher Mental Processes.* Cambridge, MA: Harvard University Press, 1978.

Wolfe, Thomas. *Look Homeward, Angel.* New York: Scribner, 1952.

Woolf, Virginia. *The Waves.* New York: Harcourt Brace, 1931.

Wordsworth, William. *The Prelude/Selected Poems and Sonnets.* New York: Holt, Rinehart &Winston, 1948.

Wright, Richard. *Native Son.* New York: Grosset & Dunlop, 1940.

RESOURCES

Most of the books listed here are histories or seminal reports on American education. The Cremin is highly respected, the Freire work is a landmark in literacy education, and the Gilligan takes a close look at adolescent girls.

Boyer, Ernest L. *High School: A Report on Secondary Education in America.* New York: Harper & Row, 1983.

Carter, Kathy. "The Place of Story in the Study of Teaching and Teacher Education." *Educational Researcher* 22 (January–February 1993): 5–12,18.

Cremin, Lawrence A. *The Transformation of the School.* New York: Random House, 1961.

Cuban, Larry. *How Teachers Taught: Constancy and Change in American Classrooms, 1890–1990.* 2d ed. New York: Teachers College Press, 1993.

Dixon, John. *Growth Through English: A Report Based on the Dartmouth Seminar.* Urbana, IL: NCTE, 1967.

Freire, Paulo. *Pedagogy of the Oppressed.* New York: Continuum, 1981.

Gilligan, Carol, Nona P. Lyons, Trudy J. Hanmer, eds. *Making Connections: The Relational Worlds of Adolescent Girls at Emma Willard School.* Troy, NH: Emma Willard School, 1989.

Goodlad, John I. *A Place Called School: Prospects for the Future.* New York: McGraw-Hill, 1984.

Greene, Maxine. *The Dialectic of Freedom.* New York: Teachers College Press, 1988.

Powell, Arthur G. et al. *The Shopping Mall High School: Winners and Losers in the Educational Marketplace.* Boston: Houghton Mifflin, 1985.

Ravitch, Diane. *The Schools We Deserve: Reflections on the Educational Crises of Our Times.* New York: Basic Books, 1985.

Schlechty, Phillip C. *Schools for the Twenty-first Century: Leadership Imperatives for Educational Reform.* San Francisco: Jossey-Bass, 1991.

Spring, Joel. *American Education: An Introduction to Social and Political Aspects.* New York: Longman, 1988.

———. *The American School 1642–1990: Varieties of Historical Interpretation of the Foundations and Development of American Education.* New York: Longman, 1990.

CHAPTER 2

WHAT IT TAKES TO BE A TEACHER

In order to arrive at what you are not
*   You must go through the way in which you are not.*
And what you do not know is the only thing you know
And what you own is what you do not own
And where you are is where you are not.

— T. S. Eliot, "East Coker" (***The Four Quartets***)

From Expert Learner to Novice Teacher

Being and becoming a teacher

It was a late afternoon in the fall of my first year of teaching. The students had all gone home, the buses had lumbered off, most of the other teachers had packed up for the day, but I was still mopping up details from the day and working in my classroom. I took a break and stepped for a minute into the long corridor of the first floor. I looked down the hall and saw the row of closed classrooms and a few locker doors left ajar. Some stray student books littered the corridor; a few papers had fallen out of notebooks and had not been swept up. I smelled the rubber stuff the janitor sprinkled on the floors to help with the cleaning and polishing and heard the distant voices of the few teachers and students left in the building.

This was school at the end of the day, and I was a new teacher. But standing alone in the quiet corridor, something made me recall, for a strong pulse, a view of school I had repressed for many years. Right then, I felt and remembered how school had for a brief but important period in my life often scared me, terrified me. School had been a place not of success but of failure and disapproval. I felt my stomach tighten as I remembered three specific, chaotic years.

It was when my family was in crisis, and I came to my elementary school, more often than not, with clothes askew, hair uncombed, and, more to the point, homework incomplete and tests not studied for. My teachers made their disapproval clear, my grades fell, and no one at home was available to help. I managed as best I could, but for most of those three years, I feared and hated school.

I looked around me, down the hall, in the building where I was now teaching—it was, yes, that same place, that familiar, alien, scary place: school. What in the world, I wondered in a sick rush, was I doing *as a teacher in a school*? Was I going to be one of those people who had succeeded in so frightening me for those three years? Was I going to spend five hours a day, five days a week doing to others what had been done to me?

It was a jarring, dislocating moment in my early teaching career. Because I could not deal directly with it or make sense of it in my new context as a teacher, I chose to set that bitter, but accurate, memory aside and literally move on. I went back into the classroom and got to work on a stack of papers. For years I could not think the incident through as I could not really understand it, and I did not want to consider what its implications might be. It was only much later I recognized what was happening: I was shifting, and it wasn't easy or pleasant, from student to teacher. I knew in that moment that school, which had not always been a wonderful place for me, was now my place of employment and teachers, who at one point in my life had terrified me, were now my professional colleagues. I had to make a new vision, which I did, that school was my home and I was a teacher. I also realized later that I could call upon my memories of being a frightened child to help me understand my students for whom school was also hostile and disapproving. The dislocation became actually a positive force, and I accepted my memory—school-as-scary-place—as an asset in understanding.

You may have no such mixed memories in your history, but regardless, there is no way to soft-pedal the fact: the shift from student learner to teacher learner is a tough one. It is no small exaggeration that the world looks very different on the other side of the desk, and for some novices it is almost a loss of innocence to confront the classroom with the chalkboard *behind* you. Making that transition is a difficult one under the best of circumstances; you have had some success in school or you would not envision becoming a teacher, but the shift from a member of the class to the principal organizer of the class is not automatic or, as in my case, a graceful event.

Teaching is also, as you suspect, a tough profession. One indication of its toughness is the limited number of longtime members of the profession: the number of teachers with twenty years experience has dropped 50 percent from 1965 to 1980, and 40 percent of those teachers say they would not enter the profession again (Fuhrmann, 176).

So why do teachers stay in the classroom?

One of the widest studies of the profession, *Schoolteacher*, by Dan C. Lortie, which involved almost 6,000 teachers, gives somewhat of an answer. Lortie found that teachers' overwhelmingly greatest satisfaction is the interaction with students; other "rewards" such as salary, community status, security, summer vacation time, and freedom from competition are much lower on the scale (105). Lortie calls what teachers cited as the interaction with students a "psychic" reward (103ff.), and it is true for many veteran teachers and is why they continue to meet first period every morning.

But *becoming* a teacher is a different matter, and often the psychic rewards are not as apparent early in the game. Becoming a teacher sometimes involves unlearning what you know or think you know—and possibly involves recognizing that what you may assume about teaching is, as T. S. Eliot writes, precisely what you do not know.

Lee Shulman, a professor at Stanford and a respected figure in the study of how people become teachers, writes:

[One of the reasons] it is so difficult to learn to teach is that, unlike many other professions, people who learn to teach learn it after having completed, in Dan Lortie's phrase, a seventeen year "apprenticeship of observation." They have spent seventeen years, more or less, and nearly 20,000 hours as observers of teaching and they've learned an enormous amount about it. . . . Another reason learning to teach is difficult, is that much of learning to teach depends on learning from experience. . . . The whole idea of learning from experience is: I do something, it doesn't work, so I try something else until I finally find something that does work. It's a kind of thoughtful trial and error, but it's predicated on two assumptions: one, we have reasonably accurate access to what we do, and two, we are reasonably accurate in identifying the consequences of what we do. But it is very difficult to establish those two assumptions.

Thus we come into the classroom with our own history as students—and a relatively successful history at that—and we assume that what we see in our own classes is not only what is happening there but that we can figure out the effects of what is happening. Sometimes we are very wrong.

Characteristics of good teachers

There are a number of studies about personality traits that teachers need to be successful, and some education or certification programs even administer personality tests to their students to ensure that students are psychologically equipped for the profession. Most teachers know, however, that successful teachers have a formidable range of personalities and that the classroom atmospheres those teachers foster can be remarkably varied. Beyond that range, however, there are a few generalizations we can make. Successful teachers:

- **Like people (young people in particular)**: Some folks even rather humorously advocate being "arrested in development" in order to be a successful teacher, but it is true that you must almost have an appetite for the age group you teach. Those who thrive in middle school, for example, express a certain affinity for persons that age and the characteristics of their developmental level.
- **Can be flexible:** You may have the whole day planned only to find that an assembly has been scheduled—with little advance warning—for all of your second-period and part of your third-period classes. You may find that your lesson plan that worked well for the morning section of a course is a bomb with the afternoon section. The two students whose reports were going to take up half the period need all the period; one of your students is upset by something and is quietly crying. Successful teachers adjust and adjust quickly.
- **Can draw appropriate conclusions from classroom observation:** Students are bored or disaffected; the small-group arrangements in third period were especially successful; over half the class did not understand the homework reading assignment. A number of factors may explain these observations, and the successful teacher makes a judgment regarding subsequent planning.
- **Listen actively and attentively to students:** Students often tell teachers nearly all they need to know if indeed the teachers have, as the biblical aphorism tells us, the ears to hear and the eyes to see. Students also will share more in class if they have the impression their comments are being really listened to. It is important to recognize the overt *text* of what our students say and the covert

subtext of what they are saying. Successful teachers make appropriate eye contact, don't interrupt, listen, and through body language get students to feel their remarks are worth attending to.

- **Have a sense of humor:** Laughter, in its best manifestation, is emotional warmth, and both students and teachers can make significant personal contact through lighthearted exchanges. You do not need to have the skill of a stand-up comic, but you do need to have a sense of play and liveliness. This, of course, does not embrace the extremes of humor, which are often best left to one's peers. The use of mocking remarks, sarcasm, or jokes at students' expense are unpleasant and often scarring, but the happiness of a more gentle humor can permeate a successful teacher's classroom.

- **Have a sense of intellectual curiosity—both their own and their students':** Truly exciting things happen in the classroom, especially when the parties involved are somewhat prepared to be surprised and pleased and intrigued. "Why is that so? If it is true, what else could be true? Does anyone know about, has anyone heard of _____ ?" are all questions that can open doors of exploration. Good teachers ask these questions frequently.

For Your Journal

Think about your personality and who you are. How would you describe yourself to others? Don't be modest; list six or so of your best traits. Then look at those traits and pick two or three that you think will *help* you be a good teacher. Why do you think those traits are important? How do you think they will function in your interaction in the classroom?

What a Teacher Needs to Do

One of my favorite books about teaching is *After the Lesson Plan: Realities of High School Teaching.* Amy Puett Emmers is a veteran teacher, and her book is both hard-nosed and compassionate. Emmers believes a teacher has four major tasks. They are:

1. **A teacher must gain students' attention.**
2. **A teacher must insist that students perform at the level of their ability.**
3. **A teacher must provide consequences for learning.**
4. **A teacher must recognize and insist.** (xiv, xv, 60)

Gaining students' attention

We all remember classes where the students were having a great time carrying on their own conversations while the teacher futilely tried to either quiet them or just talk above them. During her student teaching, Debbie Martin recalls one class:

> Third period—GAWD!!!! . . . When I asked them to pleeease quiet down for the video [we were seeing], it was as if I wasn't in the room—there was a total disregard for anything & everyone except what they were interested in. I repeated my request several times by standing in the middle of the room saying, "Excuse me, excuse me, please. Let's get quiet. Let's

not be rude to those who wish to watch the video." One student shouted, "Hey! show some respect." I thanked her and started the video.

On a longer-term basis, we also can remember semesters where we just endured a course (and a teacher), resigned that we were not going to learn or do much of anything interesting. Sometimes we wondered if the teacher noticed what we certainly knew. Sometimes we made the best of the class by daydreaming, passing notes, or surreptitiously talking with friends.

Actually this activity has been studied and researched. In an article you may find interesting, Robert Brooke discusses and categorizes the "underlife" of a classroom, a sociological term that "refers to those behaviors which undercut roles expected of participants in a situation . . . [for example] students disobey, write letters instead of taking notes, and whisper with their peers to show they are more than just students and can think independently of classroom expectations" (141). While much of this is normal classroom behavior, when carried to an extreme it can be highly disruptive and certainly can be demoralizing to class order. And when it happens in your classroom, it can be a real problem.

Emmers suggests a number of principles to help us gain—and keep—our students' attention:

- **Interest students in the subject matter and relate it to their lives.**
- **Build on what the students know.**
- **Discuss, don't lecture.**
- **Answer student questions.**
- **Provide an element of excitement through reasonable competition.** (23–47)

As you will see later in this chapter, the discovery model of teaching may be closest to what Emmers suggests. Certainly, when we care about our students' learning, it is rather automatic that we will adopt many of Emmers's suggestions in our teaching.

Insisting students perform at the level of their ability

This may seem so obvious that it is simpleminded, but the difficulty is that we are often clueless about where our students truly are in their level of ability. Test scores and grades are not the reliable indications you may have been led to believe. People also, we know from cognitive psychology, can "plateau" in their development—stay at the same level for long periods—and then make remarkable gains in relatively rapid periods of time. How do we know where they are? While students with disabilities need special help and those who are unwilling need prodding, Emmers is most concerned about our setting limits on the other students. She counsels:

> We still know very little about what actually occurs in the brain when people learn. Moreover, teachers cannot possibly be aware of all of the many factors that contribute to their students' motivation to learn. Is it really the function of teachers ever to discourage a student from attempting something he wants to do? If he can't do it, he'll discover that soon enough for himself. He certainly won't thank anybody for advance information about his shortcomings.
>
> When asked whether he knows how to do any specific task, whatever it is, a friend of mine usually replies, "Maybe I do; I haven't tried." Most people smile at his whimsy, which they do not regard as a very realistic appraisal of ability. Perhaps, though, students would

benefit if teachers could be just this optimistic. Teachers would not be requiring anyone to do what he can't. They would not be forcing anyone to do what he really doesn't wish. Rather they would be trying to extend a student's possibilities. After all, maybe he can! (87)

And perhaps the tragedy of many classrooms is not that we ask too much of our students—but that we ask too little. Certainly when we assume that a "less able" or "slower" group cannot handle classroom tasks above the level of filling in worksheets, we are not trying to get our students to perform at the level of their ability. Nor are we giving them the chance to move to a higher level.

Providing consequences for learning

There are many ways to reward learning: with praise, class privileges, posting of work on bulletin boards or publishing it in anthologies, congratulatory notes sent home, grades, awards. Once students are motivated and capable of the work level, they will perform. What about students, however, who are not motivated or not capable? While teachers need to make their best effort and attempt, rather unceasingly, to capture students' attention and motivation, there is a limit. Emmers writes:

> For teachers to blame themselves unnecessarily when students are inattentive or unmoti-
> vated is a waste of time and emotion, for it is, after all, an individual student who must
> change these conditions. Teachers can't do it for him. All they can do is try to conduct the
> kind of class in which uninterested students will at least be tempted to reverse their feelings
> about the subject. (57–58)

Beginning teachers especially feel the sting of students who refuse to engage in class. While we have an ethical obligation to do our best in a class, we also must acknowledge that teachers cannot learn *for* the student, cannot study for them, and cannot be motivated for them. We can create the classroom atmosphere that emphasizes all students should—and can—do their best, but we cannot ensure that everyone is engaged all the time. For students who, despite our best efforts, resist working in our classes, often we have no choice but to give them the grades they have earned. And just showing up is not enough; if we make that a sufficient standard, we certainly cannot expect that students will do anything resembling work once they cross the classroom threshold.

Recognizing and insisting

Besides the three tasks listed above, Emmers also articulates a teaching principle that is worth lingering over: *recognizing and insisting*. She writes:

> At the opposite extreme from those students who for whatever reason can't do the work are
> those who are capable but won't do it. While there are various causes for students' not
> working, or at least not working as much as they should, most . . . think they can get by
> without doing the assignments. They are also convinced that what they neglect won't make
> much difference in their lives. (68)

Again, our students come largely by compulsion—which can make the relationship in the class a difficult one. On the other hand, a student's very presence in a class can imply that she or he is there to learn; as teachers we recognize that. We can also insist that we be allowed to teach the reluctant students as well as the others. Class is for learning; participation, in some form, is a way towards that learning.

Perhaps one of the worst things we can do with our students is ignore them, minimize them. We need to let students know we know them and that they are in our classes; while they are there, we need to insist upon their participation. Indifference is, ultimately, killing. We have an obligation to see and recognize our charges and to demand from them as much as we can—we must insist on their learning. To do less is to turn our backs on them and, ultimately, on ourselves.

FOR YOUR JOURNAL

The four tasks that Emmers believes teachers should address are similar to many such lists. If we use what she counsels as a springboard for discussion, how would you rank or prioritize those four tasks? Which is the most important? Why? Which seems the least important? Why? Remember to think more from a teacher's point of view than a student's.

Five Models of Teaching

Adopting a teaching model

My own teaching model was shaped, first, by what I had experienced as a student and, second, by the experience of my own students as I myself became a teacher. What I remembered—and treasured—from my favorite teachers was their ability to set a stage for discovery and talk. The best of my teachers seemed interested in what we had to say and let us grope through many wrong turnings to find out what indeed was not only important to us but what was true. From these teachers I felt I had had an opportunity to learn, to find on my own. And I remembered the learning, which was *my* learning, not someone else's.

It was learning to love the questions, for, as seers have often pointed out, we are often not ready for the answers. I still am not ready for some answers—that, by the way, is part of the wonderful discovery of teaching; it is a self-renewing enterprise when it is at its best, and, with our students, we explore.

My students helped me develop a model of teaching. Most of them, even the more traditionally polite, had a highly limited patience with listening to *me*. At the extreme, I found students who not only were impatient about listening but who would just not do it. They needed to be involved and active and to find on their own. It was, essentially, an instructional issue for them as much as it was a discipline question.

I found that asking, not telling, was almost always more powerful. Students had to make their own meaning of events or text or writing; it became *our* class, not just mine, and when it was ours, many discipline problems seemed to evaporate. The nonclass-related chatter diminished, and talk revolved around the subject.

When teachers are not interested in their students, when their own telling is the most important, we have a classroom as described by a student, Susanna Field:

> [My English teacher] could have improved her class by coming closer to the students. She could have been more interested in what we had to say. (Because she was not interested, we cared to say nothing.) . . . Also, she could have arranged the desks in a circle, so then we could all discuss with each other, rather than facing the front of the room and merely listening to the teacher.

Thus I set for you a model of teaching that is almost wholly based on asking and constructing events and opportunities for students to find the meaning. It is a skill that takes some practice; it takes patience, yet it, I think, yields probably the only learning that is worth our energy. If we want students to know facts, they need to consult information sources. If, however, we want students to think and explore and weigh and argue, they need an environment and an arena to come up with their own learning. A popular aphorism states, "Give a person a fish, he eats for a day; teach a person to fish, he eats for a lifetime." We must teach our students to fish, not keep handing them the dead ones *we* have gotten from the stream.

There are, in essence, a number of models of teaching—ways of teaching—that are not so much correct and incorrect, right or wrong, but that reflect different philosophies of instruction and approaches to students and appeal to different personality strengths of teachers. Some of this is individual and essentially neutral in character; some of this is part of good practice. There is, however, an essential approach to teaching that is beyond the kind of individual aspects unique to each of us, teaching as discovery, and that model will be presented here as a goal toward which you should strive.

One book on the subject, Bruce Joyce and Marsha Weil's *Models of Teaching,* presents four groups of twenty-five separate models of teaching. The following is a stripped down version of five models you may need to consider in your own teaching. Please note that some of this is developmental; you will naturally be attracted to certain models early in your career. Some of this also is hierarchical; I see the later models as superior to the others. Teaching as telling is the earliest model and the one we want you to move away from. It is also a very necessary step for a beginner: the other models will come, I believe, for you, as they did for me and for many other teachers, with time.

In his study *Twenty Teachers,* Ken Macrorie sees teachers, regardless of grade level or subject matter, as those doing "good works" in the classroom. In the award-winning *The Making of a Teacher,* Pamela Grossman describes a number of beginning teachers and discusses especially how many of them try to replicate their English major experiences in college with their high school students. Robert V. Bullough, Jr.'s *First Year Teacher* explores the experiences of a beginner and her attempts first to survive the classroom and then to truly become a good teacher. *Sometimes a Shining Moment* is former teacher Eliot Wigginton's account of how he got his students to research the community and publish the findings in the now famous *Foxfire* books; social studies teacher Stuart B. Palonsky writes of the strain of teaching in a book appropriately entitled *900 Shows a Year.* In *Home of the Wildcats,* Joan Cutuly writes of some of the hard struggles of teaching. There are dozens of good books about teaching and teachers (some of which are also cited in the resources section at the end of the chapter) and, as you get deeper into this business, you may not only want to read them, you may want to add your voice to the collection. Almost all of these accounts, however, include some of the following models of teaching.

Teaching as telling

When you first thought of being a teacher, one of the early images in your mind was probably that of you standing in front of a class and telling students about a novel or poem, explaining to them a concept or idea, and writing on a chalkboard while students listened to you or watched what you wrote. The sun is shining through the classroom windows, the room is attractively furnished, the students are quiet, and there you are, at the podium, teaching. You are teaching eloquently, and the students are rapt with attention, taking notes and asking, only occasionally, a salient question on the issue. It is an orderly scene, and you are at the head, faced by interested, attentive students.

For many people getting ready to enter the classroom or even for some veteran teachers, teaching is telling, the teacher talking and the students listening. Certainly for most of us early in our career, teaching was a great deal of telling, although as many later found, the longer we taught the farther we moved from this model of teaching.

If this is your image of what middle school or high school English teaching is, I want you to think about it for a minute. Consider: Who is doing the talking? Who is making the connections? Who is giving the examples? Who is in charge? Who is the active one? Shifting the scene: Who is doing the listening? Who is receiving the connections, the examples? Whose mind may be wandering everywhere? Who is the passive one?

How does the teacher know, especially if he or she speaks for a long period—an entire class period—if the students understand, have questions, already know all of the material, part of the material, can extend the material beyond what the teacher is discussing? Is asking "are there any questions?" or checking to see that students are silent or taking notes sufficient to answer this concern?

Clearly I see severe limitations in the model of teaching as telling; I think it is inefficient, overused, and encourages a great deal of student passivity and intellectual laziness. And, from a teacher's point of view, it is exhausting: the teacher is the center and the one upon whom all are dependent. To take that responsibility, undiluted, five periods a day, five days a week, is a recipe for burnout as well as a waste of teacher resource.

Being a talking head is my not my idea of teaching; and I have lost faith in the idea of students being a *tabula rasa,* a blank slate upon which the teacher writes. Similarly, I am concerned about the idea of what Brazilian educator Paulo Freire criticizes as the "banking concept" of education where the teacher makes knowledge deposits into students' heads. These ideas of teaching are often attributed to the factory model of the western Industrial Revolution where education was considered analogous to manufacturing; the students were the raw materials, the factory was the school, and the teachers were the workers who shaped the students into some sort of product, or educated person. All these ideas, teacher as knowledge knower, student as knowledge receiver, sound fairly logical and, indeed, some of them are deeply rooted in our culture. The models, however, are largely based on a few assumptions that we need to examine seriously:

- **Teachers' functions are largely to funnel specific pieces of knowledge to students.**
- **Students' functions are largely to absorb that knowledge, much as they would read a book or view a film.**
- **The reception of such knowledge is active and efficient and also incorporates critical assessment of that knowledge.**
- **The giving of such knowledge is tailored to students' experience, prior knowledge, and difficulties with the subject.**

Many teachers just don't agree. The major problem with teaching as telling is that it is overwhelmingly a one-way street: the person doing the work, including making many of the learning connections, is the teacher, not the student. Listening is rarely that active of an experience, and listening for long periods of time is downright wasteful, if not impossible to sustain, for most students. A teacher who talks most of the class cannot tailor the knowledge or the insight to all of his or her students; students, moreover, do not have the experience of questioning, arguing, and putting into context what they are hearing if the overwhelming activity is simply receiving another's talk.

This is not to say that there are not times when a teacher needs to give students instructions, history, major points. Some of those times, judiciously chosen, are when students need background before they can begin to approach a subject. There is a place for the brief lecture on the use of imagery in modern poetry, for the uses of the semicolon, for the difference between alliteration and assonance. But, very soon after that lecture, it is time for students to take the information and use it, question it, incorporate it, illustrate it, *something* it so that the knowledge does not become someone else's point but their own. As one young man in student teaching, using his first student groups as an effort to help him break the teaching-as-telling mode, wrote:

> **Tuesday, April 3**
> English Literature Class: 3rd Period was motivatingly scary. The students worked in groups (another way for me to cut down on talking). I feel I am actually getting the message of why it's ineffective to talk too much to students. They received their instructions, played some, and talked some, and laughed, and joked, and worked some. And when the groups were presenting their answers, they did it as if they had actually learned what I had intended.
>
> —RONNIE FLEMING

Teaching as inspiration

I have taught a number of students who were rather successful in their own school careers and, understandably, took that skill with them into their new lives as teachers. For many of these students, however, they also took their ability to "wing it" and used that ability in the classroom. While there is surely a place for inspiration—changing the direction or focus of an activity in response to what happened in a previous class, or, indeed, what is happening in that very class at that very time—I urge you to reconsider the model of teaching as inspiration. Teaching as inspiration must grow from the planning that has already been done. Planning, as we will discuss in this chapter, is really the foundation to good teaching, and while no one can realistically map out everything that will happen in every class—nor should they—relying on inspiration and waiting until the last minute to pull a class together won't do you or your students much good.

Teaching as inspiration is based on the following assumptions:

- **Getting students excited is more important than leading them to some sort of intellectual conclusion.**
- **Things always have a tendency to "work out" in a classroom setting.**
- **The freshness of inspiration is always superior to the certainty (read *dullness*) of planning.**

Certainly, as I said before, there are times when it will strike you that an activity could change or be added to right here and right now, and that will help you with your classes, but relying solely on teaching as inspiration will not substitute for mapping out instructional activities before class. Teaching a short story you have not read, asking students to do exercises you have not reviewed, showing a film you have never seen, or making up a classroom activity on the spot is part of poor planning and can—not always, but can—result in some tense classroom moments and some instructional gaffes. Further, it is likely that some smart student will know just how unprepared you are.

Part of your job as a professional is to come to class prepared; relying on inspiration is a sloppy way to run your teaching life.

Teaching as maintaining a creation

In the opening of Nancie Atwell's *In the Middle*, she describes herself early in her career as an organizer and planner who carefully, minutely created a class and its organization and then, essentially, maintained that creation throughout the year. With the best of intentions, she set a complicated system "in motion" and simply made it endure throughout the school year. Atwell writes:

> I confess. I started out as a creationist. The first days of every school year I created; for the next thirty-six weeks I maintained my creation. My curriculum. From behind my big desk I set it in motion, managed and maintained it all year long. I wanted to be a great teacher—systematic, purposeful, in control. . . . I didn't learn in my classroom. I tended and taught my creation (3).

A teacher such as Atwell describes herself is indeed in control and manages a classroom much as one would manage any system. As she writes in another article, "Sitting there at my big desk, developing new assignments and evaluating the results, I remained oblivious to . . . my students' ideas, experiences, and expertise. I remained in charge" ("Everyone Sits," 35).

Teaching as maintaining a creation is based on the following assumptions:

- **Teaching has more to do with systems and patterns and rules than with the shifting demands of learning.**
- **Once a classroom organizational pattern is established, it can successfully guide an entire semester or year of the class.**
- **A teacher can successfully anticipate student needs to the point that any organizational pattern that he or she establishes will be durable for a fixed pattern of time.**

The problem is, of course, what Atwell describes: *I didn't learn in my classroom.* It is not just spineless sentimentality or softheartednesss that leads us to believe that, yes, our students can teach us. Indeed they do—different ways of approaching and different aspects of knowledge. As Atwell describes, we can, and should, shift to another model:

> These days, I learn in my classroom. What happens there has changed; it continually changes. I've become an evolutionist, and the curriculum unfolds now as my kids and I learn together. My aims stay constant . . . but my practices evolve. . . . What I learn with these students . . . makes me a better teacher. (*In the Middle*, 3)

While setting a class's agenda is part of teaching, we have to strike a balance between being the organizer and being the dictator. The latter is not only inefficient—all responsibility falls on the teacher—but it also often means that the students' interest is not captured and capitalized upon. Being in charge, absolutely, always, can stifle our students and box us into an unshakable role as sole authority. Planning and organizing can become a trap: we fall so in love with our own system for our classes that we neglect to revise, adjust, change, to accommodate our students.

Teaching as discovery

We now come to the model I believe will be the most enduring for you as a teacher. A teacher who uses discovery:

- Doesn't necessarily avoid questions to which there is no answer or mind saying, "I don't know."
- Lets students talk.
- Allows pauses in the talk—just like in a real conversation. This means there are periods of silence in the classroom.
- Asks, asks, asks and falls out of love with telling.
- Starts teaching with where the students are, not where the book is or where the teacher is.

It is not as efficient, as many suppose, to be told the point and then find the examples to support it. It's like being told the punch line and then trying to recreate the joke to fit the end, like being told the answer to the algebraic equation and being asked to reconstruct the problem. Using the discovery method, we learn and internalize that learning by finding the point ourselves, by making it our own, by saying it, by stumbling toward it. We avoid overt didacticism, as our knowledge is not our students' knowledge, our revelation about a poem or play or language principle is not our students'.

If we adopt this teaching model, we must stop asking our students to admire the fine conclusions we have reached or to be in awe at our knowledge of any given subject. Instead, we allow them to lurch through to their own. This is the major health in the act of teaching. I often wonder if, actually, it is the only one.

Teaching as a reflective practitioner

It is important that you add into your teaching life the concept of reflecting on what you do in your classes and what your students do and what seem to be the outcomes. The aphorism, "Those who do not know history are doomed to repeat it" may have some bearing on this discussion: if you are unaware or do not consider not only why a class was unsuccessful but why it was *successful,* it would seem virtually impossible for you to progress in your teaching life. In fact, the whole idea of a teacher being a researcher within the context of his or her own classes is a large part of being a reflective practitioner.

The field of reflection can be summarized, perhaps, by four very salient questions. Researcher Bud Wellington cites them:

1. **What do I do?** ("observational description of practice")
2. **What does this mean?** ("principles of theories-in-use . . . which underlie and drive the described practice")
3. **How did I come to be this way?** ("forces our awareness beyond the classroom . . . correctly reveals educational practice as essentially political")
4. **How might I do things differently?** ("gives us the call to action") (5)

Wellington notes that these questions "are not intended as rhetorical . . . for casual consideration over tea. Rather, they are intended to raise consciousness, to challenge complacency, and to engender a higher order of professional practice" (5). When we ask these questions about our classes and our teaching—before we embark on a class or after it, as evaluation and follow-up—we are being reflective about our models of teaching. When we alter our teaching in response to the answers to the questions, we are being responsible and responsive.

Teaching *The Color Purple* and the Five Models

So, let's take a piece of literature and look at it from the point of view of each of the five models.

Pulitzer Prize winner Alice Walker's *The Color Purple* has become popular in some high school English classes. While its mature themes and frank language make it unacceptable in most middle school settings (and, indeed, those factors can also prevent it from being used in secondary schools), it is nevertheless on a number of reading lists across the country. The novel is a strong one that deals with important questions; it uses an intriguing form (it is an epistolary novel, written as a series of letters). *The Color Purple* is also characterized by direct language and a powerful and gripping plot.

If the teaching model were **teaching as telling**, a teacher using *The Color Purple* could more than likely engage in the following activities:

- Give students a brief lecture on the definition and characteristics of the epistolary novel and ask them to find examples in *The Color Purple* to illustrate those characteristics.
- Cite the major themes of the novel and ask students to find illustrative incidents.
- List the major characters of the novel and ask students to define their roles.
- Give students worksheets with important quotations and have students explain why those quotations are significant.
- Tell students about the history and importance of the Pulitzer Prize and then have them justify why the novel deserved the Pulitzer Prize.
- Review the parts of a plot for students and have them identify rising action, falling action, and one climax.

If a teacher was relying upon **inspiration,** he or she might make a few notes on the novel and start the class hoping that someone would bring up important issues. The teacher would follow the students' lead and pursue whatever came up. The length of the "study" might be one day, might be a week; it might lead to other literature or not.

A **maintaining-a-creation** model would involve *The Color Purple* as part of a thematic unit or genre study, orchestrated and integrated with other pieces and following the same pattern of discussion and investigation as pieces of literature in the previous part of the unit. The topics to be discussed would be strictly established as would the time spent on each topic or activity. It would not be unusual for the test on the novel to be written before the actual teaching of the novel.

A **discovery** model would look different. Instead of the teaching as telling questions listed above, instead of meticulous mapping out of the topics and time and even testing, the teacher would change the focus and emphasis to exploration and discussion. What topics would be lingered on and for how long and what the final evaluation would be would not be immediately established; it would rely on the students. With that as a conceptual frame, the teacher might:

- Ask students about the form of the novel: Was it difficult? Was it helpful? What would happen if the novel were not written in letters? Can you rewrite one section into a narrative form and then compare and contrast the dramatic effect? What is gained? What is lost?

- Ask students about the theme(s) of this novel: How do you know which are the themes or theme? Which seem the most/least important to you? Why?
- Ask students about the characters: Who, by the way, is this novel really about? (Celie? Shug? Mr.?) How do you know? How can you tell? To what extent is it important to decide? Why?
- Ask students to select three quotations that seem important: Why are these quotations important?
- Tell students that some critics have suggested *The Color Purple* just doesn't deserve the Pulitzer Prize, that it was given to Alice Walker largely because she is African American and the committee wanted to redress past discrimination in the award structure: What do you think of that argument? To what extent do you think this novel deserves / does not deserve the Pulitzer Prize? If you were giving a literary prize, what would you select as criteria?
- Ask students to determine if there a climax to this novel: Is there more than one climax? How do you know? Why do you think that? What, by the way, is a *climax*?

A **reflective practitioner** would consider what to do and why in teaching *The Color Purple* and would be sensitive to options (how might I do things differently?). If a reflective practitioner used the discovery activities listed above, he or she would be attentive and make adjustments; the Pulitzer Prize question, for instance, which assumes that students have an interest in literary awards, may be tedious to answer and puzzling. It also raises the spectre of racial discrimination and might be difficult for some classes, especially if the teacher is of a racial majority making the inquiry of a class largely of minority students. Adjustments would need to be made. These could be reflected in the class immediately and in future plans to teach the novel.

For Your Journal

Pick a piece of literature or a skill and consider it from the point of view of the teaching models. If you were to teach it by *telling,* what would you do? If you were to rely on *inspiration,* what might be the shape of the lesson? If you taught the concept in the frame of *maintaining a creation,* what might you ask students to do? Finally, if you had students *discover* the concept, how would you structure the class? Then, as a *reflective practitioner,* what questions would you ask yourself about any or all of the above teaching models and their effectiveness?

It Didn't Work

Teaching as considering instructional options

Another aspect of teaching, especially beginning teaching, is the seductive—but false— idea of teaching as correct and incorrect. Beginning teachers, like beginning anything, tend to think in terms of *right* and *wrong* when it comes to classroom practice. Having sat in on the classes of dozens of student teachers for some ten years, I have yet to find a novice who is not concerned about what he or she did that was in terms of *correct* and *incorrect*. It's maddening news for the beginner, but it's true: there is very little right and wrong in this business. It is, actually, almost wholly as a matter of options, the choice of any one of which yields different outcomes.

Teaching is not right or wrong, things don't just "work" or "not work." It is, both happily and unnervingly, much more complicated than that.

Let me explain: if we could hypothetically assume a lesson plan that would be identically presented to two different classes of students in the same grade in the same school, the outcomes and learnings of those classes would be, despite all efforts of the teacher, very different. The variables are crucial: not only are the students different but their "mix" is different; the sheer number of students is different; the time of day of the class period is different; different things happened the day before in class; and so on. Some of those factors are choices made by the teacher of subject matter and methodology, but some are simply indigenous to school and the varying classes a teacher deals with every day.

And also, as experienced teachers know—sometimes intuitively, sometimes through bitter trial and error—the same lesson plan, technique, or instructional approach cannot be used successfully with all students semester after semester or even from period to period. This may come as an unhappy surprise if you were hoping that after the first year or two your lesson or unit plans would become sort of unchangeable blueprints on which you could rely for many years. Certainly experience will be helpful to you as a teacher, but you will not be able to replicate from year to year or semester to semester entire class plans. Change and adjustment to the many factors that go to make up a class and a group of students is part of successful teaching, and there are many factors to consider.

The variables involved

What can make a successful class? What can contribute to a less than successful one? There are a variety of components, all of which you should know and recognize. As a beginning, however, it is useful to know that there is rarely a single reason for a successful or unsuccessful class. While you may be tempted to point to one thing, it's not just you, the teacher; it's not just your students. It's not only what anyone is studying or how they are studying it or even how long they have spent on it. It's rarely just the school or even the weather. It is a little bit of all of these; every one of these factors can and does interact and affect learning outcomes and learning environment. Let's look at the variables one at a time.

One variable that can affect a classroom is **subject matter**, its **nature, amount,** and its **purpose.**

The **nature** of subject matter can be a factor because that which is familiar and that which is not can affect not only learning but student attitude and classroom environment. For example, sometimes literature that is difficult can be more intriguing to students than that which is readily accessible; on the other hand, starting with familiar material and then moving to the more difficult can give students a sense of security that they might not have if the difficult material was immediately begun.

The **amount** of subject matter is also a crucial variable in classroom success. For example, let's consider the extensiveness of material: a number of nonfiction essays might provide a successful and enjoyable study with a specific group of students for two weeks but be a disaster if stretched into a month. Likewise, a day of poetry can be wonderful; five straight days might be tedious and boring, taking all of the surprise and newness out of the genre. On the other hand, two days working on an essay may leave students puzzled and confused; three days might give them more time to revise and rework.

Looking at **purpose,** material students know has to be learned for a standardized test or because it is a curricular requirement may be viewed very differently from material they have chosen or in which they are taking a newly discovered interest. Even if that material is essentially the same in difficulty, why someone is learning something can affect attitude and actual learning itself.

Often, too, **methodology** is just not successfully interchangeable with all classes. Students, for example, who are used to working in small groups will, with direction, continue to function efficiently and productively in those groups. On the other hand, abruptly putting students who have been fed an exclusive diet of worksheets into small groups can be a disaster. In another area, verbal and assured students will often respond well to a large group discussion; for some students, however, large groups are intimidating or alienating, and the opportunity to talk as a whole class will not be successful.

Setting or school context can also affect classes. As outlined in other chapters, knowing who your students are and what their lives are like outside school can give you crucial clues about what links to establish in making material relevant and what material to select or emphasize. To give a fairly low-level example, students in rural midwestern settings may need background information if they read a short story set in New York City; Western urban students may need the same sort of information regarding poetry about Southern fields and farms.

Veteran teachers also know that at a certain **time** of the day (a split period broken by lunch, for example) or at a certain time of the year (late spring, for instance) certain activities and courses of study will be more successful than others. To illustrate, creative dramatics, which require movement and noise and expressiveness, might best be avoided when students are really excited or keyed up. The first school day after a holiday or the last period of a Friday are times when creative dramatics might not be such a good choice for a classroom activity. I think, from my experience, of the senior research paper. I have found that scheduling the completion of that project in late spring is not very smart. Most seniors by that time of year and at that late date of their high school life really don't have their minds set on research or the format of a bibliography. It is better, I have found, to schedule the completion of such a long project in the late fall or winter.

Of course, another variable is you, the **teacher**. Your degree of experience, your enthusiasm for and knowledge of any given subject, even your mood on a particular day can truly affect your classes. Imagine that you are, for example, still unsure of the difference between restrictive and nonrestrictive clauses and yet you are going to give fifth bell a ten-minute minilesson on the subject. All other things being equal, just how relaxed do you anticipate that ten minutes will be? How receptive do you think you might be to a possible barrage of questions from puzzled students? How many inventive examples do you think you will be putting on the overhead? Chances are, with the best of intentions, what you present will be tight, to the point, and not very expansive. And, as you can imagine, that type of presentation might have an effect on your students and the class atmosphere. Contrast this in your mind with a class period talking about one of your favorite plays. Can you imagine how your attitude might affect the class itself? Finally, you may have had personal issues or problems that are worrying you; leaving your own problems, however legitimate they may be, at the classroom door is a habit you may just be learning.

Of course, the **students**, their experience, background, and maturity are a powerful variable in the success of any classroom. Knowing and adjusting to your students is vital in making instruction "work."

The teaching act, as experienced teachers know and beginning ones quickly learn, is a complex event and is influenced by a myriad of variables: when novice teachers report "it didn't work," they are actually talking about numerous factors.

To recap, the problem begins with the nebulous "it." Is "it" the interest or appropriateness of the subject matter? the success of the students' activities? the teacher's instructional methodology? the students' learning outcomes? the students' responses and general satisfaction?

We also need to look at the even more vague "work." What didn't "work"? Did the majority of students fail a test? Did the students seem confused about a concept? Did class discipline disintegrate? Was the teacher simply dissatisfied with the lesson or unit?

There are a number of variables involved, and while "it didn't work" is not an unimportant or easily resolved worry, it can be more readily handled with a conceptual framework that can help break teaching and learning into component parts.

A paradigm for analyzing the teaching act

Let us imagine a paradigm for learning that is, essentially, A producing B or B resulting from A:

A Paradigm for Analyzing the Teaching Act

Subject matter of this nature
        in this amount
        for this purpose
with *methodology* of this type,
in this *situation* or *setting,*
and in this *time,*
with a *teacher* of this disposition
        this background and
        these qualities,

           A

PRODUCES

these *patterns of affective and cognitive learning,*
in *students* at this level of development and maturity
        with this level of experience and
        with this kind of background.
(Christenbury, 233–39)

           B

Without belaboring what may appear as a perfectly self-explanatory model, let's look at some obvious (if not simpleminded) questions to highlight the components.

Subject matter of this nature   To what extent is the complexity of British seventeenth century metaphysical poetry accessible to all students? What kind of ethnic studies can be / should be taught in a community? What kind of student response will there be to an intensive consideration of spelling rules? Do all students need and find useful the formal argumentative essay?

Subject matter in this amount   Should a teacher present major punctuation rules in an intensive unit or intersperse them with other material? Should novels be read and taught extensively or intensively? Do students learn more producing a final draft of a piece every week or every other week?

Subject matter for this purpose   Is there a difference between teaching something as a review or because students requested it? How do students respond if a teacher spontaneously adds material to a class? If a subject is taught as part of a curricular requirement, to what degree can student interest be affected?

Methodology   Do some classes enjoy large group discussion? Do some classes respond well to small group work? Do some students seem to like silent reading and working alone? Is work at a computer successful with the majority of students? How can pair work be used?

Situation or setting   Is the last period or bell of the day appropriate for certain types of instructional activities? In what ways are the bells that are usually usurped for assemblies and pep rallies affected by the disruption? Should the approach for a split lunch period be different from that for first period?

Time   Considering the students in a particular class, are two days enough to review imagery? Is one month too long for the reading of a novel? Are three weeks sufficient for the reading of a play? How many days do students need to work on a rough draft?

Teacher   Does a teacher's experience, academic qualifications, and personality characteristics affect a class? To what extent can his or her level of confidence and ease with students be a factor in teaching success? Can all teachers readily adapt to all types of methodology?

Patterns of affective and cognitive learning   Are all groups of students equally able to understand all levels of material? Do some students understand material but remain disengaged? Can some students thoroughly enjoy some material but not completely comprehend it? Should a teacher demand emotional (or affective) responses of any kind? A mix of cognitive and affective? Cognitive only? When? Why?

Students   Do some students, regardless of chronological age, seem more mature than others? What forms does this maturity take in the classroom? Do "above average" students react differently and learn differently from "disadvantaged" students? Are urban and suburban students alike in their instructional needs? What about students for whom English is a second language?

Now that you are completely depressed and overwhelmed by the above questions, know that they are the issues that veteran teachers perhaps never fully answer but do learn to consider, especially when we wonder why something didn't "work" in the classroom. Knowing the questions in this case may be more important than knowing the answers, and it may help you when you know that a class didn't go well or, yes, just didn't work.

Playing a game with teaching variables

So let's play a game with the teaching variables. Let's imagine you know everything *but* the type of learning that may occur. Thus, you will have six variables and will need to speculate or predict *one*. You will need to work in a group of three.

First, the group will need to prepare index cards representing the six categories of variables discussed on pages 47–49. To begin, let's simplify the game and imagine that the subject matter is a short story and that the discussion will center on the other five variables and that short story.

Using a different card for each variable under each heading, write out the variables and place them in six piles of three.

(I) Subject Matter (nature, amount, and purpose)   Cards one, two, and three: a seven-page modern American short story in the anthology, part of the school curriculum

(II) Methodology   Card one: reading the story out loud and following it with a large-group discussion. Card two: reading the story for homework and doing a short journal entry / writing response as a prelude to small-group discussion. Card three: reading the story silently the previous day and then discussing it in small groups

(III) Setting (period / day of week / time of year)   Card one: first period, Monday, early fall. Card two: fifth period, Friday, late spring. Card three: third period, Wednesday, winter, assembly day.

(IV) Time   Card one: all of the period/bell. Card two: two consecutive periods/bells. Card three: two nonconsecutive periods/bells (e.g., Monday and Thursday).

(V) Teacher   Card one, two, and three: you. (When you are further along in your career you might want to consider including two of your colleagues; you will then know teaching "styles" a bit more intimately.)

(VI) Students   Card one: class of 18, considered average. Card two: class of 31, considered high ability. Card three: class of 22, considered reluctant learners.

Once the cards have been written out, have a group member shuffle the cards in each category and, in turn, select one card from each of the six categories. When you are through, each member of the group should have six cards, one card representing subject matter, one representing methodology, and so on.

Now, silently study what the fates have given you and imagine that this mix is your class. Spend about five minutes and make a few notes to yourself. Then in the group, go around in a circle and have each person briefly present what his or her variables are and what, regarding the success of teaching this short story, the person guesses would be the possible results.

Factors each member of the group should consider include: What, given the best guesses you can make, do you predict about learning outcomes with specific students? What problem areas (if any) do you think you would need to be aware of? What adjustments do you speculate you might need to make in the classroom?

Even if your assumptions and predictions are off-center, it will give you a chance to consider, given the components of a teaching act, what kind of effect this combination of variables might have upon the learning of these hypothetical students.

As a variation, make up your own game and, in your group of three, brainstorm for a minute the possible specifics that could be placed under each of the six categories. To get you started, look at the following as *Subject Matter* suggestions:

Card one: a 250-page nineteenth-century British novel, required by the county curriculum.
Card two: ten modern American poems in the anthology.

Card three: a three-page persuasive essay written to the school principal on a subject the class has selected.

Card four: the 500-year history of the English language presented by the teacher who studied—and loved—history of the language in college.

As before, write each variable in each category on a separate index card; provide at least three or four variables in each of the five remaining categories: **methodology**, **setting**, **time**, **teacher**, and **students**. Repeat the procedure of choosing six cards, spending time to consider what has been "dealt" you and writing on what you have and what you speculate about learning or classroom outcomes.

While certainly this game is about as hypothetical as it gets—you are making a number of assumptions about students and schools that are largely speculative and, in some cases, based on not much experience or knowledge—it does give you a chance to think about variables and issues of options and change within the classroom.

Deciding that an instructional pattern just "doesn't work" is rarely the case. You must try to get an eye for the variables; while the class may not have "worked," there may be more reasons or different reasons than you might automatically assume.

FOR YOUR JOURNAL

Write a response to the teaching game above. What did you learn from it? What were your assumptions and predictions?

Planning Your Teaching

Creating activities with teaching

There are excellent books available on planning and a number of books on writing objectives. There are also, especially from the National Council of Teachers of English (NCTE), hundreds of journals, books, and newsletters with teaching activities (*Notes Plus* may be of especial interest). While these resources, and the good ideas of your fellow and sister teachers, will often help you with your planning, you need to know how to do it yourself. In general, then, you need to plan a class with the following headings in mind:

- **Objectives:** Why are your students doing this activity? What do you want them to learn? know? understand? feel? appreciate? What's the point?

- **Method:** How are you going to get these objectives across? Will the students write? discuss? work in small groups? read and then respond? act something out?

- **Materials:** What will you need? cards? books? films? overhead? tape recorder? art materials? props?

- **Outline:** What will be the general procedure for the class? what comes first? second? What is the timing for each section?

- **Evaluation:** How will you judge if students have learned? understood? appreciated? If you give a test, what will be on it? If students write, what will be the content and focus? How long will it be? If students discuss, how can their contributions be evaluated? by frequency? importance? originality?

You also need to remember three principles of creating activities: simplicity, relevance, and specificity.

Simplicity   Thinking about *The Color Purple*, you would want your students to do something that is fairly small scale. Asking students to research statistics on African American families in the novel's era, for example, or bringing in a local social worker to discuss incest is probably more complicated than necessary and, further, deflects attention away from novel. When designing activities you need to keep the focus direct and simple.

Relevance   It may seem outrageous, but some beginning teachers might think that any assignment would be adaptable to *The Color Purple*. The perennial interest in Africa and its heritage is, actually, of peripheral significance to the novel, as is the issue of sexual orientation. In addition, having students research the Pulitzer Prize would also not be relevant to the work itself. Activities need to be directly related to the novel and its study.

Specificity   If you want students to write, tell them the general direction and the length. Similarly, if they are to do an art project based on the novel, list the components needed. While too many specific directions can be stultifying, giving students no directions ("write about what the novel meant to you"; "draw a picture based on *The Color Purple*") is unfair. Such vagueness will also, as you may imagine, lead you into difficulty when you have to evaluate and grade such assignments. Further, specificity in assignments will help *you* clarify what you want from students and also make you consider how long students need to complete successfully the activities.

For Your Journal

Let's imagine your ninth grade students have read that famous—and still controversial—short story, Shirley Jackson's "The Lottery." Sketch out a plan for teaching it to your students in a single fifty-minute class period. Use the headings listed above and the concepts of simplicity, relevance, and specificity. Share your ideas with a friend; what is similar? different? What do you think you could add or delete?

Discipline

Most people getting ready to enter a classroom for the first time, especially after having completed courses on teaching and having read books on students and classroom management, expect that they will be able to quickly establish an orderly atmosphere and run a classroom fairly smoothly. This expectation, however, is rarely fulfilled, and some novices are bitterly disappointed that they were not "taught" what to do or how to react in real classroom situations. The fact of the matter is that no class or book can teach a beginner or novice what to do and how to do it in every specific instructional incident. Even a very successful student teaching experience is no guarantee that the first year in the classroom will go smoothly in the discipline arena.

Discipline seems a simple concept, but it is actually very complex and is the sum of a number of variables, not the least of which is the beginning teacher's rather nascent perception of what is acceptable behavior and what is not. School context is important here, as are school rules. In certain schools there is a surprising level of informality that is expected and acceptable; in other schools, the opposite may be true. What you assume to be polite or respectful behavior between teachers and students and students and students may not, indeed, be what your students assume. The only way to determine this is to watch and learn, ask and adjust your own expectations—and, yes, you have the right to have those expectations—to the reality of your school context. And, of course, if for whatever reason you find the school context antithetical to your beliefs, you need to change schools or school systems.

In addition, in the beginning of anyone's teaching, the fit between what a teacher thinks is happening in a classroom and what is actually occurring is often not exact.

Thus a beginning teacher may honestly feel that the entire class is out of control when actually two or three students are being disruptive. A novice may think that her tone of voice was sufficiently commanding when, in actuality, it barely could be heard. The teacher may be frustrated that students, although instructed to raise their hands to be called upon, simply call out answers, and unaware that he routinely accepts answers from students who do not raise their hands and thus reinforces the behavior.

Having someone observe your classes, watching other teachers' classes, and trying to become more self-perceptive are three ways to establish a more clear view of what you are doing in your own classroom. Also, though they are as general as anything you will read in any similar book, the following principles may help you establish and maintain good discipline. They are not magic, and implementing all of them will not automatically ensure a well-managed class, but they are sensible and common sense.

Be firm; be fair   Once you decide on a procedure or a consequence for behavior, stick to it. Of course, be sure the procedure or consequence does not favor or punish in an inequitable manner. Thus if something goes for one student, it must go for the other, and, unless it is an unusual circumstance (a judgment call in and of itself), you should not be talked out of or into anything different for different students.

Be consistent   If it's a rule on Monday, it should be a rule on Wednesday. Constant change confuses students and confuses you. While there are often real and compelling reasons for altering classroom procedures or consequences, don't do it willy nilly.

Use "I" messages   As much as you would like to tell a student that he or she is the problem, phrasing statements such as "*I can't accept this behavior in class,*" or "*I would appreciate / prefer that you sit down*" helps students see the issue as an issue, not as a direct attack on them personally.

Single out students but don't humiliate them   Often, talking with or disciplining individual students—not the entire class—is sufficient to change a disorderly atmosphere into an orderly one. Be aware, however, that such attention to individual students needs to be done thoughtfully. If you wish to talk to a one student, take him or her out in the hall or meet them before or after school; don't discuss their behavior in the presence and hearing of their peers and their class.

Use praise and rewards   Students need praise for working well or for working better than before. Students are people, too, and they often appreciate positive attention from you. Students also respond to rewards, rewards that can range from something class-related (you can have a choice on this procedure; you can have ten minutes of free time in this class) to something more tangible (pencils or pens; a copy of a paperback book).

Offering praise and rewards to students if they achieve or continue to achieve can be helpful. While certainly we would all like to think that students come to our class and study and work without the need for reward, that is often not true. Judiciously used, praise and rewards can help students stay on track and stay out of trouble.

Make your students too busy to misbehave   A class that starts on time and in which much happens is a class where a student will have to work to get in trouble. While you do not want to assume that students might have misbehaved just because the class was not sufficiently organized or rigorous—some incidents will occur regardless—you can head off a lot of trouble by establishing a productive, busy atmosphere.

 FOR YOUR JOURNAL

Discipline is a large issue for most beginning teachers. Which of the above principles seem to you to be the easiest to enforce or adopt? Which seems to be the hardest? Why? What do you assume will have to happen in your classes before you have what you feel is an acceptable and orderly environment?

A Few Other Things: Openings, Voice, Body, Touch, Dress

Openings

One of the most important days of teaching is the first day of class. How you set a tone and deal with students that first day can make the rest of the year or the semester a smoother one. Being organized, relatively calm, and prepared your very first day gives students the expectations that this is how you will be the rest of the year. Getting ready, therefore, for the first day may actually take some time: leaving tasks until the last minute—when presemester school meetings and paperwork may interfere—is not a good idea.

But what, besides the handing-out-of-books administrivia, should happen the first day? There are a few things:

1. You need to think of what is important to you and the classroom and **establish and communicate rules or general principles.** If you want students to evince certain behaviors or attitudes, the first day is the day to mention them. Use positive language; giving students a list of *don'ts* is a surefire route to a negative start.

2. You need to **arrange the room** in a way that reinforces what will be going on in your classroom. This includes bulletin boards and artwork, study areas or reading areas, and a quiet corner for a class library. Desks should be positioned (in rectangles, circles, or squares) so that students can see each other for large-group activities. When students need to work individually and/or in small groups, desks should be positioned accordingly.

3. You need to **provide an introductory activity** that will let students get to know each other as well as you. Activities can include:

- **Interviewing each other and then introducing the other person to the class.**
- **Drawing a coat of arms that represents interests and then sharing it.**
  Students draw a symbol or series of symbols that represent the importance they give the following (number 5 is the most metaphorical):

  > 1—Outside Interests or Hobbies
  > 2—Family
  > 3—School
  > 4—Reading
  > 5—My Essence

My Coat of Arms

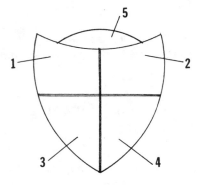

- **Writing a letter of introduction to you the teacher and/or to peers.**
- **Filling out a brief interest inventory and then sharing it.** Providing fill-in-the-blank statements can help, such as:

  When I am alone in my room I like to _____ .
  My favorite possession is _____ .
  What I like best/hate most about English class is _____ .
  My friends value me because _____ .
  School would be better if _____ .

These activities are ways of letting students establish who they are and who the others are. While every minute counts, the time spent on these activities will give you useful information about your students and will highlight their crucial importance in the success of the classroom. Your sharing something about yourself will also help students connect with you as a person, not just a teacher. If students do a coat of arms, for instance, you do one, too.

4. You need to begin to **learn and use all your students' names**, being very careful to pronounce them correctly or, within reason, to use their preferred

names. What is on the roll books may not be what your students want to be called, and your sensitivity to their names will establish a positive and immediate bond.

5. You need to **tell students about the class** and how you envision what you will be doing together. Don't forget to use humor and positive terms and enthusiasm. If students think the class will be interesting or fun, they are more likely to work with you and with each other. If you also stress that students will have a say in the class' organization and procedural rules, students will feel that the class is not just yours, the teacher's.

6. Finally, while it may seem hard to do both at once, you need to **establish that you are in charge of the classroom and that you are a friendly, pleasant person.** Smiling and looking at your students as if you are happy to be with them will, frankly, reassure many of them. On the other hand, being pleasant does not mean that you are a pushover; classrooms need order to proceed, and you are in charge of that order. I am sure you have heard the old saw about not smiling until Thanksgiving; while many teachers actually take that as serious advice, I think it's silly. You are a human being working with other human beings. Not showing a pleasant demeanor is, to me, self-defeating. Your class is not boot camp, it's school, and you and your students should have a good and productive time together.

Voice

Most of us in this culture associate a commanding presence with a relatively deep voice. While many men have an edge over many women in this department, it is somewhat of an exaggeration. It helps, however, to use an authoritative or relatively professional tone when trying to get students' attention, particularly, say, at the beginning of a class. Know also that if you speak over students or shout at them—and you'll be tempted—you are establishing an atmosphere that is hard to break or retract. If you use a quiet voice, they will, too.

And trust the power of silence; constant talk from you is not helpful; pauses and silence can get students' attention effectively.

Using your body

Do not believe people who tell you that to be successful in keeping a class in order, you must be big or tall. The key here is *presence*, and people who are short of stature—both male and female—can have tons of it, and tall folks can have none of it. Remember your body is a tool and one that you can use effectively. Moving around a class, standing near a student, standing erect, using your eyes to scan a room or to catch a student's attention, using your hands to gesture appropriately can all send messages to students that indicate care, attention, or discipline.

When I taught some years ago in a high school where discipline was an ongoing issue, I made it a practice to stand at my class door and greet or smile at each student as he or she came in the room. It established my presence, it made immediate, individual contact with each person, and, further, students had to pass by me—acknowledge me—in order to enter the class. Thus the signal of standing at the door was both a personal touch and an order measure.

Similarly, walking around the class can help students—although not to the extent where, in one of my classes, a student told me *just sit down*. My pacing (and in this class, that's just what it was) was making her nervous, and she decided to give me some advice and to attempt to save her relatively shattered nerves. While I wasn't particularly thrilled to be criticized, I listened, and I learned from that encounter to be more aware of my own movement and to move a bit less frenetically.

The personal touch

Touching is contextually and culturally determined. While much of what we do in class is pretty personal—write about how that makes you feel; discuss in your group if anything like that has ever happened to you—it does not give us a license to invade our students' private space, i.e., their bodies. My personality characteristics are that I am affectionate in speech and gesture, but I try to curb that enthusiasm. It is smart to know students and classes before one ever touches—even in the relatively neutral locations such as forearm and upper arm.

For sure, if you are having a conflict or disagreement with a student, *do not touch them* while you are discussing the issue; it may be seen, rightly or wrongly, as an act of hostility or aggression, and you may get—and deserve—a disproportionate reaction.

Male teachers need, especially in this era of heightened sensitivity, to be extremely cautious about touching female *and* male students; while culturally the reverse is generally not quite so true for women, it is still good advice. While we are human, and some of us have been raised in families where touching is customary, know, however, that our affection and care is not always reciprocated, and it is an imposition on our part to force a student to accept our gesture, however well meaning. Know before you reach out to touch.

Dress for context

Dress is another context issue. You need to look around you and see what the other teachers come to school wearing. Do not model yourself after the one person on the faculty who everyone thinks is weird or who most assume is repressed or stuck up and who, others assume, illustrates that by his or her clothing. You can be weird and stuck up or whatever—later in your career. In the beginning, without wholly sacrificing your own individuality, it is best to take the middle of the road in attire. Frankly, you have enough to concern yourself with without adding your sartorial choices to the mix.

First of all, with the above in mind, try to dress in a way that seems comfortable to you. If, as a woman, high heels make you feel silly, wear flats. If you feel stupid in flats, by all means, wear those heels. For women, the restrictions regarding pants and dresses are often real ones: if no one in your school wears pants (or dresses), understand that you will be noticed if you come to school in such. If, as a man, ties just mean awful stuff, wear a jacket and shirt and no tie. If dress shirts seem stultifying, try more informal ones. Again, if you feel like you can't teach or talk with any authority without a tie, put one on.

Real teachers wear clothes that make them feel attractive, comfortable, and professional. Look at your closet, check out the other teachers, and make your choices. By all means, however, remember that you are a teacher and not one of the students. That may take some wardrobe adjustment for some of you, but you'll get over it.

I taught in Iowa for a year and came to my first classes dressed as I would to teach in my home state, Virginia. I found my students were truly intimidated by what I assumed to be standard attire; they asked about my clothes before class, and I would often see them checking me out. Accordingly, I put the suits and silk dresses and pumps in the back of the closet and came to class in flats, trousers, and sweaters and jackets. My students noticed the change immediately and made approving comments about my "looking nice." They seemed happier; there were fewer comments about my being from "the East"; I felt their ease and was happier in the classroom.

Back in Virginia, when I wore the *dashiki* friends had brought me from a Caribbean trip, my African American students took time to remark on my appearance. They liked my wearing an interpretation of African fashion, and it made me, to them, seem more personal. These kinds of things may also happen to you; students react to our appearance and can also give us invaluable advice about something so personal as how we dress.

For Your Journal

Pick two teachers you either have in your current classes or can observe for a class period in your school. Do a case study (no names, please). How would you describe the teachers' personal mannerisms and body language? voice style? touching? dress? What seems effective? less effective? If you could write the teachers anonymous notes of praise or advice, what would you tell them? Why?

Teaching as Failing

This section may be one you'd like to skip; the idea of failing in the classroom may come a bit close to home. As a beginner, you may rightly fear that a great deal of your teaching will be failing. Actually, while that is true, it is also true of veteran teachers, as one of my favorite articles outlines. Richard Hawley opens his essay with almost uncomfortably harsh truth:

> Whenever a teacher enters a classroom to engage students in the process of increasing their understanding of some subject, some process, some created thing, some event—that is, whenever a teacher enters a classroom to teach—he or she risks great failure and, regardless of his or her gifts, *experiences* that failure to a significant extent. (597)

It is daunting and distressing to think that each class will reveal your failure as a teacher, but Hawley is on target. The poet T. S. Eliot wrote in *The Four Quartets* that "The only wisdom we can hope to acquire / Is the wisdom of humility: humility is endless" ("East Coker," 126). Hawley tells us:

> Human beings generally dread the prospect of speaking authoritatively before a group. The dread is greatest when the group being addressed is not particularly receptive or welcoming, when they do not anticipate being pleased. Teachers play to tougher houses than actors do. They also play to them in more intimate settings, and the scheduled run is generally longer, regardless of the reviews. An actor, often with reason, may blame a flat performance on his material. Teachers are less able to do this; it is rarely Euclid's or Melville's fault that a class has fallen flat. Teachers move among their audiences, address them, converse with them. Any inattention, boredom, hostility is clearly visible before them. Because there are normally no co-stars or supporting players, the experience of teaching imperfectly is essentially a private matter. And again, because failure is by nature humiliating, we tend to keep it to ourselves. (597)

For this reason more than any other, it is necessary that we become reflective teachers and also that we find a teacher friend, teacher buddy to bounce ideas off. Joining in a professional organization can literally be a lifesaver, as with friends it is possible to share what we have done and not done well.

But beyond the concept of failing, there are two other factors intertwined with teaching and failing. Both deal with defenses against classes that "did not go well." The first is blaming the students, the second is blaming the method. The latter, I hope, has been addressed somewhat with the section on "it didn't work." And do remember, although the bumper sticker, "Of all possible worlds / we only have one" is true of our earth, it is just not true of teaching. Of all possible methods, we may indeed only choose one at one time, but there are a universe of ways to approach a given instructional question. But let's look at the other approach—blaming the students.

Blaming the students

Blaming the students is counterproductive and probably has a lot to do with teacher frustration. While you will have in your career many "difficult" students—which often means they are insufficiently prepared for your class, culturally different from you, learning disabled, emotionally disturbed—it is a trap of the first order to blame classes that do not go well upon the students. As a beginner, you will, by a grim custom of the schools, often be given the youngest and least tractable students and classes. Tempting though it may be, you cannot afford to blame failure on them. You must continue to find a way to teach, enthrall, seduce, illumine them *where they are*. Decrying their lack of attention, preparation, or ability does no good—it is cursing the darkness. Be a lighter of candles, not a curser of the dark; it will save energy, and, further, you and your students just might surmount the problems and learn.

This is not a perfection business: it is an approximation only, and in a rather mystical sense, we teachers are rarely given to know exactly what the outcome of our classes are—what students remember, retain, what comes back to them years later, is really outside our control. It is also really not reflected by the grades they earn, the tests they take, the essays they write, or even our memories of who they were and what the classes in which they enrolled were like.

Some stories

Like many teachers, I remember incidents with students that make me squirm: times I misunderstood, mistrusted, did not pay attention to an individual.

I lost all patience with Florean Witcher who, even after being repeatedly advised, just would not look up the term she needed in a book's index. She had the book in hand and knew how to spell the term. I was losing patience. Florean had a legendary temper, and after her third request for help and my third identical reply (*look it up in the index*), she pulled furiously away from me.

I saw the anger—and the frustration—and in a well-meaning but misplaced gesture, I tried to stop Florean from storming to the other side of the class. It was winter, and, as was her custom, she had on her coat even though we were inside. In one of those fateful split-second decisions, I reached for her coat's belt to keep her from moving away. But Florean did not stop, and the belt ripped from its tie. Florean, I, and the class froze; Florean's right hand went into a very convincing fist and, indeed, she was fully capable of flattening me for, in essence, tearing her clothing. She didn't, the moment passed, and I both apologized for damaging her coat and offered to repair it. The apology was accepted, the offer to repair was declined, and the atmosphere cooled.

I then renewed the index discussion and found out that Florean would not look up her term in the index because she had never even heard the word *index*; I was asking her to look something up in an igloo for all she knew. We both became calm and business-like, Florean learned what an index was, and *I* thought, first, about trying to anticipate students' background and knowledge and, second, about making split-second decisions involving touching and restraining angry students.

And I slowly learned other things. How could I have insisted that Linda Kern's self-confessed nervousness about giving a report in front of the class was overestimated and all that she needed was to just get up and *do it*? She tried, she started, and succeeded, as she had warned me, in becoming so overwhelmed by the experience that there, in front of all of us, she turned and, in her terror, vomited her lunch on the classroom floor. On my knees, as Linda and I cleaned up the remains, I thought about listening to my students.

I could not ever stop the social bullying and name calling of the physically slight, but very smart, Tho Dang—the first of the Vietnamese refugees to come to my high school and the first student I had ever taught for whom English was a second language. I also just did not rattle the school's resources sufficiently to get the help he needed to negotiate my "remedial" English class. Tho struggled on his own—and successfully— without me. He passed all his usage tests with triumph, but it was not due to me, his English teacher, but to his own very hard work and a tutor in the Vietnamese commu- nity. When I complimented him on his high scores, he was polite but noncommittal. He knew, I knew, I had not taught him.

There is a roll call I have—as all teachers do—of students I have failed in the sense that I did not live up to my obligations as teacher.

Like many teachers, I also have had students, years later, tell me brilliant insights or words of advice or encouragement I gave them—good, serendipitous deeds that were wholly individual and that were so context-dependent that I do not often remember, at least not in the same way as the student. But, nevertheless, a number of students have cited crucial incidents in which I, evidently, played an important role.

The failures are dramatic, the good stories are heartening, but some of teaching is a bit more mixed. I also must recount the memorable—and utterly typical—incident when a former high school student of mine, who was then in college and functioning as a summer hostess in a local restaurant, stopped me in the restaurant foyer with exclama- tions of pleasure and recognition. I was with a group of friends and, actually, rather pleased to have an audience for my student's greeting and such obvious delight. When she wanted to tell me what she remembered most about our class in English those years ago, I glowed with pleasure, somewhat confident that my friends would now hear some stellar incident from the class. I braced myself to accept what she would recount; my friends smiled at each other and at me in pleasant anticipation.

"Oh yes," she recalled, her eyes lighting up with pleasure, "I just never forgot when you told us about your wedding cake and how you decided on it and had it spe- cially ordered."

My dismay, if not my disbelief, was immediate and total; was that, I asked her, what she had remembered?

"Oh yes," she gushed enthusiastically, "it was made entirely of *cream puffs,* and you had ordered it from that new French restaurant."

Well she had me. My wedding cake *had* been made of cream puffs and ordered specially from a new, local French restaurant. But, good grief, had I ever spent class time telling students about my *wedding cake?* About *cream puffs?* What in the world was I thinking to talk about a wedding cake? Even as an aside? Where was my brain that day? Where was my lesson plan?

I squeaked a thank you and quickly moved with my amused friends through the foyer and out of the door. My wedding cake—on which I had evidently actually spent class time—was what my former student remembered. Humility is endless.

Hawley sums it up well:

> Failure—real failure—is palpable everywhere in the teaching process. We need to name it and to face it, so that we may continue. If we insulate ourselves sufficiently with defenses, we may go unhurt, but we will teach nothing, while providing students models of flight and disengagement. Acknowledging failure and acknowledging defenses, we may come to know as much about our business as the medieval scholastics knew about God: what he is not and that he is necessary. Now off to class. (600)

And perhaps that is one encouraging aspect of this business of teaching; there is always another class and more students and, thanks to the fates, another chance to teach. As a teaching friend of mine says, "Teaching is the *only* profession where we can clear away all the failures at the end of the school year and start afresh in the fall."

A final word from a poet (and student and teacher)

Henry Taylor, a Pulitzer Prize winner, wrote a poem I like to share with my students. It's about failure and domination and a terrible incident in a long-ago but not long-forgotten math class. It presents a bright but not truly confident student and an insecure, overbearing teacher. But the last part of the poem is even more powerful for us, because Taylor, now a teacher himself, writes of what all of us teachers know; we all fail each other and, to a certain extent, we must forgive each other in the classroom:

Shapes, Vanishings

1

Down a street in the town where I went
to high school twenty-odd years ago, by doorways
and shadows that change with the times, I walked
past a woman at whose glance I almost stopped cold,
almost to speak, to remind her of who I had been—
but walked on, not being certain it was she,
not knowing what I might find to say.
It wasn't quite the face I remembered, the years
being what they are, and I could have been wrong.

2

But that feeling of being stopped cold, stopped dead,
will not leave me, and I hark back
to the thing I remember her for, though God knows
how I could remind her of it now.
Well, one afternoon when I was fifteen
I sat in her class. She leaned on her desk,
facing us, the backboard behind her arrayed
with geometrical figures—triangle, square,

pentagon, hexagon, et cetera. She pointed
and named them. "The five-sided figure," she said,
"is a polygon." So far so good, but then when she
    said,
"The six-sided one is a hexagon," I wanted things
    clear.
Three or more sides is *poly,* I knew, but five only
is *penta,* and said so; she denied it,
and I pressed the issue, I, with no grades
to speak of, a miserable average to stand on
with an Archimedean pole—no world to move,
either, just a fact to get straight, but she
would have none of it, saying, at last, "Are you
contradicting me?"

                 3

A small thing to remember a teacher for. Since then,
I have thought about justice often enough
to have earned my uncertainty about what it is,
but one hard fact from that day has stayed with me:
If you're going to be a smartass, you have to be
    right,
and not just some of the time. "Are you
contradicting me?" she had said, and I stopped
breathing a moment, the burden of her words
pressing down through me hard and quick, the huge
weight of knowing I was right, and beaten. She
had me. "No, ma'am," I managed to say, wishing
I had the whole thing down on tape to play back
to the principal, wishing I were ten feet tall
and never mistaken, ever, about anything in this
    world,
wishing I were older, and long gone from there.

                 4

Now I am older, and long gone from there.
What sense in a grudge over something so small?
What use to forgive her for something
she wouldn't remember? Now students
face me as I stand at my desk, and the shoe
may yet find its way to the other foot,
if it hasn't already. I couldn't charge
thirty-five cents for all that I know
of geometry; what little I learned is gone now,
like a face looming up for a second out of years
that dissolve in the mind like a single summer.
Therefore,
if ever she almost stops me again,

I will walk on as I have done once already,
remembering how we failed each other,
knowing better than to blame anyone.

—Henry Taylor
The Flying Change

And so, off to class.

FOR YOUR JOURNAL

As you think about your teaching career, what is the one area more than any other
in which you would hope you would not fail your students? Is it intellectual? emotional? social? Would it have to do with something inside the classroom? outside?
If you could ask your teaching Fairy Godmother to keep you from one area of failure, what would it be? MAKE A WISH—

REFERENCES

Atwell, Nancie. "Everyone Sits at a Big Desk: Discovering Topics for Writing." *English Journal* 74
(September 1985): 35–39.

———— . *In the Middle: Writing, Reading, and Learning with Adolescents.* Portsmouth, NH: Boynton/
Cook, 1987.

Brooke, Robert. "Underlife and Writing Instruction." *College Composition and Communication* 38
(May 1987): 141–53.

Bullough, Robert V., Jr. *First Year Teacher: A Case Study.* New York: Teachers College Press, 1989.

Christenbury, Leila. "A Paradigm for Analyzing Components of the Teaching Act." *English Education* 11 (May 1980): 233–39.

Cutuly, Joan. *Home of the Wildcats: Perils of an English Teacher.* Urbana, IL: NCTE, 1993.

Eliot, T. S. *The Complete Poems and Plays 1909–1950.* New York: Harcourt Brace & World, 1952.

Emmers, Amy Puett. *After the Lesson Plan: Realities of High School Teaching.* New York: Teachers
College Press, 1981.

Freire, Paulo. *Pedagogy of the Oppressed.* New York: Continuum, 1981.

Fuhrmann, Barbara Schneider. *Adolescence, Adolescents.* 2d ed. Glenview, IL: Scott Foresman/Little
Brown, 1990.

Grossman, Pamela L. *The Making of a Teacher: Teacher Knowledge and Teacher Education.* New York:
Teachers College Press, 1990.

Hawley, Richard A. "Teaching as Failing." *Phi Delta Kappan* 60 (April 1979): 597–600.

Joyce, Bruce and Marsha Weil. *Models of Teaching.* 3d ed. Englewood Cliffs, NJ: Prentice-Hall,
1986.

Lortie, Dan C. *Schoolteacher: A Sociological Study.* Chicago: University of Chicago Press, 1975.

Macrorie, Ken. *Twenty Teachers.* New York: Oxford University Press, 1984.

NCTE. *Notes Plus.* Urbana, IL: NCTE, 1990 and years following.

Palonsky, Stuart B. *900 Shows a Year.* New York: Random House, 1986.

Shulman, Lee. S. "Learning to Teach." *AHHE Bulletin* (November 1987).

Taylor, Henry. "Shapes, Vanishings." In *The Flying Change,* 14–15. Baton Rouge, LA: LSU Press,
1985.

Walker, Alice. *The Color Purple.* New York: Harcourt Brace Jovanovich, 1982.

Wellington, Bud. "The Promise of Reflective Practice." *Educational Leadership* 48 (March 1991): 4–5.

Wigginton, Eliot. *Sometimes a Shining Moment*. Garden City, NY: Doubleday, 1985.

RESOURCES

Many of the books listed below are stories of being and becoming a teacher; the Mohr book is a practical guide to being a teacher/researcher; the Moffett is a classic you will not want to miss; the Milner is a comprehensive teaching text, and the Tchudi is still one of the best "handbooks" for teaching around.

Glatthorn, Allan A. *Learning Twice: An Introduction to the Methods of Teaching*. New York: HarperCollins, 1993.

Kozol, Johnathan. *On Being a Teacher*. New York: Continuum, 1981.

McAndrew, Donald A., Marilyn Graves, Laura Toki, and T. Collin Wansor. "Three Routes to Becoming a Good English Teacher." *The English Record* 4l (3) (1991): 10–16.

Milner, Joseph O'Beirne and Lucy Floyd Morcock Milner. *Bridging English*. New York: Macmillan, 1993.

Moffett, James. *Teaching the Universe of Discourse*. Portsmouth, NH: Boynton/Cook, 1983.

Mohr, Marian M. and Marion S. Maclean. *Working Together: A Guide for Teacher-Researchers*. Urbana, IL: NCTE, 1987.

Natkins, Lucille G. *Our Last Term: A Teacher's Diary*. Lanham, MD: University Press of America, 1986.

NCTE. *NCTE's Position on the Teaching of English: Assumptions and Practices*. Urbana, IL: NCTE, 1991.

Raphael, Ray. *The Teachers' Voice: A Sense of Who We Are*. Portsmouth, NH: Heinemann, 1985.

Ryan, Kevin, ed. *The Rollercoaster Year: Essays by and for Beginning Teachers*. New York: HarperCollins, 1992.

Silberman, Charles. *Crisis in the Classroom*. New York: Random House, 1970.

Small, Robert C., Jr. and Joseph E. Strzepek. *A Casebook for English Teachers: Dilemmas and Decisions*. Belmont, CA: Wadsworth Publishing, 1988.

Tchudi, Stephen and Diana Mitchell. *Explorations in the Teaching of English*. 3d ed. New York: Harper & Row, 1986.

Wolfe, Denny T., ed. *Guidelines for the Preparation of Teachers of English Language Arts*. Urbana, IL: NCTE, 1986.

CHAPTER 3

STUDENTS

When I think back
On all the crap I learned in high school
It's a wonder
I can think at all
And though my lack of education
Hasn't hurt me none
I can read the writing on the wall

—Paul Simon, "Kodachrome" (*There Goes Rhymin' Simon*)

No One Ever Said It Was Going to Be Easy

It seems like a terrible thing to say, but one of the many reasons teaching is difficult is students. On the other hand, students are also, inescapably, the only lasting reason to teach or to stay in teaching. What is this paradox?

Interacting with students is the heart of the teaching process: when that interaction is lively and relatively smooth, the joys of teaching come easily to mind. When, however, the interaction is strained, awkward, or even unpleasant, then teachers often wonder why they got into this business in the first place. Teaching is, as you suspect, a terribly *intimate* business, and when we and our students are not in sync, the level of discomfort can be frighteningly high. While the days and weeks of teaching can go by in a very routine manner, there will be days when things go wrong between teachers and students and when the entire enterprise becomes remarkably difficult. It is, first, that students are in groups and identify in ways different from adults (see Penelope Eckert's *Jocks and Burnouts* for a fascinating look at social categories in high school); it is also that some students don't identify very much at all.

And, indeed, that is the conclusion of many people who have been through high school and middle school: they remember the "crap" Paul Simon celebrates in his song, and they wonder how they ever survived the experience.

If you have been a visitor in a teachers' lounge recently and no one particularly worried about your presence there, the remarks you overheard might have surprised you. In many teachers' lounges across this country, in countless school workrooms and offices, relatively sharp things are said about students by teachers, and unflattering remarks are made. Much of that talk is the release of tension by people who interact intensely and over sustained periods of time with large groups of young people. Thus, much of that talk means little. Some of it, though, can be cynical and cruel. The latter is not worth your sustained consideration and often comes from adults who are over-whelmed and very tired and disappointed by the entire enterprise of teaching. But where in the world does the former come from?

The cynical comments come from the difficulty of teaching as we define it in this country in the public school system: teaching people in same-age groups, teaching people in groups, and the political act itself of teaching people. Some of this has been discussed in previous chapters, but the fact that these patterns can make teaching difficult is prob-ably not very surprising to you, especially when you recall your own life as a student.

While no one wishes to paint the nation's classrooms as the proverbial "black-board jungle" (a notorious phrase that emerged from a 1950s novel and subsequent movie of the same name), it is naive to expect that your teaching career will not have some hard moments. Teaching students can be a tough business; it can have ugly times. Some of my former students—males and females—are in jail; some are dead. Some are hard to remember fondly.

The Tough Times of Teaching: Apathy and Violence

For all of the wonderful experiences I have had in the classroom and the countless satis-fying and even exhilarating encounters with students, like many teachers, I have also had my share of rough moments.

Fighting student apathy is part of my history as a teacher: I have been unable to motivate every student in my classroom. Some, for a variety of reasons, have refused to engage, be involved, or attempt to do assignments. Some slipped in and out of my class-room more like ghosts than real people, only temporarily there, perched, just waiting to move on. Some were so quiet, so removed, I almost forgot they were on my roll book and, after some months of trying to get them involved, I turned my energies and efforts elsewhere.

Despite my attempts, my energy and enthusiasm, I have seen students turn away from an activity, a learning contract, a book. I have had students who have, without exaggeration, done virtually nothing in class for days at a stretch. I have asked students to sit up in class and not sleep, to open books that have remained resolutely shut, to bring a pen or pencil or paper to class, to get up and actually *sit* with their group. I have had students who made themselves so unobtrusive in class that very soon after our time together I could not begin to recall their names.

I, like many teachers who have taught for some time, have also had more dramatic difficulties with students. I have been threatened physically, cursed, and had my car damaged. I have had my locked classroom broken into and test materials stolen. I have had bulletin boards I assembled and for which I bought or made the artwork defaced or vandalized. Some of this was directed at me personally; some of this was directed more generally.

I was hit "accidentally" in the act of shielding a slightly built student from the class bully; sadly for me, the larger student's fist went into my stomach but, thankfully, not into the other kid's face. While standing in the hall during a class change I was slammed into a door by a student I did not recognize and who was trying to get away from a pur-suing assistant principal. On hall duty I was knocked out of the way while walking a con-fused and drug-dazed student to the school infirmary; his friends, observing the scene, feared any intervention and did not want a teacher involved. The student was taken away from me forcibly and spirited somewhere across the school campus.

When I was taking over a hospitalized colleague's study hall, I was warned that the group had been a "problem" in the past. Sure enough, the second day of my assignment I was backed up against the classroom door by a student who wanted to leave the room before the bell rang. Cheerfully, I stood at the door, but the encounter changed character quickly; the game became one of seeing whether the student could frighten me by producing a lighter and threatening to set my long hair on fire. With his face inches from mine and his arm blocking my movement, the student, with a fascinated and repelled audience behind him, watched to see whether I would back down. I did not, would not; there seemed to be too much at stake. But I was scared. In this case, the fates were merciful: the lighter stubbornly refused to operate (did the student know this? was this part of the game?), the bell finally rang, and study hall ended.

The reasons for these events vary: some involve individual students and their responses not only to teachers but to situations; some reasons involve reactions to school as an institution and teachers as representatives of that institution. Many arise from students' response to situations not related to schools or teaching; students can "act out" against family or community problems and can do that acting out in school. While you may have many serene years in the classroom without anything such as the above happening to you, student apathy, physical and verbal assaults on teachers, and the occasional flare-up of anger or hostility are actually fairly commonplace in schools across the country. Vandalism is an issue for school systems, as is maintaining an atmosphere not only of relative civility but of some form of mutual intellectual engagement.

But why does this occur? Why in the world would such an atmosphere exist in school?

We need to look at how school is an alien place for many of our students and why the we/them dyad can be one of the most damaging of relationships. You, the beginning teacher, are *them*. Many students see themselves absolutely as *us*. For some students that will mean withdrawal, apathy; for others it will involve a more active and combative role. For both types of students, school is foreign territory, and they come with their defenses up, committed to getting over, getting by, and ultimately, mercifully, getting out.

Two Researchers on Students: William Glasser and Linda McNeil

There are two books you might want to know about, Linda McNeil's *Contradictions of Control* and William Glasser's *Control Theory in the Classroom*. Both researchers have studied schools and students and conclude that, in Glasser's words, the whole game needs to change. Glasser, a psychiatrist, sees schools as places where students do not feel part of the process:

> The problem is that at least half of all students are making little or no effort to learn, because they don't believe that school satisfies their needs. To make school harder—to increase the length of the school year or the school day, to assign more homework, to require more courses . . . is not going to reach those students. . . . We can't do anything *to* people, or really even *for* people, to get them to produce more. We have to change the school itself, so that students look at it and say, "In this school and with these teachers I can satisfy my needs, if I work hard." (656)

For McNeil, the enterprise has become seriously poisoned at the source—at what teachers actually present to students in the form of content. McNeil writes that teachers, in an effort to maintain a semblance of power or control in school, actually diminish what they teach—their content—and create "brief, 'right' answers, easily transmitted, easily answered, easily graded [in order to accommodate] to a school where their only power came from the classroom" (157). Glasser advises cooperative learning to counter this lack of control. For McNeil, however, Glasser's control theory has some insidious implications:

> Adults who visit high-school classrooms are often struck by the dullness of the lessons. Those who visit systematically note the overwhelming prevalence of boring content, dull presentations and bored but patient students. . . . The dull presentations are not caused merely by poor teacher preparation or teacher burnout, but by deliberate, often articulated, decisions teachers have made to control the students by controlling the content. . . . Defensive, controlling teaching does more than make content boring; it transforms the subject content from "real world" knowledge into "school knowledge," an artificial set of facts and generalizations whose credibility lies no longer in its authenticity as a cultural selection but in its instrumental value in meeting the obligations teachers and students have within the institution of schooling. . . .
>
> As the course content is transformed into 'school knowledge,' there is little incentive for the student to become involved in that content. It is there to be mastered, traded for a grade and, as some students have said, deliberately forgotten afterward. (191)

For McNeil, "the very relations within classroom[s] and within schools will have to be transformed" (215) for real knowledge and school knowledge to become one. And this leads us to one of our great concerns, the alienated student.

The Alienated Student: Not Always Who You Think

Susan Beth Pfeffer, a writer of adolescent novels, has lightheartedly defined what she calls the "basic rules of teenage life." Some of them include: *My Family Is Awful, Anyplace Would Be Better Than Here,* and *It Is Inconceivable That I'm Going to Survive This Awful Moment.* Her most important rule, however, is: *I Am the One True Outsider.* Pfeffer notes: "No matter how popular teenagers might be, they always know that they and they alone are the one true outsider" (6).

Even though Pfeffer is being humorous, the issue is a serious one. Certainly it is a hallmark of many young people to feel the outsider, the only one, the stranger. Adults have a tendency to smile at this feeling, knowing that, in some measure, it is rarely a perennial condition that persists into mature years. On the other hand, the power of feelings of alienation cannot be minimized by us as teachers in the classroom.

In a series of issues of the *English Journal,* a number of teachers wrote about their experience in the classroom with what they termed "alienated" students. Daniel A. Lindley, Jr., wrote "we know who they are, and we know what they do to us, the alienated ones, those students so far removed from our values, our beliefs, our whole way of life" (26). Lindley asked teachers to distinguish between the "possible" and the "impossible," and certainly we know that a teacher can control or influence only certain aspects of school and life that might contribute to a student feeling alienated. Certainly we cannot bring students home with us, give them money, trade places with their parents, get them off drugs, make them motivated, or even learn for them. But we can, within our classrooms, make contact with them as human beings and provide opportunities for them to succeed and participate.

A National Center for Educational Statistics study, called the *National Education Longitudinal Study,* looked at 25,000 eighth graders and, two years later, followed the students up when they were tenth graders. The study cites six "at-risk" factors that may help determine whether students will drop out of school:

At-Risk Factors for School Dropouts

living in a single parent family
having a yearly family income less than $15,000
being home alone more than three hours a day
having parents with no high school diploma
having a sibling who has dropped out
having a limited English proficiency
(United States Department of Education)

Notice that family income is only one of the risk factors; notice also that most of the factors are not under the control of the school.

Characteristics of the alienated student

For many students, school and our classes are arenas where they do not feel safe or a part; they do not want to be there. While there are always exceptions to the following generalizations, these are the students who only put in their time in school, who want to be left alone, and who will occasionally "act out" if pushed or challenged. Alienated students, both the truly apathetic and the more combative, do not talk a lot in large group discussions, do not do much homework, do not see themselves as any part of the life of the school—either during the day or after the last bell. Listen to this description Johnathan gives of himself in high school:

> I was what I think one would call a "problem child.". . . In my junior English class . . . I sat in that back corner of the room as always. I could never stand the feeling of people looking at the back of my head. This class was a little strange for me because there was not one person in the room that I was friends with. And, of course, I never participated in class discussions. This meant that I never spoke in class, I never said a word.
>
> This has been, over the years, a very typical situation for me. And once the silence starts it becomes increasingly difficult to say anything. The silence builds such a momentum that in order to utter one word I would be facing a mountain of shame, and at once losing my anonymity, drawing attention to my paralysis.
>
> One day in this English class we had a test. I had forgotten to bring a pencil. Class had already started, the door was closed, I was trapped. I thought about asking the people near me for something to write with; I thought about asking the teacher. Instead, I just made writing motions with my finger the entire period and turned in a blank test, face down, quickly as I left the room.
>
> The next year English class was better. One of my best friends was in the class, and he sat next to me in the back corner of the room. I still never said anything in class. The other students were just faceless heads, masters of all social situations. The teacher was someone whose gaze I averted for fear he might think I was interested and call on me. I didn't have to worry.
>
> —Johnathan Morris

Alienated students are often like Johnathan, the ones who, at least in class, are likely sitting by themselves, who are apt to try to sleep or otherwise withdraw from the life of the class, who are absent from school more than the average, who consistently forget or lose their instructional materials. With some exceptions, these are the students who just don't turn in major assignments and who don't complete even minimal parts of tests. These alienated students are those who are termed "at risk" and who are often extreme underachievers.

Jeffrey Landon describes a young woman he encountered in his student teaching who fits the at-risk description and whose behaviors outside school as well as in it are cause for concern:

> Jewel is a sophomore, six feet tall, and she walks hunched over to disguise both her height and her chest. Her skin is the color of an acorn, and her cheeks are acne-scarred. I have never seen her talk either in class or out; in class, she is almost invisible.
>
> I have read two short essays by Jewel. In the first she talked about Christmas, and how it depressed her. Her parents live in another city, but she hasn't seen them in 2 years. She writes, "they are to busy." She thought she would see them on Christmas, but it didn't work out. Instead they sent her a yellow dress 2 sizes too small for her body.
>
> On New Year's Eve, Jewel injured herself, falling down some stairs while holding onto a butcher knife. It was called an accident by her grandmother (who she lives with). Jewel required many stitches. Apparently, she had accidently (and repeatedly) punctured her stomach and sliced open at least two veins in her arms. . . . In another essay comparing herself to a figure in literature, Jewel wrote, "I always wanted to have a happier life, but that won't happen I guess. I don't want to hurt myself, because I care about myself. But sometimes I can't stop what they do."

Sources of alienation: students who don't fit the norm/ students who do

While it is a gross generalization to assume that any minority—of race or sex or ethnic heritage—will necessarily feel alienated in a majority culture, it is an occasional consequence. Caucasian students in predominately African American student bodies, Latino students surrounded by Anglos, Asian Americans in a sea of Caucasians—and the reverse of each—can feel a certain sense of aloneness. Students for whom English is a second language can also feel much apart from school culture. Moslem and Jewish students are often the exception in a student body of Christians; Roman Catholic students can be a small proportion of a largely Protestant group.

Because of school boundary disputes, it is not that frequent that student socioeconomic status is often greatly at variance within a single student body, but schools whose boundary areas include students from widely differing economic classes face special challenges.

There is also some recent research evidence that gender is even more powerful an alienating factor than we had previously suspected. Researcher Carol Gilligan has found that female students seem to lose a sense of confidence and assurance as they move through the middle school years and begin to become silent in our classes and doubtful of their intellectual strength as they become high school students. Female students begin to perceive and become troubled by the contradictory roles they will face and are currently facing as women. Often they will not participate vigorously in class and will not challenge either male students or the teacher. In fact, in a recent survey of 2,400 girls and 600 boys in fourth through tenth grades, "adolescent girls experience genuine, substantial drops in self-esteem that far outpace those reported by boys [and have] less confidence in their academic abilities and fewer aspirations to professional careers" (Bower, 184).

Finally, alienated students can be those who are learning disabled, for whom reading and writing and speaking are difficult because of perceptual or neurological impairments.

Yet, we cannot assume that all the alienated students over whom you will worry or with whom you will have difficulty are students who are predominately racially or ethnically in the minority or are students who live at or below the poverty level. While you will be teaching people who can be categorized in that manner, not all of them will be what we are defining here as alienated students. In addition, many of your alienated students will be people who, by this society's definition, are in the mainstream and who, materially at least, have substantial advantages.

While not all of the following factors mean that a student will feel alienated, it is helpful to remember, once again, the great range of pressures that confront young people. It is too easy for us to look at those youthful, clear faces, those expressive clothes and hairdos, and assume that what is in our students' lives is equally cheerful and well balanced. The appearance can often belie the reality.

What kind of students will you be teaching who might have reason to feel alienated in school?

You will be teaching people who are parents, who have their own babies at home. You will be teaching people who have parents who are in the midst of divorces or bankruptcies or emotional breakdowns. You will be teaching people who feel they live, despite material comfort, in emotional poverty. You will be teaching people who are finding identity in gangs, who are trying to see if sexual intimacy can lead to psychological intimacy, who are escaping with drugs or alcohol or even compulsive shopping. You will be teaching people who are repeatedly told that they have everything—and who feel that they have nothing. You will be teaching people who, at their age, profoundly suspect that life doesn't hold a whole lot for them—and, for sure, that school is not going to help them make it any better. You will be teaching people who are told that getting into college is the most important goal of their lives and who know they will never make it—and people who are sure they will get into college and question whether that will mean very much at all. You will be teaching people who are told that this is the best time of their lives—and who wonder, if that is true, what in the world the succeeding years hold.

You will be teaching people in the great and dramatic process of growing up, a growing up that often is marked as much by fear and danger and unhappiness as by joy and discovery. For some of our students the latter feelings are intermittent and transitory, lasting a few days or weeks; yet for others, the feelings are relatively permanent. For Faye Girardi, a student preparing to teach English, alienation came from a cultural shift:

> I graduated from an upper middle class suburban high school in the San Francisco Bay Area. I had been a student there for two years, having spent ninth and tenth grade at Ghana International School, a private English-style school in Accra, Ghana. Entering a new high school in one's junior year is tough, but in addition to the routine practice of becoming acclimated, I also experienced severe culture shock. . . . The school environment in West Africa was a nurturing and protective one. . . . My fellow students numbered . . . around 25, and we were together the entire school day. . . . We were multi-cultural and accustomed to socializing with many different nationalities and ethnic groups.
>
> By contrast, the suburban high school to which I transferred at the beginning of my junior year was far from a nurturing and reassuring environment. Suddenly I was worried about makeup, clothes, the prospect of dating, finding friends, learning the new music or the latest fashion—the list was almost endless. We changed classrooms constantly: we even changed our clothes and showered during P.E.! The prospect of learning the unwritten and unspoken

codes of conduct at Campolino High School seemed an impossible feat. The students were extremely competitive amongst themselves and uncooperative with each other. I could find very few outward differences among us, and it became clear to me in the first days of my junior year that conformity was my ticket to acceptance. This was a new concept for me.

I remember my parents telling me that the high school experience would prove to be the best experience of my life. It often felt barely manageable. Even though it has been . . . years since I attended high school, I still compare hardships in my life with the one of entering high school in the United States as an eleventh grader.

For Beth Hagy, it was a different sort of cultural shift:

I am the new kid in the tenth grade class. There are only fifty-six students in the whole grade and half of them are in my first period English class. The majority of this English class is either taking a nap because they have had to get up early to do the farm chores and were too tired to even bother bathing so the room reeks of corn meal and cattle, while the minority passes the latest Harlequin [romance] to one another at warp speed which defies and offends my snobby English class upbringing. I contemplate switching to the second section to see if the odors and tastes in books are a step up, but that means rearranging an already miserable schedule. . . . I had come from a very large junior high school [and] kept forgetting that I was in a small town in which the Baptist church and the triple x rated movie theatre sat directly across from one another. No one wanted a free thinker. No one was interested in learning nor did some of the teachers care to teach. They all lived on farms and were more concerned with farming and whether the basketball team would win the district than how to learn or how to teach.

While hindsight may make such observations soften, at the time the school world of these young people was frightening and alien.

Sources of alienation: teachers/administration/school size

Another, perhaps hidden, source of alienation is not only the shapes of our students' personal lives and the composition of the student body itself but you, the teacher, and your school's administration.

It is likely that you, the reader of this book and the beginning teacher, are Caucasian and middle class. It is also likely that you are a female. Further, it is also probable that most of your colleagues in your school will share these characteristics. In other words, you the teacher and your school administration are largely homogeneous in class and race. While this is not to imply that Anglo teachers cannot deal effectively with non-white students or that female teachers are limited in their connection to male students or that middle-class values are always at odds with those of other classes, the issue is that the power structure of schools—of which you are or will soon be a part—is usually over-whelmingly represented by the white, middle class, and female. When your students are different, there can be conflict and misunderstanding, issues that while not your sole responsibility, are nevertheless your predominant responsibility to attempt to bridge. Carol Smith Catron remembers the magic of a teacher who seemed to bridge that gap:

Junior year I had [a teacher] who I loved. My favorite thing about her class was that there were no favorites. We had everyone in that class from a guy named Wendyl with a pierced nose and chains on his boots to a girl named Julie who was head of the cheerleaders and won every beauty contest to come her way. And then were all the people in between, like me. I felt like I was this teacher's favorite person in the world. So did my friend Vanessa, and my fiance, John. And, no doubt, Wendyl and Julie felt the same way. There were no "shadow" people, or people who dominated every discussion. Everyone was called upon in class and every one's answers were given respect and consideration.

Within her class, the teacher Carol Smith Catron recalls made all of her students individuals. On the other hand, you must remember that the way middle and secondary schools are organized, you will be seeing upwards of 120 students a day in a school of anywhere from 1,200 students to 2,000. While many schools attempt to ameliorate the drawbacks of such "largeness," kids can, as a recent NCTE booklet notes, feel "lost in the crowd." It is quite possible to hide in such large configurations and, quite possibly, to feel even more apart and disengaged.

Let us turn to some students whose stories are based on real people and, in one case, on a composite of two people; I taught them, and they are all, in their own ways, alienated students.

Three Students: Marianna, Antoine, and Marc

Once I had a student who had very pale skin and pale, wispy blonde hair. She had a pretty, sweet face with watchful eyes that would widen enormously. She was shy, had no friends I could discern, and ate alone in the cafeteria and walked alone between classes. She was, at sixteen, undergoing a difficult period in her own life and with her alcoholic mother. When she took an overdose of pills between classes, the rescue squad came and carried her from the girls' bathroom floor to the hospital. A month later, she returned to school and was placed in one of my classes. I knew her recent history but was cautious about treating her differently from the others. But equal treatment was hard for two reasons: Marianna was virtually incapable of speaking above a soft whisper. Almost no one in the class, even those sitting right around her, could hear her comments, and no one, including me, her teacher, could induce her to raise her voice. But it got even more complicated because when she turned in her first writing assignment, I realized I was in the presence of one of the brightest students I had ever seen in my teaching career. Whispering and writing, the troubled and brilliant Marianna was in my class.

Once I had another student whose almost angelic features, mocha skin, and dark eyes belied a volatile temper. It was never clear to most of his teachers and even many of his friends what would "set off" Antoine, or why he would decide at a given juncture in class to raise his voice in question, protest, or complaint—or stalk out of the classroom, slamming the door behind him. When he did his work, Antoine was a wonderful student, and he could be a strong addition to any class discussion. He was aware, smart, and explosively under pressure.

One day he came into class ten minutes late, a fairly usual behavior. But in the missed ten minutes, Antoine had not heard the class introduction of why the day's reading, the South American short story, was paired with the Biblical story of the Good Samaritan. Standing up to announce, "This is no religion class," Antoine once again stalked out and slammed the door behind him. Not very much later, no one was happy—but no one was terribly surprised—when, one Saturday night, Antoine returned to an after-hours club for retaliation. Antoine's father, who had taken him to the club, had been insulted, the story went, and Antoine went back to the club ostensibly to retrieve his coat—but actually to shoot the owner dead. On bond and awaiting trial for murder, and later after he was convicted, awaiting the beginning of his jail sentence, the volatile and very bright Antoine was, like Marianna, in my class.

And once I also had a student who didn't exactly look like James Dean—he was too stocky and his cheek bones weren't as prominent—but wanted to act like him. When he bothered to come to school (he attended only about two-thirds of any given week) Marc either would not bring his books to class or, when he did bring them, would not open them. He would not answer questions, turn in homework, take tests, or do much of anything but slouch in his desk and watch the class. Whenever he decided he had "had enough," he would get up and walk out. He was moody, abrupt, and in the middle of his fifth year of a well-known and tempestuous love relationship with a class-mate. His sole interests were Angie and motorcycles; the rest was irrelevant. When Angie, pregnant, withdrew from school, Marc stayed to get more Ds and Fs. Putting his face down on his desk with his jacket pulled over his head, bereft of his girlfriend, Marc was also in my class.

Teacher reaction to the alienated student

In a newspaper some years ago, I read a study of nurses and their critically ill patients that I think has some bearing on teacher reaction to alienated students. Researchers found that registered nurses would spend a considerably shorter period of time interacting with and caring for patients who were critically, often terminally, ill. The researchers concluded that because such patients were less rewarding to deal with, the nurses, more than likely unconsciously, spent less time with them. So it is, too, with us as teachers. In fact, the subtitle of the Lindley article on alienated students, "For Teachers of the Alienated," is "Defenses Against Despair," which, while a rather melodramatic phrase, captures the intensity of the issue. Most of us will tend to avoid the truly alienated student because he or she is often not rewarding to be with. We can make a number of efforts, but it is not axiomatic that they will be successful. And, in fact, some teachers, fearful of "burn out," make it a point to be less than fully engaged with such students. Others have experiences that confirm that the school, as it is currently organized, cannot be effective with such students.

For example, it is with no little shame that I recount my encounter with the alternately vacant-eyed and occasionally giggling student I had and whose behavior was a complete puzzle to me. Her hair was unkempt, her skin blotched, and her clothes were held together by a dozen or so safety pins. Even in my less than affluent school she stood out as poorly, inappropriately dressed. She insisted, though, that she had big plans for the immediate future: she would be on a bus to Hollywood the next week. The movies were her goal, she asserted, and she was only in my class as something to pass the time before she set out for California. And her instructions to me were equally direct: she told me to leave her alone, put her desk away from the others, and not speak to her. She would not cause me problems, she assured me, if I would just cease and desist.

As I recall, that's just what I did. She dropped out of school in a month or so, for the system's resources and my energy were no match for her problems.

For a colleague of mine facing a different situation, there was also little recourse but, in this case, she made a better effort than I had with the student described above:

> Nothing prepared me for the day two of my students who had killed a cat wore the bones to school around their necks. One gleefully described how he had killed the animal while his classmates alternated between disgust and laughter. I asked him why he had killed the cat. He told me that his god was calling out for a sacrifice. A week later he wore the cat's skull to school on a string, complete with a red cross painted on top.
>
> I exhausted all of the channels possible—guidance counselors, department chairman, administration. The facts seemed to be that unless the two had killed the animal on school property, there wasn't anything that could be done.
>
> Tell that to the cat.

Tell that to the parents in the school district.

Tell that to the next teacher who hasn't a notion how to handle this. . . . If we can't deal with students in crisis we are potentially turning them away from possibly the only place where they may be influenced positively. If we sit in class and fervently hope that [such students] will drop out, we are being woefully shortsighted.

On the other hand, caring is just not enough; for these students there needs to be attention to different sorts of strategies to bring them into the life of the classroom. And, as in the case of my Hollywood-bound student, we are not doing our job if we just, as I did some years ago, give up and turn away.

Guidelines for dealing with the alienated student

Perhaps it is more a sense of degree than kind when we think of guidelines for dealing with alienated students and an effort to individualize our approach with them. Certainly there is no magic set of activities that will turn apathetic students into involved ones or calm the disaffected student. Certainly many of those students do succeed with minimal—even no—intervention. For many of them, however, extra help is necessary, and we need to do more than just leave students alone. Here are a few guiding principles:

- **Refuse to ignore your alienated students:** let them know that you know they are there in the class and that you are aware of them and their performance and want to see it improved. **Things to do:** speak to these students every day, make eye contact with them, ask them how they are doing. Do not avoid them, since it only reinforces their behavior.

- **Maintain expectations for the alienated student's academic performance:** regardless of the origin of the "problem," the student must be held accountable for his or her own achievement. **Things to do:** remind these students where they are in terms of assignments and deadlines; look for opportunities to tell them when you genuinely expect they will do well or be interested; praise them when they have earned it, without letting them know you really feel "it's about time."

- **Use performance contracts to shape behavior:** written contracts can define behavior and goals for students. **Things to do:** you and the student agree that answering so many times in class will equal such and such a reward, that so many assignments completed with such and such requirements will equal thus and such grade; you establish a written contract or form, and both you and the student sign and date it.

- **Make deals:** make deals all the time, on large issues (such as the performance contracts listed above) and small, giving students a sense that they can exert some control over their fate. **Things to do:** tell the students that if they turn in homework two days in a row they can go to the library for half the period; if they answer questions on Monday you will not call on them on Tuesday; and so on.

- **Remember that variety in curriculum and flexibility in instructional style is probably more important to your alienated students than to others:** the lack of choice can be numbing to the alienated student. **Things to do:** tell the student, you can read either this or that; you can do one of these four projects.

- Finally, without creating a wholly artificial situation, **try to structure activities where the student can be engaged and can legitimately succeed.**

With Marianna, whose whispered, virtually inaudible speech was a problem in class, the first step seemed to lie in her great strength in writing. I encouraged her to write out her comments rather than speak, and after some discussion, on an occasional basis I asked her to read her writing aloud. I also put Marianna in group and pair work where speaking in front of many others would not be such an issue. When these two strategies seemed to be consistently successful, I initiated a step-by-step attempt to get Marianna to speak audibly in large-group discussion. Along the way I realized that I had, inadvertently, reinforced Marianna's behavior pattern not only by physically moving closer to her to hear what she had said but by asking her to reiterate her comments and then praising her rather effusively when she did repeat them. I stopped those behaviors and started calling on Marianna as I would any other student. If her speech was only partially audible, I accepted it as she presented it, although other students would occasionally insist that she speak up. The combination of techniques seemed to work, and Marianna became more a part of the class, not the pale, whispering student she had been before. This procedure took about two semesters; it was my impression Marianna gathered some confidence and seemed to shed her "speaking aloud" block. By the time of graduation she was headed to college some states away and seemed more confident.

I was not able to do anything about Antoine's outbursts of temper. While he was awaiting jail, however, his behavior became understandably subdued. We worked out a reading list/project contract that directly addressed the years he would be spending in prison, and Antoine made excursions into sociological studies on crime in America and the penal system. Antoine did the best work he had ever done in class, and his written reports were careful and detailed. As tragic and sad as his situation was, his work allowed him to pass his English class. If nothing else, he went to prison with very recent academic success, not to mention some factual knowledge of what awaited him.

Marc and I consistently struck deals. Although it was against departmental policy for juniors in British Literature to write a research paper on anything but British literature, I threw out the rules. Marc's research paper, a major part of his year's grade, detailed the history and production schedules of the Harley Davidson Company, complete with specifications and descriptions of all the current models. I used the successful research project to build on other behavior; Marc now had a chance to pass my class despite his previous academic deficiencies, and we worked out an arrangement for minimal participation. Marc agreed to answer at least twice a week in class if left alone otherwise; he was not allowed to put his head down in class, but he did not have to bring his book and could share with someone else. He was absent a great deal and would not take unit tests. He also initially refused to take the final exam, but I got Angie to intervene, and Marc did, just barely, pass for the year.

The place of the guidance counselor, the parents, the administration

It is likely that when a student shows up in your class and appears to be apathetic or disaffected—or alienated—someone else in the school is aware of that student and his or her difficulties. It is not a given, however, and when you perceive, as a teacher, that the student is displaying signs of relatively desperate behavior, you must inform your guidance staff, make an effort to call the student's parents, or otherwise alert your administration. To this day, I still worry about my Hollywood starlet; I let her slip away. I decided not to expend the energy, and it's hard to know if the intervention of a counselor would have helped her cope more successfully with reality.

In the case of Marianna, other students were well aware that she was teetering on an emotional edge and were the ones to get a teacher involved as soon as she overdosed and slumped on the girls' bathroom floor. In her case, her parents, who had problems with their marriage and their drinking, had not been heretofore helpful and, because Marianna was a student who had never been any "trouble," she had escaped most of our notice. When she returned to school, however, it was under a certain amount of supervision and care. She was also placed in a foster home through the efforts of the guidance staff.

In the case of Antoine, the school was not directly responsible: he got a gun and shot the nightclub owner on the weekend and off school property. There had previously, however, been little organized effort to intervene in what escalated into a major problem and left one person dead and one life shattered. Antoine's outbursts were not recognized for what they eventually became; instead, his behavior in school and difficulty with teachers were perceived, possibly cynically, as fairly typical for a teenage African American male.

With Marc, parents, guidance counselors, and administration were aware of his difficulties in school, and, as a strategy, all three had resorted to reward structures, threats, and a variety of punishments. All three seemed ineffective: it was only when the rules were bent, deals struck, and his girlfriend Angie enlisted into the struggle that Marc showed improvement.

One Teacher's Strategy for Dealing with Alienated Students: "Big Bucks"

The three students described above and the strategies devised to help them are representative of attempts to deal with alienation in school. In the following account, however, an individual teacher had an entire class that was relatively unmotivated and certainly apathetic. What can a teacher do about a *group* that might be termed alienated? This teacher decided to use a behaviorally oriented plan that depended on extrinsic reward; for her the solution was successful, and while it may not represent any sort of plan you would like to implement in your classroom, it is worth detailing. "Big Bucks" offers a tangible, real-life reward for school activities, and in this school context, it worked.

One of the saving graces of the second half of my teaching career in high school was the friendship and guidance of a buddy down the hall. Nancy Rosenbaum, more than most anybody I knew, could come up with systems that worked and that were directly related to a student or instructional problem. I always admired Nancy for the crafty way she could adapt a principle or a concept to her students.

We have stayed friends through the years, and we share personal and school-related news. Recently, Nancy had a crisis of sorts. She had moved to a new school and just did not like what was going on in one of her classes. Here was her situation: she was teaching Project College, an intensive reading course to prepare athletes and others who were not particularly motivated or geared to go on with their education. Built within the class were a number of field trips and guest speakers to give students an idea of what was "out there" in the world. It seemed a relatively ideal structure.

But the students in Nancy's Project College class turned out to be a highly unmotivated group of juniors and seniors. As a group, they consistently came to class late and without materials. A disproportionate number wanted to go to the bathroom immediately when class began; some of them insisted on using class time to study for what they perceived were more important tests in other subjects. They were not convinced about going to college or jobs; for a few, an athletic scholarship might be an entry ticket, but even that was a bit remote. They were not angry or hostile: they were just indifferent, disaffected, and tuned out. They did not want to do a whole lot of work; for many, even participation in field trips was declined because it would mean make-up work in other, missed classes. For a number of students in this group, very little that was going on related to what they perceived as the reality of the world. And, as Nancy knew, they might just have been right.

What to do?

It was during a routine weekend trip to the local office supplies store that Nancy had a vision. Browsing in the aisles, she spied oversized note pads with a reproduction of a $500 bill on one side and space to write a grocery list or a memo or whatever on the other. It was a gimmick to jazz up ordinary note pads, but to Nancy it seemed to open a door. Big bucks, she thought. Hmmm . . . Big Bucks. She bought a lot of them. She made some notes, did some planning, and was ready to institute a barter-and-reward system in her class, a strategy she called "Big Bucks."

The next week in class she put the stack of $500 memo pads on her desk. Gesturing toward them, she began. What, she asked her students, do you have to do to earn Big Bucks? What, after these final years in school, can you do to get those greatly desired Big Bucks? The class perked up; here was a subject they were interested in. Students brainstormed, they brought up illegal activities, they snickered, they got serious.

Okay, the students concluded, to earn Big Bucks you have to do something fairly extraordinary—or maybe something pretty well for a sustained period of time. The students knew from their class that college graduates make about $100,000 more over a lifetime than high school graduates do. They even cited some of the guest speakers they had had in their class who could command higher fees in law, interior design, accounting for just those types of achievement. And, of course, with those Big Bucks you can have at least some of what most people call "the good life"—the conversation moved a bit to cars, houses, jewelry, vacations, and the like.

Nancy then gestured toward the note pads and outlined how students could earn the $500 "bills," one at a time, for certain behaviors or achievements:

- Being on time to class four times in a row: $500.
- Showing a 10 percent improvement in score from pre-test to post-test on certain subjects: $500.
- Sharing great ideas with the class, including study techniques that really worked or memory tricks for any subject: $500.
- Quizzes with scores of over 98 percent: $500 each.
- Being exceptionally polite and pleasant: $500.
- Keeping a semester calendar for assignments and deadlines: $1,000, payable the last day of class.
- Going on field trips that required make-up work in other classes: $500.
- Meeting deadlines, getting money and/or permissions slips in before the due date: $500.

Nancy then outlined what her students could do with the Big Bucks they earned, a list that was directly related to the issues of this particular class:

- Going to the bathroom during class cost $500.
- A trip to the library to study for something else was $3,000 for half the class period, $5,000, for the whole period ("not cheap," Nancy noted, "but a bargain if you need it").
- School rules dictated that four tardies to class equaled one after-school detention; a student could be tardy to class, without further penalty, for $500.
- The big-ticket item: buy all or parts of the final exam. For Big Bucks, students could purchase their year-end Project College English exam ahead of time and study accordingly. The entire exam sold for $9,500; individual sections cost varying amounts.

As Nancy set up "Big Bucks," students could lend money to others or give their money away. They could not, however, borrow from the teacher, forge the Big Bucks (Nancy initialed and dated each bill), or get their money replaced if they lost it. And a student who had purchased all or part of the final exam could show it to others who hadn't been able to. That decision was left entirely up to the individual.

The point of this one teacher's strategy for dealing with the alienated is that it was based on an established order all of us, students and teachers, intimately understand—money. It may have been symbolic—note pads with enlarged $500 bills—it may have relied a great deal on extrinsic reward, but it took on a power and a reality of its own. And in this one class, Big Bucks reinforced good behavior, study habits, *esprit de corps,* and a very good final exam. Nancy also observed, "Most of these students had jobs, and occasionally I'd hear one remark that this was just like life; as soon as they had a payday, they'd have a bunch of bills that used it all."

What would Nancy change? She wrote:

The use of Big Bucks cut the tardies and bathroom trips even more effectively then I first thought it could. It gave me a chance to reinforce behaviors I think will help students—sharing study ideas, practicing on quizzes with each other to get the 98%, keeping a calendar so that deadlines do not totally sneak up on them, consciously thinking of the extra politeness or helpfulness that may help them in their relationships with others. It also did not make every reward a grade.

Students suggested things to earn and spend Big Bucks that I could never have thought of, and some of them were great ideas. . . . Students also can save!! During second semester, everyone's priority was accumulating the $9,500 first—everything else could wait. When they had their nest eggs, spending could begin.

At the end of the semester (and sometimes before) students could be incredibly generous with each other. One girl was the surprised recipient of $1,000 from a student who gave or "loaned" Aimee the money because Aimee needed it right then.

I never had any big quarrels or fights about money. Students did like to keep up with how much they had and how much other people had—a couple of people counted their "cash" at the end of the period every day. But the emphasis was never all money—money was a bonus.

While the administration had to be notified, Nancy wrote that members of "the administration, including the department chair, came to observe when I was first beginning with Big Bucks and were very interested and supportive" and the program then went along on its own. It is one teacher's solution to a problem in one disaffected class, a solution that relates to the class—and also uses what we so frequently refer to as the outside and "real" world.

The Average Student: Caught in the Middle

At one point in American history a large group of citizens was characterized as the "silent majority." That phrase still has some power and can be applicable to what is often termed the "average" student: the ones in the middle who are neither characterized as gifted nor alienated and who do not otherwise call attention to themselves. These students are the majority of those we teach in middle school and high school and are tracked and labeled as "average." When they are flanked either in a single class or in our teaching day by others at the extremes, it is easy to gloss over them and to forget that they, too, are a vital part of our teaching life. While most of the activities in this book are directed to them, the "average" student, it is helpful to consider them as a group with as much definition as our alienated students.

Kids who don't cause any "trouble," who largely do their assignments and cooperate, can be given short shrift by us as teachers. We need to remember that these students also require attention, praise, reinforcement, and, indeed, an acknowledgement that what the system may call an "average" student can be highly misleading. Within your average group can be startlingly original thinkers and, conversely, kids who are over their heads academically. Being seen as average is not necessarily a pleasant experience, and for some students, it can also be a conscious strategy to keep notice from being called to oneself, a way to hide. We as teachers need, as best we can, to remember to examine the labels we so often glibly place on or readily accept for our students and not lose our responsibility to our average students.

The Gifted Student: Burdens and Responsibilities

The pinnacle of success for many teachers is to be given a class of "gifted" students, those who have risen, at least at a given point in their school lives, to the top academically. Some enjoy this teaching immensely and find it very satisfying to deal with motivated, competitive, college-bound students. Such students, however, have their own special challenges, and not all of them are academic.

There is for these students often an incredible pressure to produce, succeed, and, in some cases, to be relatively "perfect" in a variety of other areas, notably social and athletic. While some of this pressure comes from parents and teachers, a great deal of it also comes from the students themselves.

It was during my teaching of Advanced Placement English that I had my most extensive contact with students who could be termed gifted. While not every one of those I taught was truly gifted, the majority were academically talented. These students needed intellectual stimulation but also needed less an atmosphere of competition and aggression than one of mutuality and cooperation. In almost all cases, the students needed to consider their own paths to success and, in the case of the AP class, the limitations—perceived or not—of their segregation from the rest of the student body.

Accordingly, I tried to use more cooperative learning with these students and, to an extent, to deemphasize what was for many of them the major motivating force of their lives, the grade. It was possible with these students to make a convincing case for postponing a tangible reward or to use participation and completion as benchmarks.

Keeping in touch with my gifted students' parents was also as important as keeping in touch with those of my less successful students and helped, in some cases, to soften the pressure from home.

And we need to remember that gifted students are as varied as all our other students. Jill Williamson recalls her AP English class and paints a portrait of the varied gifted student:

> Shawna and Amy were best friends, but their personalities were entirely different. Amy spent most of her time popping gum and cracking silly jokes and took her poetry quite seriously. Shawna worshipped her GPA yet did the very least amount of work she could to get by. And Shawna had the most beautiful head of long, wavy, red hair. I was so jealous. Jason, Jim and Jeff always became the teachers's pets. Jason was my modern-day Adonis. Jim slept most of the time but was quite charming nonetheless. And Jeff missed class frequently to celebrate Jewish holidays, and he always seasoned his speech with multi-syllabic words. T. J. was sensitive and had a quiet laugh. York had the quickest wit of all of us and had seven brothers and sisters. Greg was our token burly, slow-witted jock, and Sean was our token surfer dude. Jennifer came from a broken home and her expression was blank most of the time, yet she wrote the most eloquent and creative short stories. John was my favorite classmate. On the outside he was a Virginia gentlemen, but secretly he spent quite a bit of time drawing phallic symbols and telling dirty jokes. He was also a terrible speller. Nikki was my manic-depressive friend who spent way too much time reading Ayn Rand and stopped coming to school about halfway through our senior year. I was the class spelling champion.

Students as varied as Jill's friends in her AP class will be in your class, too.

The Delicate Contract with Students

Dealing with and getting along with your students is a central priority of teaching; depending on your personality, while you may not enter into any sort of lovefest with your students, there needs to be a sense of mutual respect and care and feeling on both sides that this endeavor is worth embarking on. While indeed school is compulsory and your language arts class is required, there is also a necessary mutuality to this business.

Regardless of the "level" of the class, the degree of alienation, giftedness, or averageness, students can refuse to cooperate. What if, we might wonder, they gave a class and nobody came? What if the teacher asked a question and nobody, but nobody—ever so sullenly or ever so politely—answered? What if a test was distributed, and nobody picked up a pencil and took it? It is a delicate contract because, indeed, there is little we can do if students, at the extreme, absolutely refuse to cooperate or, at the not as extreme, change the class expectations until they are virtually meaningless. This lack of faith can occur with any level of students, and in some ways it is a teacher's worst nightmare.

A story from Horace's Compromise

Theodore R. Sizer, who may one day be termed one of the great educational prophets of the latter part of this century, had a vision of sorts while doing field research for *Horace's Compromise,* a book which I love and from which I take a lot of wisdom. Sizer has been a secondary school teacher and principal and a university professor and dean; he knows school and students and has ideas about how school should be structured. He does not have it all figured out, however, and even with his years of experience, he continues to go into schools and talk with students and teachers and principals. During one of those visits he experienced an incident in a school parking lot that took him by surprise, and it's worth sharing:

> I arrived by car at the school at 7:15 A.M., thirty minutes before the first bell. It was a cool day, and the first arrivals to the large high school I was visiting were gathered in clots in the sun outside, around the low, meandering structures that housed their classrooms. Parking

lots and hard-used lawns encircled the buildings. There were no sidewalks in this neighbor-hood, even though it was quite built up; the school property was ringed by small houses and business establishments. Everyone came to school by bus or by private car. . . . I found a place and parked.

It was immediately clear from the stares I received from nearby students that I had picked a student lot, not one for staff or for visitors. . . . [The students] leaned against [their cars] or sat on them, chatting. Many drank coffee out of paper cups. Some smoked furtively as I drew near; though unfamiliar to them, I was wearing the drab coat-tie-slacks uniform of the school administrator who might admonish them.

My instinct was to snicker at the parking lot scene. . . . My condescension disappeared, however, when I paid more attention to the students gathered around [their] vehicles, kids observing the visitor who had taken a space on their turf. Their attitude was in no way men-acing, but it was freighted with an absence of interest. I was an object to be observed and, if they were smoking, to be mildly reacted to. . . .

These were older students, drivers. In their easy chatting among themselves, in their self-absorption and nonchalance, they showed self-assurance bordering on truculence. They had their own world.

My reaction was nervousness. I tried to smile a sorry-fellas-but-I-didn't-know-where-the-visitors'-parking-lot-was message, but it did not come off. I felt the awkward outsider, at distance from these composed young people. Even as I knew that at the bell they would enter the buildings and engage in the rituals of dutiful school-going and that they would get more boisterous and engaging as the early morning mist over their spirits parted, I also knew that these were considerable people, ones who would play the game adult educators asked them to play only when and how they wanted to. The fact that many of them, for a host of reasons, chose to go along with the structures of the school did not lessen the force of the observation: they possessed the autonomous power not to.

In this sense, kids run schools. Their apparent acquiescence to what their elders want them to do is always provisional. Their ability to undermine even the illusions of certain adult authority and of an expectation of deference was admirably if benignly displayed by the students on that parking lot. A less benign challenge can be made by students in any classroom when, for whatever reason, they collectively, quietly, but assuredly decide to say no. The fact that most go along with the system masks the nascent power that students hold. Few adults outside the teaching profession understand this. (138–40)

So how do we make sure that the students in our classes do not say no, do not decide not to participate?

It is, indeed, a delicate contract. We need, I think, to remember four things:

1. **We need to be reasonable, to offer students activities that are meaning-ful, doable, and have real connection to skills and knowledge.**

2. **We need to articulate why what we are studying or writing or reading or discussing is important.**

3. **We need to listen to students and to accord them the same courtesy we would accord our friends.**

4. **We need, finally, to remember that school, enduring as a concept, is perennial largely because the majority of students have come to our classes over the decades with a certain hopeful belief that they will learn from us and that the learning will make their lives better.**

Two Students: Tanya and Barry

Despite my stories of difficult students and failed expectations, I have to end this chapter on a positive note. An exceptional benefit to teaching—a benefit that perhaps I have not emphasized enough—is that working with students is often close to magical. Not every month, not every semester, not even every year, but often, often enough to keep you going, you will meet and work with students who shape and positively influence your life. You will remember these students and even keep in touch with some of them—as I still do with two I have written about in this chapter, Marianna and Angie. You will receive from these students kindness, consideration, and often genuine affection. They may make you laugh, and they will make you feel, perhaps as only those who work with the young can regularly feel, that the world is indeed a big and exciting and glorious place.

And beyond the parting hugs and handshakes and occasional tears, beyond the letters of appreciation and the little gifts from classes and groups—the necklace from the literary magazine staff, the locket from Advanced Placement, the coffee mugs and blank journals and books and glass apples and pens from the homeroom, the junior class, individual students—beyond all the little tokens and tributes that I, like most teachers, have received over the years, beyond the tangible gifts are those moments when your students often reveal to you their trust and friendship.

I have chosen, of those students, two who affected me in memorable ways.

Tanya and I kept a running argument going for three years; first in sophomore homeroom, then in a junior English class, then, her senior year, in my Advanced Placement where she was one of a handful of African American students in the pilot course. She was terribly bright and very sarcastic, and while I knew she was both vulnerable and talented, she could occasionally bring out the worst in me, her teacher. I loved Tanya's spirit, but she also had a way of asking the wrong question at just the wrong time, of challenging at precisely the vulnerable moment when the class was ready to have one bright member take on the teacher. Sometimes I could appreciate Tanya's wit and verve and really admire it: with the roll of an eye or a quip or just a well-timed question, Tanya could turn a class around. Sometimes, however, she tried my patience.

A good student for her sophomore year despite some run-ins with other teachers, Tanya became a *very* good student her junior year and learned to play the politeness game. In Advanced Placement during her senior year, she was aggressive in discussion and bright, and I especially enjoyed her writing. She and I tried to rise above our differences.

And it was Tanya who called me at home late one night with a very adult and truly serious personal crisis. She called, she said, to ask my advice. I would not betray her, she said, and she wanted to know what I would do in her situation. She was brisk and almost businesslike. I was mildly stunned—Tanya and I were more worthy adversaries than friends—but I gave her what insights I had, and we talked frankly on the phone for a half hour or so.

Back in school, Tanya waited some weeks before she told me that the crisis had been resolved. I was relieved for her and, operating in a rather new sense of relationship, under a truce of sorts, Tanya and I went on to finish the semester together. She graduated with honors, and as I shook her hand in congratulation, I felt a renewed sense of affection and concern for this complicated and smart young woman who had, surprisingly, possibly all along, trusted me. Her graduation was bittersweet: while I was happy to see Tanya leave high school for a very prestigious university, I seriously doubted her chances for success. And I knew, of course, as with many students, that I would never know the outcome.

It was fully four years later when a graduation invitation from that prestigious university arrived in the mail. I could scarcely believe the name on the return address, but it was from Tanya. After four years of silence, she had sent me the news. Of course, it was typical Tanya; written on the back of her calling card was her one-line comment, teasing, jaunty, and proud: *Ha! Ha! Bet you're surprised!* Indeed I was and touched that, years later, Tanya knew that I would want to know the news.

Tanya taught me something about students and teachers, about influence that is not always obvious, and about relationships that are forged over the years. Maybe I had failed to see it all along, but my sparring partner, the bright and aggressive Tanya, had turned out to be a student with whom I shared a bond and who seemed to know that I cared. And Tanya continued her triumphs; she is now a medical doctor.

Barry was a new student to my high school who did not get along very well with school rules or policies. Very early in the semester he had been in a difficulty with a number of his teachers. Typically, he and I had had a series of confrontations in my third-period class, which escalated so quickly that I really wondered if we could stand to work together for the rest of the semester. I tried to talk to Barry, but he blew me off pretty convincingly, and I decided to exercise a rare option in our school. I asked, on the basis of personality conflict, that Barry be transferred to another teacher and another class. It was probably a cowardly move on my part, but there was something about the challenge of Barry I did not feel equal to that semester; I felt I had enough to handle with five classes and 140 students.

Regardless of my motives, Barry saw the request as an insult, and, possibly on general principles, was enraged. In a subsequent conference about his schedule—and his behavior in my class and others—he assaulted an assistant principal and was immediately suspended from school.

When I saw him in the halls after he returned to his classes—and his new English class—I stayed clear; Barry was one student who I had crossed and, inadvertently or not, my transfer request was the precipitating event that resulted in his suspension. Barry, I suspected, would be more than willing to retaliate. But the year went on quietly, and I saw little of him.

It was, then, with some serious trepidation that I found myself, with other teachers and students, on a bus with Barry. My school had arranged a modified Outward Bound experience, and I was one of a dozen teacher volunteers to go into the mountains with students who had been, for varying reasons, identified as at risk. The Outward Bound day was an exercise in communication and trust building, centered around physical tests of strength and endurance that were performed in teacher/student teams. Barry, of course, was a prime and logical candidate and was, with some of his friends, on the trip.

When we began the Outward Bound day, I had no control over the activities or grouping. There was some risk in some of the "events," and participants were warned about the danger of falling or slipping—teamwork was essential to preventing injuries. At any rate, teachers and students were randomly placed in teams for varying tests of strength, agility, and trust building. My team's turn came to scale a horizontal crossbar held twelve feet above the ground by two vertical uprights. The whole structure, crossbar and uprights, had no ropes, no handholds, no ladders, and certainly no safety features such as a net. As luck would have it, I was selected to be the first to be launched over the top and handed down to an opposing team working on the other side. I hated the look of this activity, the height and the possible danger, but I just couldn't be the teacher/coward of the team.

Fearfully but doggedly, trusting my team members as I was encouraged to do, I climbed up the back and on to the shoulders of a volunteer. Standing on his shoulders and balancing the best I could, I stood up and reached for the crossbar, twelve feet above the ground and some two feet above my head. I jumped, grabbed for dear life, threw a leg over, hugged the cross bar, and desperately looked to the volunteer on the other side to help me get down.

I must have been more concerned about breaking my neck than I had realized, because I hadn't noticed the members of the other team. I literally couldn't trust my eyes—on the other side of the crossbar and the only thing between me and the void was my former student Barry.

He reached for me. I had a real sense of fatalism, twelve feet above the hard-packed earth, and possibly for that reason I felt I had to say something. Who knows, it might have been my last words before I went to the hospital with my broken leg or arm or both, and anyway, Barry and I had not talked since he had been removed from my class and suspended.

I looked at him. Barry was expressionless. It's a long way down was all I could think. And then I just blurted out what was really on my mind, "If you want to get even, here's your chance." Certainly here was his chance: this was one of the most dangerous of the day's activities, and the accidental slip and fall of a volunteer, though regrettable, would not necessarily be that suspicious. Some of these facts had been outlined before this trip; I knew it, and I supposed Barry did too.

For an eerie moment Barry remained expressionless and silent but then, twelve feet in the air, he smiled, shook his head, and grabbed my arms. Not gently—but not roughly—he delivered me safely to the members of his team—and the ground. I did not look back as I walked away and went on to the next activity, but I remember my legs were shaking.

Later that day during a break I went looking for Barry. I found him, sat down with him, and we talked. I thanked him for not dropping me, and that opened a very intense twenty-minute conversation. Barry was, as I guess I should have known, about as decent a person as I had ever met. He hated school, he didn't get along with his parents, he worried about his life and his girlfriend. I told him I was sorry about what had happened in my class; he told me he was sorry too. We shook hands, went our separate ways to finish the day, and, later, when we saw each other in the halls during the remainder of the semester, we waved and smiled. We were, in a way, friends who had done something together, shared something important. I almost hoped I would have Barry in class the next year, but his parents moved out of the area, and I never saw him again.

I never forgot Barry or that day, though, and I think about how frustrated and angry he probably was, how tempted he could have been to have an "accident" with a hated teacher, and how he, with every temptation to get even and every possibility he could get away with it, refused to. To this day I wonder, if given a similar situation, I would have resisted as he did. I learned something from Barry, something about doing the right thing regardless, and his example stays with me after all these years.

Despite the biting accuracy of the Paul Simon song quoted at the beginning of this chapter, most of our students, like Tanya and Barry and many others, believe that we, their teachers, not only know something but are people of good will and will treat them fairly.

And, in a way, the belief of the young in us, their teachers, and their belief in what we represent, the power of education, is both heartening and heart breaking. It is the essence of optimism and faith, and, unfortunately, it is often not confirmed by experience. If we take this business seriously, however, we are bound, to the best of our abilities, to never disillusion our students or dishonor what is nothing less than a sacred trust. This can be a hard assignment, this stuff of teaching, but the people before us in our classrooms and the lives they represent are briefly, yet profoundly, entrusted to us. As daunting—terrifying even—as that may be, it is also our little piece of immortality.

 ## FOR YOUR JOURNAL

Think of your middle and high school friends or of some students you may have recently observed. Can you find ones who possibly could be characterized as "alienated"? "average"? "gifted"? What behaviors do or did those students exhibit? What kinds of assignments or teachers appealed to them? did not appeal to them? What variations or refinements would *you* make on the three categories of students presented in this chapter? If you care to, how would you describe yourself, in middle school or in high school, in relation to those categories?

REFERENCES

Bower, Bruce. "Teenage Turning Point: Does Adolescence Herald the Twilight of Girls' Self-Esteem?" *Science News* 139 (March 23, 1991): 184–86.

Eckert, Penelope. *Jocks and Burnouts: Social Categories and Identity in the High School.* New York: Teachers College Press, 1989.

Gilligan, Carol, Nona P. Lyons, Trudy J. Hanmer, eds. *Making Connections: The Relational Worlds of Adolescent Girls at Emma Willard School.* Troy, NY: Emma Willard School, 1989.

Glasser, William. *Control Theory in the Classroom.* Harper & Row, 1985.

Gough, Pauline B. "The Key to Improving Schools: An Interview with William Glasser." *Phi Delta Kappan* 68 (May 1987): 656–62.

Lindley, Daniel A., Jr. "For Teachers of the Alienated: Three Defenses Against Despair." *English Journal* 79 (October 1990): 26–31.

Lost in the Crowd: A Statement on Class Size and Teacher Workload. Urbana, IL: NCTE, 1990.

McNeil, Linda. *Contradictions of Control.* New York: Routledge and Kegan Paul, 1986.

Pfeffer, Susan Beth. "Basic Rules of Teenage Life." *The ALAN Review* 17 (Spring 1990): 5–7.

Rosenbaum, Nancy. Personal Interview with Author. June 1991.

Simon, Paul. "Kodachrome." *There Goes Rhymin' Simon.* CBS/Columbia Records, 1973.

Sizer, Theodore R. *Horace's Compromise: The Dilemma of the American High School.* Boston: Houghton Mifflin, 1984.

United States Department of Education. *National Education Longitudinal Study of 1988: A Profile of the American Eighth Grader.* Washington, DC: United States Department of Education, 1990.

 RESOURCES

These sources extend the subjects raised in this chapter; the Rodriguez and Rose books are personal and interesting portraits of individuals dealing with school.

Barbe, W. B. and J. S. Renzulli, eds. *Psychology and Education of the Gifted.* 3d ed. New York: Irvington Publishers, 1982.

Brooks, Charlotte, ed. *Tapping Potential: English and Language Arts for the Black Learner.* Urbana, IL: NCTE, 1985.

Laycock, F. *Gifted Children.* 2d ed. Glenview, IL: Scott Foresman, 1982.

Rodriguez, Richard. *Hunger of Memory: The Education of Richard Rodriguez.* Boston: David R. Godine, 1982.

Rose, Mike. *Lives on the Boundary: The Struggles and Achievements of America's Underprepared.* New York: Penguin, 1989.

Sizer, Theodore R. *Horace's School: Redesigning the American High School.* Boston: Houghton Mifflin, 1992.

Steele, Claude M. "Race and the Schooling of Black Americans." *The Atlantic Monthly* 269 (April 1992): 68–78.

CHAPTER 4

TEACHING LITERATURE
THEORETICAL ISSUES

And gladly wolde he lerne and gladly teche.

—**Geoffrey Chaucer, "Prologue" (*Canterbury Tales*)**

The Fear of Not Knowing Enough

I am back in my high school, standing in a wide and empty corridor. It is time to go to class; in fact, I am late, and behind the closed doors are other students already seated and working. I need to go to class; I have a test today. Funny thing, though, I have not been to class in months, have done no homework and no studying. I know I am going to fail the test, fail the course, and not graduate from high school. I just hate that class; I don't understand the subject and have avoided it until now. Right this moment, however, I would give anything to have been working all along; the feeling of fear and impending doom is overwhelming.

This, of course, is my dream, my special, recurring anxiety nightmare. Like many people, this dream comes periodically to visit me, and I think it stands for fear of failure or worry about achievement and preparation. While you may not have such recurring dreams, you are probably a bit apprehensive about how much you know as you prepare to enter the classroom.

There is hardly a one of us on the eve of teaching or in the first few years in the classroom who felt that she or he knew *enough*. All of us are haunted by the worry that we are ill prepared, underread, insufficiently educated, ignorant about a number of crucial areas. And the fact is, we probably are. Bluntly put, the amount and depth and breadth of knowledge that we need to be fully conversant with all aspects of language arts is just not possible for most of us to achieve in the preparation years before teaching. It is also not reasonable to expect that level of expertise in the first few years.

The fallacy, however, of the fear of being ill educated is the unspoken assumption that our reading and study should really be completed by the time we become teachers. Most teachers know that the first year in the classroom simply marks the start of a new phase of education and, indeed, that we will never "own" pieces of literature or facts about language or grasp writing principles so firmly as when, year after year, we handle and manipulate and use and create activities based on those elements of language arts. We have to, it is true, *be* a teacher from the very first day; but as veteran teachers know, we do not have control over all of our subject matter for some years to come. As the title of this book insists, we also continue to *become* teachers, and that includes expanding our knowledge and our skill in the classroom.

We do, as Chaucer reminds us, not only "gladly teche" but also "gladly lerne" (1. 308). And for those who see Chaucer's oft-quoted phrase as more of a definition of a political stance regarding teaching, it is, interestingly enough, also a pure practicality: teachers, in order to teach, really must continue to learn. The two activities are, unless one makes a conscious effort to resist, symbiotically related.

The idea that you don't know enough, that your learning is continuing—possibly, in one sense of the word, just starting—may be a depressing thought for you. If you look at it another way, it also might be relatively heartening. It would be, in the long run, horrifically boring if you could really know everything, master everything almost immediately. There might be more surety than you are feeling now but how emptily the teaching years would stretch before you! There is also the undeniable benefit (especially in literature) of discovering with your students and thus seeing somewhat with fresh eyes. Those thoughts may be most of what sustains you during the first few years in the classroom when, with mounting panic, you realize that you will occasionally be teaching something over which you yourself have only the most marginal control.

Take heart, new teacher, and forge ahead: the excitement of learning will probably outweigh the sheer fear. You will also have the pleasure of watching your own tastes change and expand as you add to your storehouse of learning authors and ideas and techniques. Unless you are very different from almost all teachers, you will, as the years go on, become far more accomplished—and educated—than you can really imagine right now.

And, of course, it almost goes without saying: if your own education has left you deficient in some area, it is your responsibility as a teacher, as a professional, to make up that deficiency. And, at this stage in the game, it really doesn't matter whose "fault" the deficiency may be; you didn't take the course or the teachers were not effective or you just didn't think the information was that important. It is, however, up to you to get yourself up to speed.

If you are confused about assonance and alliteration, look them up and learn them; if you've never gotten point of view straight, start studying now; if you don't know the difference between the Middle Ages and the Enlightenment, you can read about them; if somehow you've missed the major American twentieth-century novels, select a reasonable number and set aside some weekend time to enjoy them. If the distinction between phrase and clause eludes you, if you are not certain what a parallel construction looks like, you can learn it. You will now gladly learn as well as gladly teach. It comes, happily, with the territory.

FOR YOUR JOURNAL

This is an entry you may want to keep private; it is for you, not anyone else. Right now, at this point in your life, make a brief list regarding your knowledge of literature, language, and writing. At the top of your journal page make three columns:

What I Know I Really Know; What I Sort of Know; What I Know I Need to Know. Now look over the three columns; which is longest, which shortest? In the "What I Know I Need to Know" column, which one or two items do you think you will absolutely need in order to deal with your students? absolutely not need for some time to come? What of the items can you learn this week? this month?

Literature: The Heart of Language Arts

As writing became more valued in school instruction, and computers and word processing took a more prominent place in the classroom, there was a fear that literature would be dethroned as the "queen" of the language arts curriculum. Certainly the days of literature always occupying the lion's share of the curriculum are somewhat on the wane. But literature, the reason most of us are English teachers—and the area with which we are usually the most familiar—remains the backbone of English language arts.

As I talked about in Chapter 1, most of us entered this profession because of our love of literature. Many of us are convinced that reading is, of and by itself, a good thing to do, and we want to encourage our students to engage in it and be captivated by its magic. Many of us also associate with literature an experience that moved us and that was represented in fiction, nonfiction, poetry, or drama. We have favorite authors, lines, scenes that we carry with us much as other people carry recollections with them from their childhood. Literature is, for many of us, a cosmic memory bank of sorts, and the conflicts and characters and metaphors of our favorite books can take on a deep and highly personal resonance.

While not all of our students will appear to react with the same enthusiasm regarding all the literature we read and respond to in the classroom, literature is, for most of our students, the most enjoyable part of language arts. It is an opportunity for them to literally lose themselves in a book. Students also find themselves in other characters as well as being able to live vicariously other lives and in other eras. Finally, reading literature can be, for students, an opportunity to experience the sheer art of a well-crafted plot, the delineation of a character, the unfolding of an important theme.

Four Reasons for Reading Literature

Escape

Many of us have used—and still use—reading literature as an escape. While some might interpret that behavior as a negative, it can also be profoundly positive: books allow us to leave ourselves and go somewhere else. It is an old-fashioned phrase, antiquely put, but Emily Dickinson's belief that "there is no frigate like a book" is indeed apt; a book, like no other vehicle, is stunningly equipped to carry us somewhere else.

While it is the younger readers who seem to have the most consistent experiences with "losing" themselves in reading, many of your middle school and high school students will still know that experience. It can continue on through our reading lives, especially when the book involved is, for whatever reason, of gripping interest to us. The power of escape and its relation to reading is often ignored in classrooms; letting students read for sustained periods of quiet time can give them space in their day—space they might not otherwise have—to let a book enthrall.

Finding yourself

As mentioned above, there are a number of other appropriate reasons for your students to read literature. Looking for oneself in characters is important to all readers, especially young readers, and helps to account, in part, for the popularity of literature featuring young adult protagonists. Indeed, our students will often read with an overarching concern in mind: how is this character different from me? how alike? Would I do the same? think the same? While such an intense interest in the relation of the characters to the reader may seem excessive to an older reader (and it may not be something you do a lot now in your own reading), it is important to remember that for many of our students, the questions of how they are individually related to the characters peopling the pages is of paramount interest. We need to use this connection, not stifle it, and we need to encourage students to compare and contrast characters and characters' choices to themselves.

Learning about other people, other places, other times

Another great reason to read is that like the escape that Emily Dickinson's "frigate" gives us, books take us to other places and other eras. Nonfiction tells us about a variety of aspects of our universe, and there is virtually no limit to where fiction can be placed—outer space, foreign countries, under the ocean, during an earthquake, in the midst of a battle, during prehistoric times, in the future, fifty years ago. And, of course, literature can be set in a place very much like the one you live in and can occur this year, this month, right now, and can tell us about some very everyday aspects of our lives.

This leads, interestingly enough, to a philosophical question: how much reading should be from the familiar (that which is directly reflective of the student's own life), and how much should be clearly outside the student's experience? While it seems a species of stupidity to stuff suburban students with literature that is set exclusively in rural towns or to give later-twentieth-century teenagers novels only about nineteenth-century adults, we need to be wary of, even for the best of reasons, confining students to what they "know."

The primary issue is that our students are learning in our classes; while they know a great deal, there is a great deal that is relatively new to them and that books can provide. To give inner-city students only literature set in very large urban centers or, more specifically, Latino students only books about living in the *barrio* or athletes only books about playing sports or girls only books about romance is narrow-minded and limiting and plays more on stereotypes than on any possible comfort of familiarity.

While, for example, I have often wondered about eighth graders truly appreciating Ernest Hemingway's widely taught *The Old Man and the Sea,* there may be a real justification for giving the novel, as it is across this country, to thirteen-year-olds. What the aging Santiago, an illiterate fisherman living in pre-Castro Cuba, faces out there in the ocean—and in himself—has a certain amount to say to any reader, including a young person. Given a choice, I probably would not use *The Old Man and the Sea* with my eighth graders and would prefer a strong young adult (YA) novel on a similar theme (such as Gary Paulsen's *Hatchet,* a survival tale of great power, or Brock Cole's *The Goats,* in which two young people run away from summer camp and find food and shelter and a new sense of self-esteem, or Jean Craighead George's *Julie of the Wolves,* the story of an Eskimo girl's survival in the Artic wilderness). On the other hand, I can also see the benefits of having a thirteen-year-old contemporary American look at the choices and problems of a pre-Castro Cuban fifty-year-old. It is a powerful novel, and it speaks across the years.

It's an ongoing issue, and while you need to be sensitive to your students and what they will tell you they like and don't like, especially with regard to relevance, remember it's also your job to, yes, "expose" them to as much as possible. Something may catch fire and emerge later in their lives; balancing those two demands may be hard, but it is not impossible.

Aesthetic appreciation

Because you have been reading a while and have, further, taken a large number of college English classes and spent time looking at the structure, content, and message of fiction, nonfiction, poetry, and drama, you have acquired a certain familiarity with the territory of aesthetic appreciation. You know how to spot foreshadowing and define a climax; you can see how characters are foils for one another and how themes are repeated and restated; you know imagery and understand the power of figurative language.

It is, you must admit, a certain amount of fun to notice the craft of an essay, the turn of a line of poetry, the skill of a novel's climax. The problem in many language arts classrooms, however, is that that is often *all* a student is asked to talk about or write about or even value. Gone is the interest in interest (did you escape with this book?); the concern for character (how different is the protagonist from you?); the consideration of other place/other timeness (what about this setting? this time?). Often, by placing our entire emphasis on aesthetics—how a piece of literature achieves what it is—we can destroy the reading and the pleasure of literature. It goes back to a cynical statement cited in Chapter 1, "English class ruined every good book I ever read."

If there is a hierarchy to the four reasons for reading literature—if one is valued as a more "mature" skill than another—aesthetic appreciation is, for most people, at the top. And indeed, aesthetic appreciation should be a focus of older readers. Nevertheless, this is misleading and, possibly, the source of many students' unhappiness with English language arts classes. While we may want our students to have some appreciation, we do them and the literature a great disservice if we confine all of our discussion and attention—and testing—to that one aspect of the reasons for reading. Which leads us to literary criticism and another reason you need to spend a great deal of time with your students and their response to all aspects of literature, not only the pure aesthetics.

FOR YOUR JOURNAL

Looking at the four reasons for reading literature, think about when and how you can relate to each reason. Perhaps a specific novel or novels might stand out as being the major example of reading to "escape," of "finding yourself," and so on. What do you remember about yourself as a reader and each of the four reasons for reading? Can you link any pieces of literature to specific reasons? Are there books you read that, for you at least, fulfill all four of the reasons for reading?

Schools of Literary Criticism: Why You Should Care

It may seem that in school you were just taught literature; you read a short story or a poem in class or for homework and discussed it or wrote about it or took a test on it and that was that. Actually, whether you were aware of it or not, the way you were taught literature was based on a number of philosophical assumptions and schools of literary criticism. Certainly, as an English major you are quite aware of literary criticism and of its impact as you read and talk about literature. Whether in middle school or college, literary theory can have a powerful effect. Raman Selden in *A Reader's Guide to Contemporary Literary Theory* writes that:

> One can think of the various literary theories as raising different questions about literature. Theories may ask questions from the point of view of the writer, of the work, of the reader, of what we usually call 'reality.' (3)

What that "reality" is can certainly vary according to the interpretation of the theory. For example, if you look at any literature from the perspective of **feminist theory**, if you realize that many times gender has shaped literature in powerful—and often not immediately apparent—ways, you see it very differently than you would otherwise. Taming the wilderness, hunting the white whale, going to war, ascending the throne, finding a mate, all take on a distinctly gender-oriented cast, and these activities, which are still certainly "privileged" over the domestic aspects we associate with "female" life (cooking, tending a child), take up the predominant time in literary air space.

The contemporary popularity of Kate Chopin's *The Awakening* is somewhat a case in point. The story of a woman who literally awakens from her traditional role as a wife and mother, the novel languished in obscurity until almost seventy years after its 1899 publication date. While termed "poison" by nineteenth century reviewers, *The Awakening*'s subject matter is now very acceptable to readers, and the novel is highly rated.

But to turn to the four major schools of literary criticism: if your teachers spent a great deal of time giving you information regarding the era the literature was written, the context in which it occurred, and who else was writing then, those teachers were concentrating on **historical** or **literary background**. For some teachers, that background is of less interest than the life of the author; if you remember being asked to pay attention to a writer's birth and death dates and other such information, your teachers were probably emphasizing **author biography**.

As a third approach, many of us were taught through the approach of what has been called the **New Criticism**. According to New Critical theory, where and when and even by whom a piece of literature is written is ultimately irrelevant. In New Critical theory, literature is considered a piece of art; very little other information is important or even of interest. This was a highly influential way to approach literature and was used almost exclusively in colleges, filtering down to the high schools, for some decades. The focus of New Critical approaches was largely on close reading of the text and aesthetic appreciation, one of the reasons for reading that I outlined above.

Finally, yet another way to approach literature—to ask students to relate literature to themselves, their lives, and what else they have read—is termed a **reader response** approach, and the emphasis here is on what the reader him- or herself brings to the piece. Gone is the interest in historical context, the author biography, or the aesthetic twists and turns as major concentrations. Using a reader response approach, what teachers ask of students is how the literature intertwines with what they know, who they are, and what they believe. Clearly, a reader response approach does not involve the factual information of a literary or historical emphasis; it does not address the author's biography and the New Critical aesthetic considerations. Reader response contends that most readers approach pieces differently, can have a shift not only from reader to reader but through a person's reading of the same text at different times in his or her life.

The Four Schools: What To Do?

There are valid reasons for all four approaches and, given a perfect world and more than enough time (to paraphrase Andrew Marvell's "To His Coy Mistress"), we as teachers would skillfully combine all four (and possibly add others, such as feminist theory), shifting our emphasis in response to the demands of the literature and the interests of our students. Such blending and adjusting, however, are not possible in most classrooms. Thus we need to ask ourselves as teachers: what is served by each of these four approaches?

New Critical approaches to literature came about because of serious dissatisfaction with extensive concentration on historical context and author biography. Whether the poem was the first or the last of a writer's career or was written after the artist's mid-life nervous breakdown seemed not only irrelevant but also to deflect from the consideration of the work itself. Whether the literature occurred in response to some historical or topical event seemed equally irrelevant. Certainly there are clear exceptions to this: students probably need to know, for example, why Jonathan Swift was so outraged by events in Ireland that he would write the scathing "A Modest Proposal." Students might also need to understand that Nathaniel Hawthorne's *The Scarlet Letter* is not a historically accurate account of the Puritans but is a highly selected, highly filtered, nineteenth-century interpretation of a period of history. Do they need, however, to know Swift's or Hawthorne's biography? On the other hand, the colorful and tragic life of Edgar Allan Poe often seems to inspire students to wade through his dense prose and to attempt to understand it; the incidents surrounding Samuel Taylor Coleridge's "Kubla Kahn," whether reported truthfully by Coleridge or not, are intriguing to most readers and lend some further depth to the magical, mysterious poem.

The problem comes when such information usurps—and it can, very quickly—the point of the reading. If students spend the bulk of class time learning about history and biography, where is the time to actually engage with the literature? This leaves us with New Criticism and reader response, and many argue it is the latter to which we should be paying most attention in our middle and high school classrooms.

Reader Response

Many of us reared in New Criticism in our undergraduate and graduate training learned to love the close reading of poetry and prose. In this reading we adhered to a consideration of literature as a relatively isolated object to be discussed and analyzed, almost as one would turn a multifaceted object such as a cut diamond and consider it from all points of view. The diamond itself would not be altered by the turning and handling; it would retain its entire integrity as an object. Thus the New Criticism, as defined in John Crowe Ransom's 1941 book of the same name, was literature without the influence of the reader, the historical context, or the personal history of the author. Yet for all its obvious advantages over other forms of literary criticism, many of us reared in this tradition found when we became teachers that the technique did not often translate well. For many of us, in first period on Wednesday morning, our tenth graders were struck dumb at the prospect of close, analytical reading divorced from personal or historical context, and some, we found, were even repelled. What for us was a celebration of the intricate art of literature became, for our students, a repugnant dissection of an already difficult text, robbing it of joy, making it a task, not a connection to life. We did not fully realize what Louise Rosenblatt, the major voice of reader response theory, calls in her seminal book, *Literature as Exploration,* the "responsibility to the students as well as to the discipline" (ix).

I discovered reader response out of my own failure to entice my students to celebrate what I perceived to be the great craft of literature. What I think I had forgotten is that that appreciation came to me after, sometimes long after, I had experienced how a novel or a short story could make me feel, could tell me about my life, my problems, my capabilities. Louise Rosenblatt tells us three things:

1. **The literature itself must have some connection to the students' lives.**
2. **The approach must, in order to capitalize upon the students' lives, be inductive.**
3. **Students must be involved, must be engaged to the point where the discussion leads them, as Rosenblatt writes, "to raise personally meaningful questions . . . [and] to seek in the text the basis for valid answers"** (ix–x).

The undergirding principle is that text is a becoming, as critic Roland Barthes describes it in *Image-Music-Text* (*De L'Oeuvre au Texte*) something that is "held in language, only exists in the movement of a discourse . . . *experienced only in an activity of production*" (157). Text is, for Barthes and for many others, "the very plural of meaning . . . [dependent upon] the *plurality* of its weave of signifiers" (159). Thus, *signifiers* are not just readers; they are those who, in their time and place and with their individual backgrounds, make manifest the meaning of the text. While the students may be diverse, the signifiers are different and their weaves of patterns varied; their engagement with the literature is real and alive.

Characteristics of a reader-response classroom

In a recent study, I taped and analyzed classes of two teachers who use a reader response philosophy in teaching literature. The teachers, in two different schools in different sections of the same urban area, had their students discuss a trio of contemporary poems. A detailed look at what was said within the classes revealed five characteristics of a classroom that uses a reader-response orientation:

1. **Teachers encourage students to talk extensively.**
2. **Teachers help students make a community of meaning.**
3. **Teachers ask, they don't tell.**
4. **Teachers ask students to make links to personal experience.**
5. **Teachers affirm student responses.**

I also found that the discussions refute two common objections to the implementation of a reader response methodology in the classroom: first, that attention to student response to literature will deflect seriously from any literary analysis of the work itself; and second, that a reader response approach, in and of itself, takes too much instructional time to be efficient—it is quicker to tell students than to ask them to explore their own interpretations or reactions to a text.

Following is a brief look at the two classes and their discussion of the following three poems on young people and their fathers:

Breakings

Long before I first left home, my father
tried to teach me horses, land, and sky,
to show me how this kind of work was done.
I studied how to be my father's son,
but all I learned was, when the wicked die,
they ride combines through barley forever.

Every summer I hated my father
as I drove hot horses through dusty grass;
and so I broke with him, and left the farm
for other work, where unfamiliar weather
broke on my head an unexpected storm
and things I had not studied came to pass.

So nothing changes, nothing stays the same,
and I have returned from a broken home
alone, to ask for a job breaking horses.
I watch a colt on a long line making
tracks in dust, and think of the kinds of breakings
there are, and the kinds of restraining forces.

—Henry Taylor
An Afternoon of Pocket Billiards

Those Winter Sundays

Sundays too my father got up early
and put his clothes on in the blueblack cold
then with cracked hands that ached
from labor in the weekday weather made
banked fires blaze. No one ever thanked him.

I'd wake and hear the cold splintering, breaking.
When the rooms were warm, he'd call,
and slowly I would rise and dress,
fearing the chronic angers of that house,

Speaking indifferently to him,
who had driven out the cold
and polished my good shoes as well.
What did I know, what did I know
of love's austere and lonely offices?

—Robert Hayden
Angle of Ascent

Black Walnuts

The year my father used the car for hulling
was the best. We cobbled the drive
with walnuts gathered in baskets
and cardboard boxes, then rode with him
down that rough lane, forward and backward,
time and again, until the air was bitter to breathe
and the tires spun in the juice.
For years after, every piece of gravel
was dyed brown, and the old Ford
out on the open road would warm up
to a nutty smell, especially in winter
with the windows closed and the heater blowing.

Crouched over hulls mangled green and yellow,
we picked out corrugated shells
even the car's weight couldn't crack
and spread them on the grass to dry.
My father, on his hands and knees, happy
over windfall, talked of how good
the tender meats would taste; and in that moment
I wished with all my heart that he might live forever,
as leaves ticked down around us
and the fresh stain darkened on our hands.

—Neal Bowers
North American Review

Teachers encourage students to talk extensively　　If engaging in a transaction with literature (having students make the literature their own) is an instructional goal, then students must be able to join in a conversation. This is to be distinguished from a series of responses to a teacher's question, responses that are ultimately regulated, guided, and abbreviated within the class context. Students must, if they are to thrive in a reader response classroom, really talk, converse, speak at length, pause, argue, question. They should not be confined to one-word, one-phrase answers in response to a teacher's question and in a pattern determined by the teacher. In a reader response classroom, teachers encourage students to talk extensively.

In the two classes studied, the discussion is lively. Students remain on task with the three poems during the entire class period, and the teachers do not have to guide students "back to the subject." In fact, in both the classes student responses are not always one-word or one-phrase answers but extended sentences (largely in clusters of five to seven seconds with a dozen or so twenty-second responses). When students do make brief-phrase answers, they are in the context of a rapid-fire argument/discussion with other students that seem to come in response to the drama and tension of the discussion.

Teachers help students make a community of meaning　　Because each student's response will draw on individual, even idiosyncratic, personal background and experience, and because exchange and exploration is the goal, reader response teachers must be patient with factual misunderstanding. Eventually, individual misconceptions are corrected in a community of meaning. In a reader response classroom, nevertheless, paramount attention is not focused on right answers.

Accordingly, both classes studied are characterized by open discussion and exploration of multiple interpretations. For example, about five minutes into the discussion of the first poem, "Breakings," one teacher (Teacher A) initiates a discussion on a passage referring to the breaking of a colt. The colt's experience is metaphorically linked to the poem's speaker's own "breaking" by life/reality, but the teacher waits as the students struggle with the meaning. While they later (as a whole class) understand the poem's major point, it is a journey of interpretation. As in discussions outside of school, meaning is found and lost and found again:

TEACHER A: What does it ["Breakings"] mean, James?
JAMES: He learned how to be a farmer on his dad's farm and then he left first to find a new job, and he got—he couldn't find nothing better—he couldn't find nothing good—so he had to go back to working on the farm and hopefully . . . (garbled).
KAY: He left his dad and the dad wanted the son to be just like him—so he got tired of it.
TEACHER A: What do you think he's learned at the end [of the poem]?
BILL: I thought he was at a racetrack.
TEACHER A: What made you think that?
JAMAL: Because it said—the colt—he's kicking up dirt. I thought he was at a racetrack.
TEACHER A: What's he doing with the colt on a long line?
JAMES: He's plowing.
KAY: He's breaking.
JAMES: He's plowing . . . he's training.
KAY: He's training.
ANN: He's trying to get it so that he can break the—
TEACHER A: He's trying to break the colt? . . . Ann, you work with horses, don't you? Have you ever seen them when they put them on a long line—what are they trying to do?
ANN: It's a *lunge* line. They're trying to get them to—have them get used to . . .
TEACHER A: Get used to the thing around their head—what do they call that, *halter*?
ANN: Yeah. They call it a halter.
TEACHER A: So what else could they be breaking here?
BILL: Breaking him into a plow . . . getting him used to a plow.
TEACHER A: Breaking on the plow. What does a plow do?
BILL: It plows the field.
JAMES: It breaks up the ground.
TEACHER A: Does it break up anything?
BILL: It breaks up the dirt.
TEACHER A: Okay. What does this guy say about his feelings about his father?

As the discussion goes on, much is said about what the speaker feels about his father and while it would appear the students do not immediately understand the metaphorical significance of *breaking,* they eventually come to the following conclusion:

TEACHER A: What do you think this title, "Breakings," means?
MARY: Breaking of him.
ANN: Breaking the horses.
CURT: Breaking both [of them].

A community of meaning is made.

Teachers ask, they don't tell   Teachers who tell students, who talk most of the class time, do not have reader-response classrooms. It must be the students who struggle with the literature, who give the answers, and who make the meaning—their own meaning— of the text.

The major tool in these discussions is the question. While one teacher in this study does give vocabulary synonyms, and the other speaks extensively on a related aspect of one of the poems, the teachers resist almost all direct instruction. When confronted with a student question, both teachers turn to other students rather than become the answer giver.

Teacher A does not provide students with a list of preselected terms but asks twice for words the students do not understand ("Find another word that you don't know the meaning of"), asks for confirmation regarding terms ("Ann, what do they call that, a *halter*?"), and, when she actually looks up one word for a definition, asks students to give her the spelling of the word. She encourages students to struggle to find meaning themselves and, in a typical exchange, tells a student: "Look at *corrugated* in context . . . have you ever seen corrugated cardboard?" When the student responds, "That word doesn't make sense," the teacher does not correct her or argue but acknowledges the fact and tells the student, "We're going to find out why it doesn't make sense."

When confronted with a twenty-second silence regarding the meaning of "Break-ings," Teacher A gives two prompts but waits for student answers—which do come, from three students. Even when asked for clarification, the teacher turns to her students:

TEACHER A: What do you think changes in the roles that the dad and the son play? Any-
    thing?
ANDRE: What do you mean by the *roles*?
TEACHER A: Does anyone know here what I mean by the *roles*?

She receives responses to this question, as she does when she asks for an interpretation of a line in "Those Winter Sundays":

TEACHER A: He says in here, let's look down at this bottom line, "speaking *indifferently* to
    him." What do you think that means?
MIKE: Not any differently than . . .
BOB: Not in a different language.
CURT: Same as everyone, everyone else.
TEACHER A: Why would that be that significant if he's talking to his father the same as
    everyone else?
ALAN: All fathers are like . . .
CURT: It's probably that same weekend routine.
BILL: Does that mean like *indifferently* to, like than what he usually does—or just to
    everybody?
TEACHER A: I don't know . . .what do you think?
BILL: It's everybody—he should be talking to his father differently because his father . . .

Similarly, the other teacher, Teacher B, when asking "Which of these three [poems] seems to be a *father* poem?" receives two student questions: "What do you mean by that?" and "Which one do you like?" She does not answer, however, letting students argue as to the definition. And the students do subsequently argue in what is the most heated discussion of their particular class.

Teachers ask students to make links to personal experience   Requesting that students make links to personal experience is the paramount activity in reader response classrooms. In capable hands, however, it becomes more than students simply venting their opinions. While personal experience is shared and cited, the students in both teachers' classrooms also pay close attention to the text of the three poems, using it to buttress their points.

One teacher asks students on two separate instances to relate to the anger of the speaker against his father in "Breakings" and receives multiple answers—some students link their assigned household tasks (such as mowing the lawn) to the speaker; some discuss their general anger towards their parents. During the latter, three students share responses, one for twenty-two seconds.

Certainly the fact that the three poems are central to students' lives—they all have parents, if not on-site fathers—makes such an insistence on linkage of personal experience possible. All of the students have stories and opinions and a history in this area; the discussions, as cited here, might not be as rich if the topic were about building highways or going to war. Yet as the discussions reveal, the students do more than simply link the poetry to their own lives and experiences. Most of the students return to lines, concepts, and ideas in the literature and, while they relate to the text, they also do a capable job examining and even analyzing it.

Teachers affirm students' responses   Another characteristic of the methodology of a reader response classroom discussion is that teachers affirm student response to the literature. They can affirm response by overt praise or agreement, but these two classes show that the teachers reinforce their students' responses through two major instructional methods: by referring to student comments in discussion and by asking other students to respond specifically to those comments. Such actions give powerful confirmation to students that their ideas, their responses, are legitimate.

In one section of the discussion, approximately seven students respond for a total of three relatively teacher-uninterrupted minutes, taking turns looking at the phrase in question. Another student then moves the discussion to the "speaking indifferently" section and talks, without interruption, for almost one and one-half minutes.

Teacher B repeatedly moves students to respond to other student observations—at least a half-dozen times during the class period. In "Breakings," for instance, she notes: "Jim said you break the spirit of the colt. If we make an analogy here between the father and son, does that make the son bitter—as Rick said?"

The technique has the effect of inspiring students to continue to respond to each other.

From this very heated, wide-ranging argument there emerges a question of whose poem is it anyway, a discussion that is about reader response. Theresa starts the discussion, and her comment is almost lost in the uproar. The teacher does not repeat it for the class, but signals the other students to listen:

TEACHER B: Check out Theresa's remark, and let's hear if you agree.

THERESA: I think it [the interpretation of the poem as about fathers and sons or fathers and daughters] is determined by the reader and not the poet.

JOHN: Yeah, it's neutered. (Garbled voices; Teacher B calls the class to order.)

TEACHER B: Do you agree that there's a different meaning for the reader, that that's possible?

THERESA: Yeah.

RICK: Yeah. Sometimes the poem—you put these allegorical meanings [in it], then it can. But if you just write a straightforward poem, it can't be disputed then. There's, like, no second meaning.

TEACHER B: What kind of poem is a "straightforward" poem?

RICK: What the poet wants to write.

ROB: Like a descriptive poem.

KAREN: Like when he says *he*.

ROB: Like a haiku.

KAREN: Yeah.

JOHN: I think you can interpret it however you want—but you may well be *wrong* in your interpretation. Because I think the poet had a set audience in mind and what he was remembering and what he was trying to get out. So if you want to think of it as a father/daughter thing, you may be wrong, but you're welcome to your own opinion.

JIM: The poet's a man.

KAREN: But you don't know the poet.

RICK: But if the author like released what this . . . pamphlet, this book . . . is about, is meant to mean, that would take all the fun out of discussing it.

ROB: Well, you see the poet is writing for the poet himself, and that's how he is interpreting it. But other people can read it, and that's how they interpret it.

And how they interpret it, and the very excitement, the very pleasure of discussing it, is surely at the heart of this reader-response classroom.

Certainly there is a place for the literary lecture and for an author's biography. Certainly the New Critical examination of that well-wrought urn can also be an illuminating and rewarding activity. But as Rosenblatt, Barthes, and others remind us, when we consider our middle school and high school students and their engagement with literature and the formation of their joy of literature, we must allow them not only the discussion floor itself but also the authority of their own thoughts and instincts.

In my school history, I can recall few teachers who advanced the opinion that a poet's ideas might be akin to mine or any other student's. By contrast, the two teachers represented in this study allow their students joy and time, and they honor their ideas. These teachers know and convey that different readers can have different interpretations, and they suspect that poets and young people have similar feelings. What they do is not mysterious or arcane or even terribly difficult. What they do, however, is mandatory if we care about literature and about developing our students into lifelong readers.

Reader response: uses and abuses

Especially after reading the exciting give-and-take conversations of the students above, it may be hard to think of reader response being abused in a classroom, but a few cautions are in order.

Many well-meaning teachers cite Louise Rosenblatt and reader-response theory but are not sure what Rosenblatt has written and what reader-response activities mean in a classroom. Certainly reader response does not imply that any student response under any circumstances carries complete authority. Reader response asks the student to bring his or her experience to the literature, and it honors that connection. It maintains that an individual reader can shape a piece of literature through his or her own interpretation, although the limits of that shaping are relatively crucial to delineate. Using a reader-response approach in a classroom is *not* an invitation to students or teachers to:

- Ignore completely what is in the text.
- Read into the text facts or inferences that are clearly not present or not defensible.
- Insist that "well, that's my opinion" constitutes the last—and unassailable—word on the discussion.
- Reveal sensitive aspects of their personal lives in order to discuss the literature or defend their points.

A reader's response must be intelligent, thoughtful, and have some tie to the text, however tenuous that might first appear. To consider a discussion where students do not have to pay any attention to what they have read is not reader response—it's irresponsible.

On the other hand, we cannot insist that students reveal responses to literature that may violate their sense of privacy. Much literature that is worth reading and discussing deals with mature issues. Students can have legitimate responses to that literature—and experience with those issues—but prefer to keep the specifics to themselves. Asking students to make general connections or to discuss if they know of anyone else who has been in a similar situation or felt a similar way can relieve the pressure to reveal. Teacher as *voyeur* is an ugly sight; we do not want to extract from our students, in the name of reader response or any other approach to literature, personal revelations that they would prefer to keep outside the classroom.

We must attempt to create a classroom climate where students can bring their own lives and beliefs to the text. Balancing and adjusting that climate is part of the craft of the teacher. What we do not want is described by a student on the eve of teaching:

> I had the audacity to contradict (or question) [my English teacher's] view on the analysis of poetry. For several weeks we read and analyzed poems. My poor memory cannot recall specific works, but I do recall my shock and dismay when my teacher informed me that my perception of a poem, my own personal analysis, was wrong. He then proceeded to lecture the class on the correct perception. I was incredulous. Is not poetry like a work of art? Is it not there for each of us to perceive differently? Some poems are as abstract as the most modern of art. Who is to say what the poet really means except the poet himself?
>
> —DONNA JOHNSON

While some could also argue that even the poet may not "know" what the poem means, we do know that each reader needs to be respected. Donna was not crushed by her teacher's rejection of her interpretation; some of our students, however, may not be so fortunate.

A word on deconstructionism

You may as an English major also be aware of one of the many other ways of approaching literature: deconstructionism. It posits a quite different interpretation from what the preceding theories maintain. In a deconstructionist approach, according to Raman Selden in *A Reader's Guide to Contemporary Literary Theory*, a great deal of the focus is on "the differences between what the text says and what it thinks it says." Such an approach means a reader can "set the text to work against itself, and refuse to force it to *mean* something" (102). Also, to quote from Sharon Crowley's *A Teacher's Introduction to Deconstruction*:

On a deconstructive model of textuality, literary texts do not hold still and docilely submit themselves to repeated identical readings; they can be read and reread, and each reading differs from the last. Nor are critical interpretations of texts copies of an original "meaning" that is somehow housed in the original text. Interpretations, readings, differ from the texts they interpret and from each other; and having been read, they require a re-reading of the "originary" text. This is why critical readings of important texts can continue to be made, why the pages of *PMLA* will always be filled up. (20)

Deconstruction rejects historical context as necessarily important or significant and, in addition, does not accept the New Critical belief in analysis of a text in relation to its interior structure. It is not, Crowley notes, that "we cannot read a text. It is simply . . . that the meaning we derive from reading is located as much in the process of reading and in the social and cultural contexts which surround our reading, as it is in the 'text itself' " (16).

The whole approach is interesting—and relatively new—but you may want to exercise restraint with your students who are primarily relatively young readers in the sense that they have not experienced a great deal of literature. Deconstructionism may be more of a college exercise than one appropriate for middle school or secondary school readers; for that reason (and caution) it is not discussed in any depth within this book.

Yet there is a real reason to use literary theory—old and new—as an orientation to talking about our reading. As Raman Selden notes about what theory can mean to a reader:

How does all this [new literary theory] affect our experience and understanding of reading and writing? First, an emphasis on theory tends to undermine reading as an *innocent* activity. If we ask ourselves questions about the construction of meaning in fiction or the presence of ideology in poetry, we can no longer naively accept the 'realism' of a novel or the 'sincerity' of a poem. Some readers may cherish their illusions and mourn the loss of innocence, but, if they are serious readers, they cannot ignore the deeper issues raised by the major literary theorists in recent years. Secondly, far from having a sterile effect on our reading, new ways of seeing literature can revitalise our engagement with texts . . . If we are to be adventurous and exploratory in our reading of literature, we must also be adventurous in our thinking about literature. (2–3)

■ FOR YOUR JOURNAL

Pick a short story or poem or novel you have read and might like to teach. Think about it from the perspectives of the four schools of literary criticism: historical or literary background, author biography, New Critical, and reader response. Make a list of questions you might want to ask students that reflect each of the four schools. Now look at the questions you developed, and write a brief entry on which of the four schools interests you the most as a teacher/learner? Why? How do you think your students will respond?

Organizing Literature

You may find, especially in the beginning of your teaching, that you follow a textbook's organization of literature and go from Chapter 1 to June 1. You may, practically speaking, be a bit too overwhelmed to do much more creative shaping. As you become more self-assured, however, as you continue not just to be but to *become* a teacher, you will want to experiment and play with how you organize literature for your classes. Such experimentation will help you respond to what your students may be interested in pursuing. After all, ninth-grade or seventh-grade or any-grade English, even when you and your students have a literature anthology/textbook, can include many different—and wonderful—things not only to read but to discuss and write about.

Let's consider. Most textbooks are organized in standard patterns, and some of the major ways textbooks—and teachers-—organize the study of literature are by:

- **Chronology** (the Romantic Period, the Middle Ages, and so on).
- **Author** (James Baldwin, F. Scott Fitzgerald).
- **Theme** (''Discovering Oneself'').
- **Genre** (the short story).

There are, as you can imagine, benefits to all four of the patterns. Certainly in survey courses of American and British literature the chronological pattern is the most frequently used; in more general literature courses, theme and genre are popular. Some classes focus on individual writers for brief periods of study. By dipping in and out of chapters, though, by taking some pieces from one section and some from another, the organizational pattern can be adapted. Some textbooks even list in the (often unread) introduction or teacher's manual suggestions on how to use the literature in different configurations. Obviously, you can also mix up the categories and study, for instance, a more complicated version of one pattern by adding to it.

Let us consider poetry (genre) by adding to it:

- Late-twentieth-century poetry (**chronology and genre**)
- Late-twentieth-century poetry by American writers (**chronology, genre, and authors**)
- Late-twentieth-century poetry by American writers who focused on the loss of the American Dream (**chronology, genre, authors, and theme**)

What such a series of combinations may do is enrich the consideration and discussion of the literature. Making connections intellectually is what much of our reading is all about; when students are confronted with one of the combinations above, they make connections they would not otherwise see.

The pleasures and pitfalls of theme

Asking students to consider literature under the umbrella of a theme can be very helpful as students try to make sense of a poem or a novel. It can connect what could otherwise seem so disparate it is impossible to grasp. Linking, for example, a poem, a short story, and a play that come from different countries and different eras—but that all have a similar theme—may also help students see connections and stimulate questions that might not be, otherwise, so obvious. Certainly the three poems discussed in the section on reader response (''Breakings,'' ''Those Winter Sundays,'' and ''Black Walnuts'') all share, loosely, the same theme of fathers and children.

On the other hand, we need to be very aware that by asking students to see or find a predetermined theme, we can be circumventing their discovery of the literature. And

this caution regarding theme does not necessarily mean students should seek some terribly far out interpretation in the name of rampant individuality. Literature is essentially
made new by new readers, and we need to create a classroom atmosphere where, while
there is guidance, there is not a preset determination of what a work or poem just might
be about. The point is to use a framework such as theme in a rather loose manner. Your
students may see themes you have not anticipated and may possibly reject the thematic
relation of two pieces of literature—and for good reason. Announcing or insisting that a
certain piece or pieces of literature have a set theme is intellectual hostage taking.

In a similar way, the very act of defining literature in genres can also be as limiting
as it can be helpful. Let us quickly turn to the types or categories, or genres, of literature
and see what that might mean.

A brief look at genres

To briefly outline: literature is traditionally categorized into genres, which are attempts to
classify the marvelous and myriad universe of writing. You recognize the three major
terms: prose, poetry, and drama. Prose is further defined/refined into fiction (novels,
short stories) and nonfiction (essays and longer pieces).

All of this is helpful in a way, but it is misleading in others. You will find, as will
your students, that genre is tricky at best. One of my favorite activities is to make three
columns on the board, each headed by the names of the three genres: prose, poetry, and
drama. I then ask students to brainstorm characteristics that they think are appropriate
for each genre. Students rarely hesitate as most can recall with little difficulty a few characteristics of a play they have seen or a poem or a novel they have read.

After about twenty minutes of coming up with terms and descriptors and moving
from genre category to category, I stop and ask students to look, without comment or
elimination, at the lists we have made on the board. Students generally find that each
genre shares almost identical characteristics, and they realize that when you think about
it, it is truly difficult to *define* a genre or type of literature. In fact, each genre often has
the characteristics of the others; and sometimes we may feel as if we are, in this game of
definition and codification, reduced to saying, ''I can't define it, but I know it when I see
it.''

While this argument may seem negative to you, think about how the questions of
the genres can be manipulated into wonderful discussion departures. Consider these
intriguing contradictions:

- **Fiction vs. Nonfiction**: How true is fact? How false is fiction? Where can you
  draw the line between story and account? What makes fiction fiction? nonfiction nonfiction?
- **Prose vs. Poetry**: How much poetry uses flat, prose-like statement? Which
  prose uses figurative language? How compressed is language in poetry? in
  prose? What makes prose prose? poetry poetry? What are prose poems?
- **Short Story vs. Novel**: What makes a short story a short story? a novel a novel?
  Is a short novel (a novella or a novelette) really a long short story? Why or why
  not?
- **Drama vs. Fiction**: What is the drama of a play? Why isn't the dialogue in a
  short story or novel—or a piece of nonfiction, for that matter—play-like? What
  makes drama not fiction? fiction not drama?

Talking about genre in these ways can be interesting to students and can, further, get them to look more critically at what they are reading.

Cultural Literacy, the Canon, Textbooks, and the Issue of Multicultural Literature

Cultural literacy—what it is and is not, how and when and even if to transmit it, who does and does not have it—is appropriate to consider as we look at teaching literature. We as teachers need to be aware of the implications of cultural literacy as a movement, how it is related to the "canon" of revered classics, the textbook industry, and the renewed emphasis on multiculturalism.

Briefly put, cultural literacy is generally considered to be a working knowledge of the basic features of Western culture and civilization, necessary for members of this society to communicate effectively and to share a common bond. A major proponent of cultural literacy, E. D. Hirsch, Jr., defines it as the "basic information needed to thrive in the modern world" (Hirsch, xiii), but that definition only partially reflects the dimensions of the issue.

In our field, English language arts, the major turf war is over "the canon," the works of literature that are considered essential to the transmission and understanding of Western civilization. In your English major you have read a number of authors whose works are in the canon: Homer, Plato, Aristotle, Chaucer, Dante, Shakespeare, and Milton. The controversy extends and becomes hotter, though, as we move toward the twentieth century and as we notice that the traditional canon excludes almost entirely works by women, racial minorities, and those of nonwestern and nonEuropean countries. In most accepted lists of "great" or "classic" literature there is essentially only a bare nod to those writers who are non-Western, nonwhite, and nonmale.

For varying reasons, some of them copyright laws (which translates into money issues; modern works are more expensive to reprint), you will see that many of the textbooks you will be using or are using in your classrooms feature very traditional works. It costs the publishers a great deal to obtain the "rights" to reprint a more contemporary work and, further, there is much more possibility for controversy—and censorship— with such a work. Thus adhering to the canon and avoiding more contemporary and more multicultural literature can often keep a literature textbook or anthology in the very middle of the road and give it a greater chance for adoption by a state's school textbook selection committee.

The latter, while it may seem awfully remote to you at this stage in your career, actually wields a great deal of practical classroom power. When the populous state of California, for instance, or the state of Texas adopts or approves a literature anthology series, the publishing company flourishes. When, because of whatever controversy, those states and others similarly large decline to adopt such a series, a textbook company can lose millions of dollars. No one wants to go bankrupt, despite the level of their ideals: most publishing companies, therefore, make sure that the literature they include in their anthology series is noncontroversial. The stakes are high in this game, and it lends an economic dimension to what you may have felt is essentially an academic issue.

E. D. Hirsch, the major voice of the cultural literacy movement, is the author of *Cultural Literacy: What Every American Needs to Know.* Hirsch and colleagues Joseph F. Kett and James Trefil have followed up *Cultural Literacy* with an informational dictionary.

The first book outlines the need for a definition of cultural literacy and provides an index listing, now virtually infamous, of its subtitle, "what every American needs to know." The list of 5,000 items includes dates, titles, terms, and phrases in science, literature, art, politics, history, geography, and so on. The dictionary is an effort to gloss such terms with a brief description. *Cultural Literacy* was an immensely popular book, widely quoted and reviewed and, at this writing, the dictionary is scheduled for a second edition.

The question, of course, is the role of the schools. The major areas of dispute seem to be based on three assumptions:

1. **The schools should acculturalize, operating on the rather precarious given that the schools can define the content and outline of that culture.**
2. **The schools can assume that, in a pluralistic society, the dominant culture, however defined, is the unquestioning core of what we call the United States of America.**
3. **The schools should ensure that the dominant culture is mastered by all students.**

That many have not so much lost faith in these three propositions but have never accepted them as valid in the least is part of the tension over cultural literacy. There are other arguments against cultural literacy.

Superficiality

Critics of the cultural literacy movement fear that the worst of cultural literacy will encourage students to acquire lists of terms or possess only a nodding acquaintance with historical issues and literary works. In an effort to transmit an essential core of knowledge, it is tempting to give students mere "cocktail party" knowledge. There may be little room, in the broad application of cultural literacy, for thorough reading and study. Critics worry that to know the plot of a number of Shakespearian plays, in this scenario, is preferable to spending three weeks in class acting and discussing a single tragedy or comedy.

Narrowness

Those who mistrust the cultural literacy movement also fret that if students are required to adhere to the canon of Western world—and certainly through most literature anthologies that becomes a *fait accompli*—they will no doubt miss a range of writers and ideas that are either in translation or wide publication for the first time or that are just recently written. Zora Neale Hurston's *Their Eyes Were Watching God* is a cogent example of an important literary work by an African American woman that had been relatively unnoticed for many years and that is now in wide distribution. Similarly, while no one would dispute the centrality of William Wordsworth in humanity's view of nature and our relation to it, one could equally argue that the vision of Australian Patrick White or South African Nadine Gordimer, both Nobel Prize winners in literature, is worth similar consideration and study. Much of this discussion involves the use of what is termed multicutural literature in the schools, and we will take it up again in the next chapter.

National curriculum control/national testing

The cultural literacy movement, some feel, may also imply that if educators agree that cultural literacy is our undeniable goal, a national curriculum seems the logical answer, followed, of course, by a national test. Gone would be regional and local variations of writers and history, as all-important would be the transmission of the national vision. Perhaps regional writers such as southerner Ellen Glasgow and westerner J. Frank Dobie would be lost in the shuffle. Certainly all young people would, regardless of region or ethnic heritage, be required to read and know a core of works.

Content dominance

If cultural literacy, as it is popularly defined, becomes the curricular goal, critics also worry that retention of information, not skills or process discussion and thinking, will dominate the classroom. It would make little sense for students to be able to decipher or interpret unfamiliar texts given the mammoth amount of material it would be deemed essential for them to master and remember. Thus students would not so much be able to read on their own as regurgitate interpretations and knowledge of established works. While such may lend itself to standardized tests with multiple choice questions, it will not expand skills of critical thinking.

The question of what is important to read and to know, the essential heart of the cultural literacy movement, is something we need as teachers and readers to continue to consider seriously. In addition, how we approach the literature, how we choose to talk about it, what theories actually inform our teaching are also crucial. As removed as some of these issues may first seem, as truly theoretical as they may appear, they actually have very real consequences for us and for our students, and they affect our classrooms. But regardless of what stance you take on these issues of teaching literature, considering them, thinking about them, has value that will illumine your teaching, now and down the road as you make your journey.

FOR YOUR JOURNAL

If you could create your own idiosyncratic "canon" of works, what would you include as essential for all of your students to read and know? Think of the range of fiction, nonfiction, poetry, and drama and make a list of about a dozen works. No cheating! Now look at your dozen: what are your reasons for choosing each one? What do you think students will "get" from the reading of each? To the best of your judgment, how representative is your list of this country's racial, cultural, and gender diversity? What are the limits on making the list representative?

REFERENCES

Professional sources

Barthes, Roland. *Image–Music–Text*. Translated by Stephen Heath. New York: Hill & Wang, 1977.

Brooks, Cleanth. *The Well Wrought Urn: Studies in the Structure of Poetry*. New York: Harcourt Brace & World. 1947.

Christenbury, Leila. "Cultural Literacy: What Every Teacher Needs to Know." *North Carolina English Teacher* 48 (Winter 1991): 7–10.

————. " 'The Guy Who Wrote This Poem Seems to Have the Same Feelings as You Have': Reader-Response Methodology." In *Reader Response in the Classroom: Evoking and Interpreting Meaning in Literature*. Edited by Nicholas J. Karolides. New York: Longman, 1992.

Crowley, Sharon. *A Teacher's Introduction to Deconstruction.* Urbana, IL: NCTE, 1989.

Hirsch, E. D., Jr. *Cultural Literacy: What Every American Needs to Know.* Boston: Houghton Mifflin, 1987.

Hirsch, E. D., Jr., Joseph F. Kett, and James Trefil. *Dictionary of Cultural Literacy.* Boston: Houghton Mifflin, 1988.

Ransom, John Crowe. *The New Criticism.* Westport, CT: Greenwood Press, 1979.

Rosenblatt, Louise. *Literature as Exploration.* 3d ed. New York: Noble & Noble, 1976.

Selden, Raman. *A Reader's Guide to Contemporary Literary Theory.* 2d ed. Lexington, KY: The University Press of Kentucky, 1989.

Literature cited

Bowers, Neal. "Black Walnuts." In *North American Review* 273 (June 1988): 19.

Chaucer, Geoffrey. *Canterbury Tales.* In *The Works of Geoffrey Chaucer.* 2d ed. F. N. Robinson, ed. Boston: Houghton Mifflin, 1961.

Chopin, Kate. *The Awakening.* New York: Bantam, 1988.

Cole, Brock. *The Goats.* New York: Farrar Straus Giroux, 1987.

Coleridge, Samuel Taylor. *Selected Poetry and Prose.* New York: Holt, Rinehart & Winston, 1951.

Dickinson, Emily. "Number 1263." In *The Complete Poems of Emily Dickinson.* Edited by Thomas H. Johnson. Boston: Little, Brown, 1960.

Dobie, J. Frank. *Tales of Old Time Texas.* Austin: University of Texas Press, 1984.

George, Jean Craighead. *Julie of the Wolves.* New York: Harper & Row, 1972.

Glasgow, Ellen. *The Sheltered Life.* New York: Harcourt Brace Jovanovich, 1938.

Gordimer, Nadine. *July's People.* New York: Viking, 1981.

Hawthorne, Nathaniel. *The Scarlet Letter.* Brian Harding, ed. New York: Oxford University Press, 1990.

Hayden, Robert. "Those Winter Sundays." In *Angle of Ascent*, 113. New York: Liveright, 1975.

Hemingway, Ernest. *The Old Man and the Sea.* New York: Scribner's, 1952.

Hurston, Zora Neale. *Their Eyes Were Watching God.* New York: Harper & Row, 1990.

Marvell, Andrew. *Selections.* Edited by Frank Kermode and Keith Walker. New York: Oxford University Press, 1990.

Paulsen, Gary. *Hatchet.* New York: Bradbury, 1987.

Poe, Edgar Allan. *Great Tales of Horror.* New York: Bantam, 1964.

Swift, Jonathan. "A Modest Proposal." *Jonathan Swift.* Edited by Angus Ross and David Woolley. New York: Oxford University Press, 1984.

Taylor, Henry. "Breakings." In *An Afternoon of Pocket Billiards*, 3. Salt Lake City: University of Utah Press, 1975.

White, Patrick. *Eye of the Storm.* New York: Viking, 1973.

Wordsworth, William. *The Prelude and Selected Poems and Sonnets.* Edited by Carlos Baker. New York: Holt, Rinehart & Winston, 1954.

RESOURCES

There are many resources for teachers regarding literary theory. The Moffett and Scholes books are highly regarded, and the Probst book gives a readable, interesting elaboration of Louise Rosenblatt's reader response theories. The Bennett, Bloom, Cheney, and Ravitch works provide more arguments in favor of cultural literacy.

Applebee, Arthur N. "Stability and Change in the High-School Canon." *English Journal* 81 (September 1992): 27–32.

Beach, Richard. *A Teacher's Introduction to Reader-Response Theories.* Urbana, IL: NCTE, 1993.

Bennett, William J. *To Reclaim a Legacy*. Washington, DC: National Endowment for the Humanities, 1984.

Bloom, Allan. *The Closing of the American Mind: How Higher Education Has Failed Democracy and Impoverished the Souls of Today's Students*. New York: Simon & Schuster, 1987.

Cheney, Lynne V. *American Memory: A Report on the Humanities in the Nation's Public Schools*. Washington, DC: National Endowment for the Humanities, 1987.

Christenbury, Leila. "Cultural Literacy: A Terrible Idea Whose Time Has Come." *English Journal* 78 (January 1989): 14–17.

Cooper, Charles R., ed. *Researching Response to Literature and the Teaching of Literature: Points of Departure*. Norwood, NJ: Ablex, 1985.

Farrell, Edmund J. and James R. Squire. *Transactions with Literature: A Fifty-Year Perspective*. Urbana, IL: NCTE, 1990.

Jones, Anne Goodwyn. *Tomorrow Is Another Day: The Woman Writer in the South, 1859–1936*. Baton Rouge, LA: LSU Press, 1981.

Mayher, John. *Uncommon Sense: Theoretical Practice in Language Education*. Portsmouth, NH: Boynton/Cook, 1990.

Moffett, James. *Teaching the Universe of Discourse*. Portsmouth, NH: Boynton/Cook, 1983.

NCTE. *Guidelines for a Gender-Balanced Curriculum in English, Grades 7–12*. Urbana, IL: NCTE, 1990.

Nelms, Ben, ed. *Literature in the Classroom: Readers, Texts and Contexts*. Urbana, IL: NCTE, 1988.

Probst, Robert E. *Response and Analysis: Teaching Literature in Junior and Senior High School*. Portsmouth, NH: Boynton/Cook, 1988.

Ravitch, Diane and Finn, Chester E., Jr. *What Do Our 17-Year Olds Know?* New York: Harper & Row, 1987.

Rosenblatt, Louise. *The Reader, the Text, and the Poem*. Carbondale, IL: SIU Press, 1978.

Scholes, Robert. *Textual Power: Literary Theory and the Teaching of English*. New Haven, CT: Yale University Press, 1985.

Showalter, Elaine, ed. *The New Feminist Criticism: Essays on Women, Literature, Theory*. New York: Pantheon, 1985.

CHAPTER 5

TEACHING LITERATURE
PRACTICAL MATTERS

Literature is landscape on the desk; landscape is literature on the earth.

—Chang Chao, *Yumengying*

Choosing Literature

The quotation that opens this chapter celebrates the importance and centrality of literature. For Chang Chao, literature is the world, and the world is literature. This attitude is not born, I think, but made, and somehow we need to entice the students in our classrooms into the pages of books so that they, too, find literature important and central to their lives. Much of this, however, depends on us.

If we want our students to respond to literature, then it is crucial that we choose literature—or let them participate in the choosing of literature—to which they can have a response. While much of the literature you use in your classroom will be dictated by that fixture of the classroom the textbook, there are ways you can expand beyond what your text has selected for your students. There is just not time for you to duplicate or scout out a parallel text for everything, but, on the other hand, don't forget these rich and often overlooked sources of reading, sources of literature:

- Magazines of all types.
- Paperback books (from the school bookroom, students' attics or basements, secondhand bookstores, yard sales).
- Discarded or discontinued anthology series (specific pieces can be cut from them).
- Newspapers and tabloids.
- Catalogs of all sorts.
- Advertising newsletters.
- Pamphlets, booklets, informational brochures.

While we have a contractual obligation to adhere to what the school system and our English language arts department encourage or mandate that we "cover," we also need to remember that we have a similar obligation to our students to give them reading to which they can truly respond. It is not completely revolutionary to have a classroom library of materials such as those listed above and to let students read and browse through them at specified times. Devoting an entire class period to free reading can encourage students who would not otherwise spend—or find—the time. The reading can be supervised, academic credit can be given, but it can come from the *Guinness Book of World Records*, *Road & Track*, *Sports Illustrated*, *People*, *Sassy*, *Seventeen*; a maintenance manual; horror, sports, and romance novels; and technical brochures and catalogs. Real readers are omnivorous; if we insist that reading means only one thing—that is, "good" literature of which we specifically approve and the "best" literature, which appears on sanctioned lists—we are not only lying to our students, we are in our own way discouraging the young reader.

"Great books" are fine and wonderful, and certainly we would hope that all of our students would have a generous sample of experience with what, with the best of intentions, we dub as the canon of the "classics," important pieces of literature that express time-honored ideas and sentiments. On the other hand, there is a great-books mania in our culture, which is not only alienating to many of our students but is also, bluntly put, hypocritical.

The fact is that many of the people in our society who insist the loudest that our students read the best and only the best have long ago ceased reading themselves; for them reading is a museum type of exercise suitable for the young and unformed and something that must be carefully monitored—and restricted. It's like those sets of classics offered for sale with the wonderful leather covers and the gold-edged pages. It's my impression that most people who buy those sets are less interested in reading them than in displaying them tastefully on strategically located bookshelves.

By contrast, real readers—and real readers can range from those without high school diplomas to those with doctorates—don't restrict themselves in such a manner. To open the world of the printed page to our students, we must open the covers of all kinds of reading matter, Harlequin romance to *Hamlet* to *Hemmings Motor News*. Making a reader is a broad and messy business, and we need to become inclusive, not exclusive, in our own tastes and in what we offer to our students and encourage them to read. As one of my students recalls:

> [My English teacher] allowed seniors to pick out their own reading material for the remainder of the school year after spring break. I dare say she would have allowed a college-directed student (aren't they all?) to read *Chitty Chitty Bang Bang* if they had so desired, but she stemmed this with a "water seeks its own level" speech that made one want to read *An American Tragedy* just to show her.
>
> —HEATHER TALLEY

A Story: Thurman and *Architectural Digest*

At one point in my teaching life almost all of my students were reluctant readers or virtually nonreaders. I read aloud to them, I brought in carts of library books on selected topics, I took them to the library, I scouted for class materials, and I established a classroom "library" of magazines of all types and a free reading time. For two of the classes, the two I felt could productively use the periods (my other classes were just not psycho-logically ready for fifty minutes of quiet reading), I established every Friday as a time to read silently, individually. I encouraged students to bring something in, but I also kept my magazine library; most students forgot materials or, frankly, would find access to such materials difficult. But as the months went on, my collection seemed to suffice: the magazines I had scrounged from friends and relatives and back issues of my own sub-scriptions included a really broad range of news magazines, music tabloids, traditional "women's" journals, literary digests, and the occasional technical or car magazine.

It was the reaction of one of my students to this magazine reading that hooked me on its utility and importance—and, indeed, on its unpredictability. It made what I think may have been a permanent difference in the life of one young reader, and I hope that he sees the world a bit differently to this day because of his reading.

Thurman was tall, had long, blond hair that fell below his shoulders, wore sun-glasses most of the year (in class as well as out), and sported the chains, boots, and stud-ded jacket that in my school signaled his membership in a group of rather tough, white males who endured school rather than enjoyed it. Thurman lived in a public housing project and hung out with a group who had a reputation for drugs and trouble. With most of his teachers he was silent, almost mild mannered, but he actually had a strong temper and a violent streak; he had been suspended a number of times from school and, out of school, he was prone to explosions. Too many fights and a final assault conviction led him to a thirty-day jail sentence. But the judge wanted Thurman to stay in school, so the sentence was served on weekends. He checked into the city jail on Friday afternoon and checked out to return to school on Monday morning.

Thurman was in my English class and was struggling with his reading, if not his behavior. He usually wanted to be let out of our afternoon class early; between jail, his job, and his personal life he didn't feel he had much time to waste. It was a request I almost always refused, regardless of the urgency or sensibility of reasons, and Thurman would eventually settle into work. For some reason—one of the mysteries of teacher/student chemistry—we got along very well, and he became one of my absolute, all-time favorite students. After a semester or so of contact, I thought he was wonderful, and he, in his own often elusive way, seemed to like me, too.

Maybe that was why he would be one of the first to wander to the back of the room on Friday and leaf through the magazines. He seemed to have a sense of loyalty to me as his teacher and could, most times, be enticed to try something because I recommended it. After all, I had listened to his favorite rock group of the time and even, on his recom-mendation, bought one of their albums. We had, of a sort, a deal.

Loyalty aside, Thurman was not a strong reader. He stumbled over words; he refused to complete outside reading. His writing was careful but jerky and unsure. It was, however, on one of the Friday afternoon reads that Thurman intersected with *Architec-tural Digest,* the pricey journal of multimillion-dollar homes and furnishings I had scrounged from relatives who could not only afford the hefty subscription price but who could occasionally purchase some of the cheaper items featured in it. While I had been really reluctant to add the journal to my class library—its relation to almost anyone's real life was pretty tangential—there were issues and issues of *Architectural Digest,* they were free, and I needed variety.

What possible connection could *Architectural Digest,* this monument to gold-plated faucets of the stars, sunken living rooms of the megawealthy, marble and terrazzo floors of the famous, have with a hot-tempered white kid from the projects? Photographs and text, it was a bombshell to Thurman; he read intently, steadily; he borrowed copies between Fridays. He didn't want to talk about it at first; he just, ravenously, miraculously, wanted . . . to read. He looked at the pictures, read the captions, and graduated into the text. When he did talk, and it wasn't for some time, he wanted to know about such homes, such designs, such lives. He had, he admitted, no idea that the world in *Architectural Digest* had ever existed. And I could tell, thankfully, that that fact did not depress him a bit; he was filled with understandable wonder, but with a young person's optimism, he was also filled with exhilaration. This was a world of excess, to be sure, but also of beauty and grace where the aesthetic was discussed seriously.

When Thurman wandered out of my life—he did pass my class, graduate from high school, get a job, stay out of jail, and eventually marry—I felt the loss of a favorite student. But also I felt pretty good. Thurman had looked, he had read. I never would have guessed that magazine and that young man would intersect. But they did. And I felt overwhelmingly happy and convinced, once again, that hooking kids into reading is a wide-ranging, broad-moving experience. If *I* had selected reading material for Thurman, it never, in my wildest dreams, would have been *Architectural Digest*. He made the selection himself; all I did was give him a little freedom and some time to read, and then get out of the way.

I wonder if that isn't quite enough.

The Question of Censorship

Whenever a teacher uses a poem or a novel or a piece of nonfiction or a magazine or even a newspaper in a classroom, he or she is open to the question of censorship. There is—the evidence is virtually irrefutable—no piece of literature "safe" from challenge and censorship. From all kinds of popular magazines to the most revered of the classics, reading material is regularly questioned and occasionally removed from library and classroom shelves. Sometimes the courts, as high as the Supreme Court, are involved in censorship cases. Most times the challenges are handled at the individual classroom, the school, or the school board level.

While there are few of us who would relish such a battle or the attack on our professionalism, we as teachers need to be prepared to give a rational defense of why we are asking—or, as some people might think, allowing—our students to read certain materials in our classes. The American Library Association (ALA) and the National Council of Teachers of English (NCTE) have many resources available to teachers and schools regarding books that are challenged. A few that may be helpful are the NCTE's *The Students' Right to Read* and Burress and Jenkinson's *The Students' Right to Know* (both have overviews of censorship and a helpful form for those who would like a book reconsidered), Diane Shugert's *Rationales for Commonly Challenged/Taught Books* (which offers specific justifications for specific novels) and Nicholas Karolides and Lee Burress's *Celebrating Censored Books!* Also invaluable is the ALA's *Hit List. Frequently Challenged Young Adult Titles: References to Defend Them*, which gives teachers sources outside their own judgment as to what is a good book. In the meantime, however, the following five principles may help you:

1. **Find out if your school has a materials selection policy and a procedure for dealing with books that are challenged**. If it does, get a copy. If it

doesn't, raise the issue: without something in writing, schools are unprepared to deal quickly and effectively with a parental or public complaint.

2. **Find out if your department has a file of rationales for books that are taught in classes.** Making up rationales and keeping them on file is powerful ammunition when books are questioned by parents and members of the public. Printed rationales or techniques for writing your own are available from ALA or NCTE.

3. **Get a copy of NCTE's "Citizen's Request for the Reconsideration of a Work of Literature" (from the NCTE publication, *The Students' Right to Read*).** It is a workable and usable form to give parents and others who question a work you might be teaching.

4. **As you teach and select, do keep in mind what merit you feel the material has for your students.** If you really don't know why you are using something, even if it is in the mandated textbook, maybe you don't need to teach it. Conviction is important in this business, and there are so many great things from which to choose and which are highly defensible.

5. **Finally, if a work you have selected or allowed is questioned, it is in your best interest to always assume that the challenger is a person of good will.** Civility, respect, and helpfulness are characteristics you should strive for, even in such an emotionally charged situation. Remember, parents and members of the public do have the right to ask questions and receive answers. Sometimes the underlying reason for their inquiry is simply that they are uninformed or unsure about the merit of literature with which they are unfamiliar.

If your school has a materials selection policy and a procedure for dealing with complaints, and you have a rationale on hand, the issue can usually be resolved amicably. On the other hand, if you find yourself without those resources, there are others who can help you—your local education association, your local language arts association, or, as mentioned, ALA and NCTE. The attempt to censor and restrict is almost as old as writing itself; while you may have never thought of it in this way, it is an ongoing effort to keep library shelves freely stocked and students reading widely. In no case, however, should you stand alone. Censorship challenges can be emotional and scary (the Nat Hentoff YA novel *The Day They Came to Arrest the Book* tells one such story), and teachers need to avail themselves of outside resources.

Of course, there is a certain hypocrisy in the entire issue of censorship. As my student Paul Fanney writes:

> Despite some of the controversy over particular books that schools do a great job of avoiding, this practice [of censorship] does nothing to stimulate would be lifelong readers. If schools are so concerned in protecting the innocence and virtue of untrampled youth, then they should demand that Congress ban television, and that goes for news programs as well. Over the years I've noticed also how cable [TV] is inclined to show more and more skin on the screen and in very, very steamy situations. It seems to me that few tears are shed over this fact, else why are we shown so much? At least books leave something to the imagination.

When we discuss this issue, it is also almost impossible not to cite John Milton's stirring and still very apt *Areopagitica,* his defense of writing against the censor. Milton wrote this pamphlet in 1644 in response to the censorship prevalent in seventeenth-century England. Addressed to the British parliament for the "liberty of unlicensed printing," Milton thundered about protecting the reading public through "a fugitive and cloister'd vertue, unexercis'd and unbreath'd" (691). He argued that even in a restrictive, theocratic society, reading would not sully anyone; he concluded it was better to kill a person than a book—because a book was so akin to a likeness of the divine:

> as good almost kill a Man as kill a good
> Booke; who kills a Man kills a reasonable
> creature, God's Image: but hee who destroyes a
> good Booke, kills reason it selfe, kills the
> Image of God, as it were in the eye. (681)

On a less elevated—but no less compelling—plane is E. B. White, who wrote in 1949 in *The New Yorker* regarding the New York Board of Education's criteria for selecting books. The criteria are strongly reminiscent of today's concerns:

> The Board of Education has twenty-three criteria for selecting textbooks, library books, and magazines for use in the public schools. We learned this by reading a fourteen-page pamphlet published by the Board explaining how it makes its choice. One criterion is: "Is it [the book or magazine] free from subject matter that tends to irreverence for things held sacred?" Another criterion is: "Are both sides of controversial issues presented with fairness?" Another: "Is it free from objectionable slang expressions which will interfere with the building of good language habits?" (1990, 140)

White worries in his essay that "these three criteria by themselves are enough to keep a lot of good books from the schools." He goes on to note:

> Irreverence for things held sacred has started many a writer on his way, and will again. An author so little moved by a controversy that he can present both sides fairly is not likely to burn any holes in the paper. We think the way for school children to get both sides of a controversy is to read several books on the subject, not one. In other words we think the Board should strive for a well-balanced library, not a well-balanced book. The greatest books are heavily slanted, by the nature of greatness. (1990, 140)

I wish I had written that.

Young Adult Literature

There has been, certainly even before the advent of the "dime" novel in the nineteenth century in this country, literature that has been written specifically for the younger reader, the young adult, and marketed to that audience. Known first by the term *juvenile* (which has unfortunate contemporary connotations and is slipping out of usage as a term simply synonymous with *young*) and then alternately by the terms *young adult, YA,* or *adolescent,* this literature started in modern form in 1967 with the publication of sixteen-year-old Susie Hinton's novel *The Outsiders,* the gripping story of two embattled groups of teenagers, "the Greasers" and "the Socs." Realistic dialogue, a strong plot, and compelling characters are all part of *The Outsiders,* and the novel, somewhat as did J. D. Salinger's *The Catcher in the Rye,* struck a chord with young readers. The teenage novelist's first effort signaled an avalanche of writing that continues, unabated, to this day and goes by the name of YA literature.

Many young adult novels are published not as hardback (or hardcover) books but as original paperbacks. There are a number of series books, and turnover is often rapid; YA novels can go out of print with incredible swiftness.

Definition of YA Literature

What makes a YA novel? Essentially, the genre is characterized by a few components, the most important of which is the first, followed by other, more structural characteristics:

- **A teenage (or young adult) protagonist.**
- **A stripped-down plot with very few, if any, subplots.**
- **A limited number of characters.**
- **A compressed time span and a restricted setting.**
- **An approximate length of 125 to 250 pages.**

While young adults, your students, will read "classics" with teen protagonists—such as Mark Twain's *Huckleberry Finn* or possibly Booth Tarkington's *Penrod* or Louisa May Alcott's *Little Women* or even William Golding's *Lord of the Flies*—such novels are not strictly considered YA literature. Similarly, contemporary novels popular with adults and young people, such as those written by Danielle Steel, Tom Clancy, and Stephen King, are also not in the category of YA literature. Commencing with the publication of *The Outsiders* and written for and marketed to young people, the YA genre is somewhat apart. It is also a definable genre that leads students (many of whom are not ready to make the shift from children's literature to adult literature, from *Charlotte's Web* to *Jane Eyre* and *Great Expectations*) into reading and the enjoyment of literature.

Concerns About YA Literature

For many teachers, especially those unfamiliar with quality YA literature, the whole field seems unnecessary or, possibly, only necessary for students who are unable to handle the intricacies of "real" adult literature. That argument ignores the fact that many of our students just stop reading around the middle school years and never take the habit back up. Developing lifelong readers is tricky, and for some young people, the shift from elementary school to middle school and above leaves their reading far behind. YA literature can provide an important and crucial link.

How do we keep our students reading? YA literature provides a useful and quality transition. Certainly the formula fiction of the *Sweet Valley High* series, popular with middle and high school students, and *The Baby Sitters Club* series, popular with upper elementary and middle school students, are both well-known YA titles. But they are only a part of the YA genre. More challenging YA work is reviewed in national journals and newspapers, critiqued by professors and librarians and professional writers, and awarded honors and medals such as the Newbery, the Coretta Scott King, and others. And there is a startling variety in the field: poetry, short stories, plays, and, of course, novels of adventure, romance, horror, science fiction, historical fiction, fantasy, almost any conceivable area of interest. YA literature, though certainly written on a smaller scale than adult literature (look again at the characteristics of the definition), can be judged using the same literary standards we would apply to any piece of writing.

There is no fudging the fact of the matter, though: YA literature, at least in the schools, is still a stepchild and has not entered the curriculum in any widespread way. Three issues are the more than likely culprits:

1. The question of quality.
2. The concern for the classics.
3. The subject matter and language in YA novels.

The question of quality   As mentioned before, many people, especially those who have not read YA literature, worry that the novels are just not well written. Certainly those novels that earn the Newbery Award are not in this category, nor are those that make the best lists of the numerous journals that review YA literature, among them *The ALAN Review, School Library Journal, Booklist, VOYA, Horn Book Magazine, Journal of Reading,* and others. Quality YA books are also found in NCTE's *Your Reading* (for middle school), *Books for You* (for senior high school), and *High Interest—Easy Reading* (for the less able reader). The fear persists, however, especially for those who are unfamiliar with YA literature, that these "junior" novels are nothing other than monuments to mediocrity and not worth students' time. According to these critics, students will stay mired in the worst of this literature and never develop a taste for more mature works.

My experience both as a reader and a teacher does not confirm this belief. It seems to me that our students need to read a whole lot and that not all of what they read should necessarily be immortal prose or poetry. G. Robert Carlsen, a strong voice for YA literature, wrote years ago in *Books and the Teenage Reader* regarding what he called *subliterature* and suggested that students need to read such material and would move beyond it. While very little of YA could be termed *subliterature,* the point is a valid one. Our reading has to go through stages, and when we tell our students that one year it is quality children's books, such as *The Phantom Tollbooth,* and the next it is a classic, such as Nathaniel Hawthorne's *The House of Seven Gables,* we may lose a number of readers and never regain them.

The concern for the classics   Another fear is that if students read YA literature, they will not read the classics. This implies an either/or situation in which students have a highly limited time to read and does not seem to be borne out by the experience of real readers. In fact, it would appear that many readers read both genres simultaneously, just as adults relax with popular magazines and keep at their bedside a more serious novel. Pairing young adult novels with classic novels is also an effective way to use both kinds of literature, and, as detailed below, there are a number of sources that offer suggestions for taking more traditional books and putting them with quality YA novels.

At any rate, insisting that students read classics or nothing often results in the latter: students, confronted with literature with which they can make little personal connection, choose, often quietly but often permanently, to stop reading altogether—or to confine reading to only that which is required by English class. As one student describes her experience with a contemporary novel versus the classics:

> The only novel I remember in high school English that I liked was John Knowles' *A Separate Peace.* I could relate to it. I have thought of this book many times since tenth grade, and I believe that the themes and the characters had something to say to me when I was fifteen. I am a strong believer in teaching the classics of literature. But I am a stronger believer in teaching critical thought. And if that means abandoning automatically teaching Melville and Faulkner to the exclusion of anything else then so be it. . . . I think Shakespeare would be easier for a fifteen-year-old to swallow if it were "spiced up" a little with contemporary essays or poetry. There are great themes in Shakespeare that have been echoed throughout time in different manners and different mediums.   —Mitra Palmer

Pairing young adult literature and classic novels and poetry is one way to accommodate both. In a recent book on the subject, *Adolescent Literature as a Complement to the*

Classics, a wide variety of pairings are suggested based on theme, setting, and plot similarities. In my chapter on *Great Expectations,* for example, I suggest parallel readings with Robert Lipsyte's *The Brave,* Cynthia Rylant's *A Fine White Dust,* and Gary Paulsen's *Dogsong.* Other contributors in *Adolescent Literature* make similar suggestions: Henrik Ibsen's drama *A Doll's House* could be paired with Sue Ellen Bridgers' *Permanent Connections*; Zora Neale Hurston's *Their Eyes Were Watching God* and Mildred Taylor's *Roll of Thunder, Hear My Cry* would also be complimentary. The very powerful and well-written *The Chocolate War* by Robert Cormier would work well with Nathaniel Hawthorne's *The Scarlet Letter,* George Orwell's *1984,* and William Golding's *Lord of the Flies.*

Other classic/young adult novel pairings excerpted from the Kaywell book are briefly summarized below:

- *To Kill a Mocking Bird* (Harper Lee) could be paired with:

  Words by Heart (Ouida Sebestyen)

  More than Meets the Eye (Jeanne Betancourt)

  The Day that Elvis Came to Town (Jan Marino)

  All Together Now (Sue Ellen Bridgers)

  The Autobiography of Miss Jane Pittman (Ernest Gaines)

  Let the Circle Be Unbroken (Mildred Taylor)

- *The Diary of a Young Girl* (Anne Frank) could be paired with:

  Summer of My German Soldier (Bette Greene)

  The Last Mission (Harry Mazer)

  Chernowitz! (Fran Arrick)

  Gentlehands (M. E. Kerr)

  The War Between the Classes (Gloria D. Miklowitz)

- *The Adventures of Huckleberry Finn* (Mark Twain) could be paired with:

  Julie of the Wolves (Jean Craighead George)

  Farewell to Manzanar (J. W. and J. D. Houston)

  Carlota (Scott O'Dell)

  Roll of Thunder, Hear My Cry (Mildred Taylor)

  Come a Stranger (Cynthia Voigt)

- *The Great Gatsby* (F. Scott Fitzgerald) could be paired with:

  Hero and the Crown (Robin McKinley)

  Tiger Eyes (Judy Blume)

  The Moves Make the Man (Bruce Brooks)

  Izzy Willy-Nilly (Cynthia Voigt)

  The Ring of Endless Light (Madeleine L'Engle)

  Jacob Have I Loved (Katherine Paterson)

Young adult literature can of course be used by itself; if a concern for the place of the classics is an issue, however, pairing the two can be very helpful.

The subject matter and language in YA novels   The question of censorship is a very real one in YA literature. All of the hot topics—sex, drugs, suicide, parental tensions, race, poverty—are touched on in much YA literature, and often the characters speak in realistic dialogue incorporating slang and an occasional obscenity. In fact, the realism of much of YA literature may be part of its popularity with young people. Again, the issue is polarized: all good literature addresses the hot topics, but for many people, unfortunately some teachers and librarians included, hot topics are acceptable in antique dress but not in today's clothing. There is nothing Robert Cormier's frequently censored *The Chocolate War* discusses that William Shakespeare or Nathaniel Hawthorne or Herman Melville avoid. Put the same themes in modern times, however, and discuss them in contemporary language, and many people become wary and worry that young people will be exposed to something they might otherwise never learn—or will learn sometime in that distant future when they can "handle" it. Truth be told, life is not that way, and young people need truth in today's language as much as in the language of yesteryear.

A young man dies of AIDS in M. E. Kerr's *Night Kites*; young people commit suicide in Fran Arrick's *Tunnel Vision* and deal with deformity in Dennis Covington's *Lizard*. Parents are absent or disengaged in many novels; in Julian Thompson's *The Grounding of Group Six* parents pay to get rid of their children (literally—they arrange to have them murdered). There is coming of age, painful and yet inevitable, in *Bless Me, Ultima* (Rudolfo A. Anaya), *Missing May* (Cynthia Rylant) and *My Brother Sam Is Dead* (James Lincoln Collier and Christopher Collier, set during the Revolutionary War). An otherwise good student is a minor drug dealer in Todd Strasser's *Angel Dust Blues*; a young woman succumbs to cancer in Alden Carter's *Sheila's Dying*, and another seeks out her long-absent father in Virginia Hamilton's *A Little Love*. Alzheimer's is the backdrop for Margaret Mahy's *Memory,* a mental breakdown features in Zibby Oneal's *The Language of Goldfish,* and marital abuse is part of Jenny Davis's *Sex Education.* A long-absent father breaks out of prison to contact his son, only to be re-arrested and die at the end of *Somewhere in the Darkness* (Walter Dean Myers).

There are, of course, funny novels about school and friends, lighthearted looks at family and relationships. Jerry Spinelli, Paula Danziger, Walter Dean Myers, Gordon Korman, are among the many YA writers who include lighter topics among their more serious ones. Spinelli's *Space Station Seventh Grade,* Danziger's *This Place Has No Atmosphere,* Myers's *Fast Sam, Cool Clyde, and Stuff,* and Korman's *Don't Care High* are representative titles.

There are very good collections of short stories; Joyce Carol Thomas's *A Gathering of Flowers: Stories About Being Young in America,* Gary Soto's *Baseball and Other Stories,* Chris Crutcher's *Athletic Shorts: 6 Short Stories,* and the excellent collections edited by Don Gallo (*Sixteen, Connections, Visions, Within Reach, Short Circuits*) are all widely available. The point, perhaps, is a range of offerings; the more students know is available, the more likely they will find something they really want to read.

Keeping students reading is one of the gifts of YA literature; it is a powerful tool we can use both in and outside the classroom.

Using reading inventories

Asking students what they would like to read can be done orally or in reading inventories, questions that give a teacher an idea of what a student is interested in. Reading inventories can be found in a number of sources, such as *The English/Language Arts Handbook* (Stephen N. and Susan J. Tchudi), *A Guide to Literature for Young Adults* (Ruth Cline and William McBride), and *Reaching Adolescents: The Young Adult Book and the*

School (Arthea J. S. Reed). Textbooks on young adult literature such as those by Alleen Pace Nilsen and Ken Donelson (*Literature for Today's Young Adults,* the most comprehensive text in the field, now in its fourth edition) and by the Bushmans (*Using Young Adult Literature in the English Classroom*) also have extensive reading lists. Book lists, such as the ones by Nilsen (*Your Reading*), Wurth (*Books for You*), and McBride (*High Interest—Easy Reading*), are helpful, as are the recommendations of other readers (What one or two books do your students recommend that others read? Why?). Also, don't forget librarians, reading specialists, and other teachers, who can be invaluable resources for suggesting books that students enjoy and like.

A word about nonfiction

For many of our students, nonfiction, biography, history, sociology, science, are of great interest, one that transcends their interest in any form of fiction. Most of us as teachers, of course, have progressed through our English majors as readers and lovers of literature—meaning fiction, drama, and poetry—but we should not lose sight of the power of nonfiction to enthrall. In fact, the very question of what is fact and what is fiction, though actually a fairly sophisticated consideration, can lead students to understanding and debate. At any rate, nonfiction needs more attention in our classes and needs more acceptance by us as teachers.

The range of nonfiction is great: Lorene Cary's *Black Ice* is the story of a young African American girl in a prestigious, all-white prep school; Aranka Siegal's *Grace in the Wilderness* is the true story of fifteen-year-old Piri Davidowitz, a survivor of the World War II concentration camps. And there are many others: a recent Best Books for Young Adults list compiled by the American Library Association features almost three dozen titles. They range from *Kareem,* about the last year in the profession of a career basketball player (Kareem Abdul-Jabbar and Mignon McCarthy), to William Loren Katz's *Breaking the Chains: African American Slave Resistance,* a history of how black slaves fought for their freedom all through their history. Also on the list are Sheila Hamanaka's *The Journey,* a history of Japanese Americans in the United States; *The Whole Earth Ecolog: The Best of Environmental Tools and Ideas* (edited by J. Baldwin), which gives information on the environment and helping the planet; cartoonist Gary Larson's *The PreHistory of the Far Side: A 10th Anniversary Exhibit*; and Gary Paulsen's *Woodsong,* about dogsledding in the Minnesota wilderness.

For students for whom fiction or drama or poetry is not enough or is too omnipresent, nonfiction is a real and useful alternative. Lists such as those compiled by the American Library Association, booklists published by the National Council of Teachers of English, and excellent references such as Richard F. Abrahamson and Betty Carter's *Nonfiction for Young Adults* are also helpful.

FOR YOUR JOURNAL

YA novels and nonfiction are not lengthy, and you will probably be able to read one in a brief period of time. Go to your local library and browse in the young adult section; consult NCTE's *Books for You* (their senior high booklist) for recommended works or look at the Nilsen and Donelson text listed in the references section at the end of this chapter. Read a YA work and write about it briefly: how did you react to it? Who do you think would like to read such a book? How do you assess it in terms of tightness of plot, believability of characters, realism in dialogue, appropriateness of setting, importance of theme, accuracy of information? Can you think of any adult or "classic" work you could pair this book with? What similarities/differences do you see? If you have had no exposure to YA literature, look at the resources at the end of this chapter for a list of recommended works.

Teaching Shakespeare

Like most teachers, I have changed instructional strategies and emphases over my years in the classroom and, like most, I think about those changes. Some alterations, no doubt, have resulted in improvements in my teaching and understanding; some, possibly, are just changes that reflect my own shifting interests and interpretations. You will watch yourself make these changes, too, and find them renewing your teaching.

Regardless of changes, however, I have not abandoned my love of probably the most traditionally revered writer in the language arts curriculum. I firmly advocate teaching and reading Shakespeare and think every student should, in varying intensities, be exposed to the magic of his writing. I rate Shakespeare above anything or anyone else in the so-called canon of classics. I will give up time with some of the best new writers to have students read and respond to the sonnets and the plays; Shakespeare is eminently worth my time and that of my students. You will find that you teach a Shakespearian play or two almost every year; it's a staple of most English language arts curricula, and there are ways, as you will see below, to use the Bard.

As an aside, I hope that you will enjoy your teaching of Shakespeare and, if possible, develop an enthusiasm. I would hate to see anyone like this teacher, who, in Sheryl Miller's memory

> was bored with the subject; he had taught for twenty-five years or more and apparently hated it. He actually told parents on "Back-to-School" night that he never wanted to see another production of *Macbeth*; yet he taught *Macbeth* every year to his students.

We can only imagine how his students felt about Shakespeare and *Macbeth* at the end of the semester.

Giving your students background

Before we move into Shakespeare, however, let me caution you briefly about background when reading and discussing the plays. While your students may benefit from knowing something about the Elizabethan Age—the language, the culture, the politics—I have always felt it misguided that many teachers spend a truly large amount of time on that subject, taking away time from the literature. Further, what English class has not been subjected to countless lectures on *where* Shakespeare's plays were physically performed—the Globe Theatre, its construction and layout—if not asked to construct detailed models of that theatre? While nothing is wrong with some attention to historical context, again, it can usurp the major point of studying Shakespeare at all—and the point is the literature. So give that background briefly: if it takes over a third to a half of the time you have allotted for Shakespeare, you need to reconsider the proportion of your classroom time you spend on it.

And if you haven't done so yet, look at E. M. W. Tillyard's *The Elizabethan World Picture*. It is interesting, packed with information, and brief; it remains, in my mind, one of the best short works on the Elizabethan Age you could use for your own and your students' reference.

Shakespeare's language

One of the major reasons I love teaching Shakespeare is the language. Across the centuries, it stands and endures and calls. Shakespeare has crept into our conversation, our phrases, quips, and titles—from "all the world's a stage" (*As You Like It*) to "green-ey'd jealousy" (*Merchant of Venice*) to "hark, hark, the lark" (*Cymbeline*) to "double, double, toil and trouble" (*Macbeth*) to "how sharper than a serpent's tooth it is / To have a thankless child" (*King Lear*). Our students know to "beware the Ides of March" (*Julius Caesar*); they can complete the line, "Romeo, Romeo, wherefore art thou Romeo" (*Romeo and Juliet*); and "the winter of our discontent" (*Richard the Third* and as borrowed by John Steinbeck) may strike a vague chord of recognition. Most of our students, consciously or unconsciously, know some Shakespeare. On a more elevated level, the words of Shakespeare have a freshness and sharpness that is worth our students' attention and study.

For some students, however, it is a hard task to appreciate the language. Melissa Chai recalls:

> My [current] positive attitude towards Shakespeare was not present in high school; instead it took a great deal of time to develop. Probably the most obvious reason for my distaste of Shakespeare was the difficulty in understanding the language and the meaning behind it. I recall taking a lot of notes and memorizing . . . but I never really understood the plays. Since the teacher always gave us word-by-word meaning of the speeches, it was not necessary to try to interpret them myself. I was able to memorize quite well, and that was enough to get good grades.

Memorization to get good grades is not what we want our Shakespeare study to be remember for.

Using quotations to teach Shakespeare

Along with strong imagery, gripping plots, and believable characters, Shakespeare gives us, as teachers and students, an utterly ringing collection of phrases, aphorisms, and quips. There are thousands of memorable quotations from Shakespeare's plays, and they illumine not only the plays but life itself. As Pope writes in *An Essay on Criticism*, "True Wit is Nature to advantage dress'd, / What oft was thought, but ne'er so well expressed" (l. 297). Shakespeare is the essence of true wit to advantage dressed. Studying quotations can be a helpful tool to organize discussion of his plays in the English classroom.

Using quotations to teach Shakespeare:

1. **Makes students focus on the specifics of the language.**
2. **Helps students deal with the complexity of the plays by using smaller units to discuss and focus.**
3. **Provides a structuring device of part for the whole.**
4. **Encourages students to memorize—or own—the language.**

The broad range of the plays can be highly intimidating to our students. Reducing a scene to the consideration of a single quotation can help students "manage" the play and, further, consideration of the smaller idea within the quotation can help them get a handle on the larger theme. While it is, of course, a fallacy to blithely assume that the part can stand always and conveniently for the whole, a more limited observation or a more circumscribed comment can illumine a wider field. Finally, close work with a small number of quotations can encourage students to familiarize themselves with if not actually memorize the language—students can thus "own" the words of Shakespeare, and the effect can be long range and electrifying.

Quotations and scene summaries   When I first started teaching Shakespeare in high school, I used a common and pragmatic technique to help my students understand the bare bones of the action. I had students, after reading a number of scenes, summarize the events/facts by writing a one-sentence precis for each scene. Students had three choices of how they could write their scene summaries: standard English, Elizabethan English, or school slang/street talk. Each choice yielded somewhat different results and added a bit of creativity to the assignment.

The summaries in standard English seemed to be more geared to student understanding or attempted understanding of the facts of the scene. The summaries in Elizabethan English offered this same advantage, but the students' approximations were not only often hilarious, they could be wildly inventive and occasionally almost frighteningly close to the original. The summaries in the latest version of school slang or street talk were often witty revelations of the students' factual appreciation of the action; in addition, this unusual language occasionally commented subtly on the play. Obviously, however, such an emphasis on scene summaries—on what happened—tended to make students concentrate on plot, requiring them to digest and understand more of the action than the subtlety of subtext.

My teaching of Shakespeare changed accordingly. I moved away from summary to quotations. Students would pick from each scene the single line or lines they felt were the most significant. Students would then write a brief paragraph of justification, including who said what to whom, in what context, and why this quotation was chosen over others.

The instructional advantage of the above, as opposed to the summaries, was that students could then discuss what they picked and why. Putting the two or three most frequent choices on the board or overhead and opening the floor for large-group discussion or having students who chose the same—or very different—quotations work in groups yielded lively discussion and talk.

A quotation from Act V, Scene ii of *Othello*   After students have read or acted out scenes in class, it is also possible to have the class as a whole agree on a central quotation and discuss why it merits being the majority choice. Why, for example, did my students argue that, in Act V, Scene ii of *Othello*, "I that am cruel am yet merciful; / I would not have thee linger in thy pain" (ll. 86–87) was a more significant line than the famous "Put out the light, and then put out the light" (l. 7) and the even more well known "one that lov'd not wisely but too well" (l. 344)? Just what was cruel, what was merciful, and what Othello perceived as lingering in pain were part of the discussion. The light imagery and all its resonance of putting it out was not, for this class at least, of interest; perhaps the very famous loving wisely but too well comment seemed hackneyed and, furthermore, so patently false it was not worth consideration: how could this murderer be accused of loving, at least on a surface interpretation, "too well"?

In addition, students also passed up from that scene Emilia's poetic and powerful incremental repetition of "My husband!" as she listens incredulously to Othello's accounting of just how he knows of Desdemona's betrayal; students similarly gave barely a glance to the "as ignorant as dirt" (l. 164) quotation (an insult still used widely in my region); they did not select the powerful justification Iago makes for his own perfidy ("I told [Othello] what I thought, and told no more / Than what he found himself was apt and true," ll. 176–77). For these students, the "cruel yet merciful" quotation was of central importance: we discussed Othello's assessment of his own character and actions and his stubborn refusal, at this point in the scene at least, to see the truth of Desdemona's fidelity.

A quotation from Act II, Scene ii of *Julius Caesar*   To look at another quotation choice, let us turn to Act II, Scene ii of *Julius Caesar*. There are, arguably, a number of quotations students could focus on, among them these six:

1. "Nor heaven nor earth have been at peace tonight" (l. 1).
2. "I never stood on ceremonies, / Yet now they fright me" (ll.13-14).
3. "When beggars die there are no comets seen. / The heavens themselves blaze forth the death of princes" (ll. 30–31).
4. "Cowards die many times before their deaths; / the valiant never taste of death but once" (ll. 32–33).
5. "Alas, my lord, / Your wisdom is consum'd in confidence" (ll. 48–49).
6. "[A]nd so near will I be, / that your best friends shall wish I had been further" (ll. 124–25).

Most likely, the "cowards die" quotation is one of the richer in the scene. Let's look at it in detail and consider what we might discuss if a class chose it.

Caesar says to Calpurnia, attempting to calm her fears regarding his planned trip to the Senate: "Cowards die many times before their deaths; / the valiant never taste of death but once." Certainly Caesar means this of himself, and in a subsequent line he notes that death is inevitable and thus thinks it "strange" that people fear it. Brave words, indeed, but does Caesar really live them? Is this the comment of a great ruler, a man impervious to fear who is sincerely articulating that he is somewhat immune to mortal fears of death? Is Caesar, then, the valiant man rather than the coward? Does he really postpone going to the Senate not because of any doubts he might have but because he is solely acceding to his wife: "And, for thy humour, I will stay at home" (l. 56)? It is possible. But what if it is not?

Why, then, immediately following this declamation to Calpurnia, does a new, less gruesome, interpretation of Calpurnia's dream by Decius sway Caesar—not to mention the significant news that the Senate will be awarding Caesar a crown that very day? Has Caesar intimate knowledge of the coward dying a multitude of deaths? Is his comment wishful thinking on the part of a politician whose very life is often at stake when he goes in public? Is he showing off for his wife Calpurnia?

If the above is true, what are we to make of a man who pronounces certain people cowards, others (clearly himself) valiant, when it seems likely that he is tailoring his words to fit his own self-serving actions? Regardless, how does this single line illumine the character of Caesar? Is he a truly brave man? Is Caesar, on the other hand, a boastful dolt?

And if he is the latter, does that fact in any way justify his subsequent murder and exonerate his murderers? Is self-deception or lack of self-knowledge or even pompousness so serious a character flaw that assassination is justifiable? Can we absolve Caesar entirely because while he is not valiant, he really wishes he were?

The context of the quotation is also of interest; we know that immediately after this ringing declaration Caesar finds new information that sways him. What does that mean? Also, would the meaning of the quotation be different if said to a wider audience, not, as it apparently is, to a spouse in a relatively private observation?

Looking at the language, the first line is a straightforward subject/verb construction; the second line uses the unusual verb "taste" and then the rather less emphatic "but once" for the modern equivalent "only once." Having used the plural noun "cowards," Shakespeare must use the plural object of the preposition, "deaths"; "the valiant," however, does not require such a plural, and Shakespeare can use the more elevated and almost metaphorical "death." Thus cowards "die many times"; the valiant encounter the one, cosmic death.

Turning to the verbs, why do cowards just "die" but the valiant "taste of death"? How does the verb (like the noun death/deaths) exalt death for the valiant and not for the coward? Finally, is there a conceptual difference in *dying* and *tasting of death*? Is Shakespeare implying that death for the valiant is less permanent than that for the coward? What subtlety may he be implying?

The above brief consideration of a single quotation from one scene in *Julius Caesar* demonstrates how rich the consideration of just a few lines can be. Caesar's statement to Calpurnia, an offhand comment of sorts, not only illuminates his attitude toward himself and his life but also, in its language, heavily accents the dichotomy between coward and valiant. Less important than the fact that this quotation opens the play is its ultimate interpretation: just what does this comment by Caesar tell us about his character?

Acting out quotations   Certainly the use of dramatics, or performance-based teaching of Shakespeare, is also an important part of considering the plays. Students can experiment with inflection and intonation as they perform the quotations they choose, performances that necessarily reflect alternative interpretations. Miriam Gilbert, in her "Teaching Shakespeare Through Performance," recommends "deprivation" exercises: not only miming the lines rather than speaking them but also "telegramming" them or "reducing [the lines] to the smallest number of words that will convey the message" (605) and then performing them. She reminds us that "performance-based teaching needs to work toward discussion" (605) that will reveal the number of interpretations any group of students will find in Shakespeare's lines.

Quotations and tests   As quotations can be used to discuss the plays and their implications, so also can they be used with essay tests. It is possible to present a number of quotations to students, have them pick out a requisite number (for example, ten out of twenty or seven out of fifteen), and ask them to write on each one. In their essays, students should include who said the lines to whom at approximately what juncture in the play. Students should then discuss the significance of the speech and its wider meaning. Context—who is speaking to whom when—can be most interesting, and even if students are mistaken in their memory or judgment, it can invite them to consider just what that line or lines might mean and why they were spoken. The wider significance is helpful in that it asks students to consider the ramifications of the lines both before and after the actual incident.

In selecting such a list of quotations, it would seem that students should have some familiarity with the range of lines before the test; to present students a list of relatively unknown quotations—regardless of the possibility of choice—is self-defeating and anxiety producing. The point is to look at the line or lines and see context and wider dimension. Similarly, students can choose a limited set of quotations—one for each act is a possibility, a central single line is another—and write on why that quotation or quotations is/are important.

Choosing quotations

Shakespeare provides us with a universe of great lines, and every teacher has a number of favorites from the plays. For works that are for whatever reason less familiar, there are a number of handy quotation compendia, organized by author and subject, on the market or on library reference shelves. Yet rather than shoulder the burden of choosing quotations or selecting them from something such as *The Oxford Dictionary of Quotations* (whose third edition devotes seventy-six pages to Shakespeare), it seems that we as teachers can start with our students and ask them to select, from a limited range of lines, what quotations are most significant to them. Allowing students to select what is most important not only gives students control over the discussion but also encourages them to consider just what is important and what is not.

In his essay "Technical Education and Its Relation to Science and Literature," Alfred North Whitehead railed against the widespread examination of students on the works of Shakespeare; he felt it caused in 1920s England the "certain destruction of [students'] enjoyment" and resulted in what Whitehead termed no less than "soul murder" (89). Letting students choose quotations and then discussing them in context can, I think, keep the study of the plays away from the particular type of testing and parsing many of us find ourselves confronted with; it becomes more than the "words, words, words" Hamlet sighed over (II, ii, 194). The lines of Shakespeare are, like the beauty of Cleopatra, what "age cannot wither . . . nor custom stale" (*Antony and Cleopatra*, II, ii, 240). Certainly, by exploring and celebrating those lines, we enjoy the "infinite variety" (*Antony and Cleopatra*, II, ii, 241) of one of the planet's great language masters.

FOR YOUR JOURNAL

Pick a Shakespearian play you like or have enjoyed before. Pick an act and reread it; what quotations seem important to you? Why? What discussion questions could come from those quotations? Which quotations could be used to act out parts of the play? Is there any quotation students could write about? What should students focus on as they write?

More on Multicultural: Six Contemporary African American Novels

You may have heard a great deal about multicultural issues and themes and using literature from different cultures. As discussed in Chapter 4, part of the argument over cultural literacy involves multicultural literature in the classroom. While some believe that the classics—as they define those classics—are the best, possibly the only, reading source for the English language arts classroom, there is also a current feeling that all of us as teachers need to make a much better effort to use literature from every segment of American society, not just from a relatively small, sanctioned group. That, of course, includes literature written by women. If you have been through a very traditional English major, you may not have read much from other cultures (or much written by other than men) and you may find this insistence a bit scary. You may wonder not only about the breadth of literature but also possibly about the quality.

The British novelist and essayist Virginia Woolf discussed the issue of literary merit, and while she was looking at gender issues in literature and speaking to writers, her comments, from "A Room of One's Own," are to the point in this discussion:

> All this pitting of sex against sex, of quality against quality; all this claiming of superiority and imputing of inferiority, belong to the private-school stage of human existence where there are "sides," and it is necessary for one side to beat another side. . . . [W]here books are concerned, it is notoriously difficult to fix labels of merit in such a way that they do not come off. Are not reviews of current literature a perpetual illustration of the difficulty of judgment? "This great book," "this worthless book," the same book is called by both names. Praise and blame alike mean nothing. No, delightful as the pastime of measuring may be, it is the most futile of all occupations, and to submit to the decrees of the measurers the most servile of attitudes. (110)

There is, actually, very good news: not only are there many sources of multicultural literature and literature written by women, most of it is of very high quality. Further, we as teachers have an obligation to include in the classroom literature that represents all, not just some, of our students and that reflects an array of cultural attitudes and values. Hispanic writer Rudolfo Anaya terms the absence of multicultural literature the "censorship of neglect" and calls all in the classroom to use materials that are inclusive.

Of course, one of the great bullying devices of those who laud the exclusive superiority of the canon of classics was, at one point in history, the apparent dearth of literature written by women, by people of color, and by those outside the Western European tradition. When the mocking question, "But where are the great women [black/South American/African/Asian] authors?" could not be answered with a ready list of works, there was even more justification for an adherence to the traditional list. And as Betsey Brown's English teacher tells her in Ntozake Shange's novel of the same name, as late as 1959 African American poet Paul Laurence Dunbar is not an "acceptable" choice for a classroom poetry recitation:

> I'm never going back to that old school. Never. . . . [T]his teacher tried to make me think that being colored meant you couldn't write poems or books or anything. She called [Paul Laurence Dunbar] an unacceptable choice. Now she did this only cause she doesn't believe that we're American. . . . And I said that being colored didn't mean that Paul Laurence Dunbar was less than a man or not American. . . . I bet she doesn't know who Langston Hughes is, let alone Sterling Brown or Countee Cullen. (183–84)

Yet, despite its other possible drawbacks, we live in an interesting age, one of translation, publication, and distribution. Who would, twenty-five years ago, have dreamed of courses and book lists peopled with Gabriel García Márquez, Patrick White, Nadine Gordimer, J. M. Coetzee, V. S. Naipaul? Looking in particular at African American writers, we can expand beyond the small group of predominantly male authors who stand as landmarks in literature and who now, even to traditionally prepared white English teachers, would be familiar: James Weldon Johnson, Paul Lawrence Dunbar,

Countee Cullen, Ralph Ellison, James Baldwin, Langston Hughes, Richard Wright, and the Pulitzer Prize winning poet Gwendolyn Brooks. Added to these names are those of more recent African American writers and, especially, of African American women.

Touchstone novels by African American women certainly include the biographical *I Know Why the Caged Bird Sings* by Maya Angelou, the epic and "rediscovered" *Their Eyes Were Watching God* by Zora Neale Hurston, the epistolary *The Color Purple* by Alice Walker, and the episodic *The Women of Brewster Place* by Gloria Naylor. I would like to add to that list the names Paule Marshall, Toni Morrison, and Ntozake Shange. Their works can be used successfully in and outside the classroom, and some of the works feature adolescent protagonists. While all three writers are clearly grounded in the African American experience—and take as metaphor and theme aspects of being female in this culture—all three speak widely and clearly to a range of readers. To introduce our students—and ourselves—to these voices puts the lie to the narrowly defined and traditionally circumscribed canon as the sole arbiter of truth.

Paule Marshall, the child of immigrant parents who came to the United States from Barbados, is the author of a number of novels and short stories, and has recently received a MacArthur "genius" award. Two of her novels, *Brown Girl, Brownstones* and *Praisesong for the Widow,* are of special note.

Brown Girl, Brownstones is the story of Selina, who seems in constant opposition to her more well behaved sister, Ina, and her powerful mother, Silla. It is only with her father, Deighton, that Selina seems to be in harmony, but Deighton, though elegant and charming, is unable to find purchase in his strange new land. Though he loves his wife and daughters and wishes to provide for them in America, Deighton spends most of his time halfheartedly studying for new professions that never quite materialize—radio repair and then accounting and then music. Deighton, in fact, spends most of his days and nights dressing up, going out, and dreaming of owning a piece of land in Barbados. The conflict between himself and his driven, ambitious wife is inevitable, and while Selina adores her father, the family tensions drive father and daughter apart.

In *Praisesong for the Widow,* main character Avey Johnson goes, in the novel's brief space of a few days' time, on an epic journey that encompasses not only her youth in Harlem and her childhood in South Carolina, but her whole identity as a woman and a descendent of Africa. Sustained throughout, *Praisesong for the Widow* is lyrical, deliberate, and—in its use of conventions of dream, journey, and catharsis—mythic. Its themes encompass the search for identity and the unshakable bonds of our past. Avey Johnson is not only very American, she is also a middle-aged, middle-class affluent widow on a pleasure cruise with friends. Avey Johnson—conventional, unimaginative—would seem a very unlikely and uninteresting protagonist. But Avey finds her origins in one of most dramatic scenes I have ever read.

Better known than Paule Marshall is Toni Morrison, whose work has gained wide acceptance and popularity; she is the winner of both the Pulitzer Prize and the Nobel Prize for Literature. Two of her novels, *Sula* and *Beloved,* are among Morrison's best, but both are more than likely for older and more sophisticated readers. Morrison loves intertwining the most realistic of details with an almost transcendent meaning, and it is not her intention to write novels that are immediately accessible or even completely clear as to theme. She uses strong language and writes of the serious issues of existence, life, death, and sex.

The essence of *Sula* is, in some ways, summarized by the character Nel's lament in the novel's closing lines, "a fine cry—loud and long—but it had no bottom and it had no top, just circles and circles of sorrow'' (174). This short and often puzzling work is the story of a girlhood friendship between the enigmatic Sula Peace and her more conventional companion, Nel Wright. The girls grow up in Medallion, Ohio, in the 1920s, and as their lives intertwine, separate, and then come back together, there is drama, death, and a love that even profound anger cannot erase.

Beloved is a searing work and shares with *Praisesong for the Widow* mythic aspects of plot. It very gradually reveals the central horror, a woman in slavery who goes temporarily mad with the insanity of her condition and, to save her child from a similar fate, kills her. Set also in Ohio, the work takes place immediately after the Civil War and features a main character, Beloved, who is not definably real. This fascination with what is existential and what is a manifestation of the imagination marks Morrison's work and makes it rich and multileveled. Its ultimate meaning may be elusive; the power of *Beloved,* however, lies in the gradual build-up of the plot and in its incremental language.

Ntozake Shange burst on to the literary scene with the memorably titled and well-received play *for colored girls who have considered suicide/when the rainbow is enuf.* Besides being a playwright, Shange is a poet and novelist. Two of her works, *Betsey Brown* and *Sassafras, Cypress, & Indigo,* feature teenage protagonists who must make their way in a hostile world.

Betsey Brown is thirteen in 1959, and she and her family in St. Louis confront a major event in American history: school integration and the attendant problems of racism and race hatred. But, of course, a young person's world is a small one, and ''there was a preciousness to St. Louis at dawn or dusk that was settling to the child in the midst of a city that rankled with poverty, meanness, and shootings Betsey was only vaguely aware of'' (14). Betsey's family lives largely apart from the white world, and their life, while touched and saddened by the conflict around them, remains essentially serene.

As instructive as any text—and certainly more fun than most—*Betsey Brown* is peppered with the names of black luminati from the worlds of literature, music, sports, and politics. It is a veritable laundry list of African American history: Toussaint L'Ouverture, Billie Holiday, Althea Gibson, Dinah Washington, Dorothy Dandridge, ''Sugar'' Ray Robinson, Eartha Kitt, James Brown, Cab Calloway, Josephine Baker, Dizzy Gillespie, Chuck Berry, Tina Turner and the Ikettes, Jackie Wilson, Etta James, Charlie Parker, Art Blakey, Miles Davis, Little Willie John, Bessie Smith, Paul Laurence Dunbar, Sterling Brown, Countee Cullen, and the great figure who puts little Betsey to bed one night, W. E. B. DuBois, are all mentioned.

Sassafras, Cypress & Indigo, Shange's other family story, features three sisters and their mother. ''Dedicated to all women in struggle,'' the novel explores the choices and journeys of the sisters, one a poet and weaver, one a dancer, and one whose dolls can talk and who plays the violin not from sheet music or lessons but from the passions in her soul. Set in Charleston, South Carolina; New York; and Los Angeles, the novel is interspersed with pertinent recipes, spells, chants, brief plays and letters, journal entries, and lists of rules, which adumbrate the text and the dreams of Hilda Effania for her daughters Sassafras, Cypress, and Indigo: ''What she wanted for her girls was more than that. She wanted happiness, however they could get it. Whatever it was. Whoever brought it'' (57).

There is a pungency to *Sassafras, Cypress, & Indigo* that is absent in *Betsey Brown.* The novel also explores important issues of being female in American society, being creative, and especially being a black woman in what is largely a hostile environment. There is violence in *Sassafras,* and there is sex, drugs, and tough language. But the novel is honest and unflinching; there is salvation in art, not just expression, and the three sisters and their mother find their way in the world with no easy answers but only honest questions.

For Your Journal

One of the advantages of multicultural literature is that it often presents archetypal concerns and subjects in different dress, making perennial themes new and fresh. Browse through some of the multicultural works recommended in the resources section at the end of this chapter; pick one you already know or one new to you that you would like to use in your classroom. What are the advantages of this novel? To what "classic" work might it be compared and why?

Using Literature: Some Teaching Tips

There are a number of books available, especially from NCTE, that regularly provide teaching tips on specific works. Do use your *English Journal* (the NCTE magazine for secondary teachers), state language arts publications, and *Notes Plus* and similar publications for teaching ideas. Publishers also offer teaching guides, many of which are written by teachers in the classroom and by YA authors. In general, however, there are a number of principles to keep in mind when you think of using literature.

Limit your time

Covering every aspect of any piece of literature is deadening, and furthermore, real readers don't approach literature that way. Why is it in the classroom we beat poems and short stories and novels to death, exhausting every avenue of discussion and, in the process, our students, too? Think about limiting the time you spend on what your students are reading and try to fall in love with the concept that it is better to leave them wanting to discuss more, do more, than to end a unit of study with everyone cranky and worn-out and just sick of the piece. It's the extensive versus intensive debate, and I, for one, always opt for the former. I would rather range over a wide variety of works than spend significant portions of time exhausting a single piece. From my experience, extensive, not intensive, reading seems to give students a wider range of ideas and facility.

Practically, what does this mean? It means, particularly with the Godiva chocolate of literature, poetry, that less is definitely more: five straight days of poetry should drive you and your students crazy; think of a maximum of two or three, and never, never do a complete "unit" of poetry. The stuff is too condensed for most younger readers—that's middle school and high schoolers—and should be properly, happily, interspersed with other forms of literature. I also find it helpful to "drop in" a poem every week or so; duplicate one, read it aloud, briefly discuss it, and move on. Sometimes, of course, even brief discussion is unnecessary; poetry, like those delicious Godivas, needs to be sampled and savored.

With longer works, such as multiact plays and novels, two weeks—ten days of instruction—is a reasonable limit. And, yes, this means Shakespeare, too: most students' enthusiasm will flag, as will yours, if you spend class period after class period on the same, single work of literature. Even the most dedicated of classes will wilt if, day after day, you and they mine the piece for every bit of gold it holds.

Short stories, particularly when they relate thematically or chronologically to other pieces of literature, are highly useful for "breaking up" poetry and longer pieces of study. Short stories, like poems, can also provide vehicles for "self- contained" classes in which in one period, one day, students can read and respond to a piece of literature. This not only avoids homework—which in some school settings or at some junctures is difficult, if not impossible, to have all students complete—but it also provides an impact that is hard to replicate when the literature is read outside class.

Give them a context/lead them in

Many beginning teachers forget how puzzling a piece of literature can be, how it can seem, especially on first reading, to come from absolutely nowhere. They often assume that students will "get it" much quicker than is realistic; accordingly, in their classroom discussions or activities involving literature these teachers just start—often seemingly out of thin air—as if the mere act of having heard the poem read aloud or reading the short story as homework was a sufficient introduction.

Always think about how to lead your students into a piece: call it a *hook,* a *warm-up,* an *anticipatory set,* call it what you will, but do it. Give students some sort of context for what they will be dealing with, and try at the onset to help them puzzle out a connection.

For example: In Samuel G. Freedman's *Small Victories,* the story of students in New York City's Seward Park High School, English teacher Jessica Siegel uses a number of techniques. To introduce "Walden," the Henry David Thoreau essay on leaving the complications of civilization to live simply in the country, she opens the class discussion by asking, "What's a luxury?" and uses student answers to set the stage for what Thoreau would describe as going into the woods to "live deliberately" and, necessarily, without luxury. To open a unit on early American literature that encompasses writing about what the early settlers hoped for in the New World, Siegel asks her students, predominately the children of relatively recent immigrants, why their parents came to the United States. She then uses their answers to link today with the eighteenth-century first settlers of America. For "Upon the Burning of Our House, July 10th, 1666," which is about the destruction of seventeenth-century American poet Anne Bradstreet's house by fire, students write in their journals a brief description of their favorite possession. Following this, Siegel asks students to imagine their feelings about the destruction of that favorite possession. In all three cases, students are encouraged to think of a concept or an idea that ultimately relates to the literature.

In her first few months student teaching, Debbie Martin did a similar activity:

> Today I probably had my best day of teaching yet. I mean *real teaching.* . . . I wrote on the board: Defining death is a very difficult task. If a six-year-old asked you, "What is death?," what would you say to him/her?
>
> Students had ten minutes to respond. They were told that we would share answers.
>
> Which we did. I had no trouble getting students to share. They wanted me to read their writing first, but once I did they eagerly volunteered. I let those who wanted to read, read and those who just wanted to tell me their ideas, tell me.
>
> When they did so I made very little comment. I didn't need to. The remainder of the class jumped in. We even had quite a disagreement between two students in one class. As long as it was rational and kind, I let it go on for a few moments. I ended it by saying that a definition of death was often tied to religious beliefs and that in any case [it] was tied to beliefs that were very personal. Further, that if we had the time to really get into it, more than likely not one of us would agree.

We then read John Donne's "Sonnet X" or "Death, be not Proud." The relationship between the writing and the sonnet were crystal clear.

One of my students who does *nothing* said later, when I mentioned a review, "We don't need to review this one; we've practically memorized it now."

While there is a danger, as with the pitfalls of theme, that such openers, warm-ups, or anticipatory sets will steer students only too precisely into what *we* want them to see in and believe about a piece of literature, the opposite is probably more dangerous, especially for younger and unsure readers. Leaving students to founder, repeatedly confronting them class after class with literature that seems relatively contextless, is to invite disaffection and unease. The luxury of no context and discovery may be more appropriately left for college and graduate school, where more adept readers are not so confounded by what they are discussing. By and large, our middle school and high school students, many of whom are pretty new to this game of looking at unfamiliar literature, may need to be pointed in a general direction. What Jessica Siegel and Debbie Martin do in their classrooms seems to have far more benefits than disadvantages.

On the other hand, if a focused "warm-up" is too targeted for you, consider doing one or more of the following:

- **Ask your students to speculate on the title: what does it mean? How do they know? Can they provide synonyms? Can they create a parallel title?**

- **Read them the first line of the poem or the first paragraph of the prose, and ask them to write about what they expect will happen next. Ask them to share their answers and discuss.**

- **Excerpt a snatch of dialogue from the play; have a number of students read the parts, and ask students what is going on. Have another duo or trio read the same lines and ask the question again. Do the readings differ in tone and interpretation? How?**

Let them create it—within reason

A way into poetry is encouraging students to write their own; similarly, short skits can also help students appreciate drama and feel its power. Be very wary, however, of asking students to write epic poems or five-act plays; while there are some classes and some students who may be able to do it, insisting that an entire class embark upon a complete, whole work of literature may not invite creativity so much as despair. Asking students, similarly, to write an entire short story is an assignment many teachers rather routinely give, and the results are very rarely satisfactory. Unless you are committed to helping students work through the process of creating a long work, stick to more attainable goals. It is one thing to do a very short, self-contained piece; it is another to piece together prose that features, in the case of the short story, setting, characters, and dialogue, not to mention theme and a coherent plot with conflict and climax.

If you doubt the truth of this, consider what it took you to write your most recent long poem, play, or short story. What?! You've never written such a piece?

Well, actually, you are like most people, English majors or not. Few of us have attempted or completed such works. Accordingly, try it before you blithely assign it to your students on a Monday morning. It may give you an appreciation of what you are asking; in addition, it may help you define what you expect from your students. What we don't want is described clearly by Jonathan Morris, who recounts:

[In class] we were reading some sonnets. And at the same time we were being taught the form and structure. One of our assignments was to write a Shakespearian sonnet. I can't think of anything more sure to create feelings of inadequacy. At the time I had been writing poetry for a year or so, sentimental poetry, whose deity is, of course, Shakespeare. I spent days writing this sonnet, with its crucible of structure, working on it far more than the time one was expected to spend on the assignment. A few days after we turned them in [the teacher] read some of the sonnets in class. Mine was not one. I got a C and was crushed. My creativity was discouraged along with my errors in iambic pentameter.

Consider having your students create short pieces of text that are related to the original. With a chapter from a novel or with a short story, students can look at plot, setting, and character. For example:

- **Have students pick a favorite or pivotal scene. Then let them add a character, delete a character, or alter a piece of dialogue by changing a crucial word or key phrase. Ask your students to rewrite that one scene and share it by reading it aloud and discussing how it changes the plot.**
- **Have students write a new ending or a sequel by extending the ending by one hour, one day, one week, one month, one year. For some pieces of literature, what happens immediately after the final period is of great interest; for other pieces, what the characters are doing after a year is more realistic. Have students share their new endings and discuss how they arrived at them.**
- **Have students do a new beginning to the literature—in mediaspeak, a *prequel*—that begins an hour, a day, a week, a month, a year before the literature actually starts. Again, have students share.**
- **Let students change the title and rewrite the opening paragraph and/or the closing paragraph to reflect that new title. How did they come up with the new title?**
- **Have students rewrite the setting of a section. Setting can be a snooze to students, but what if a section of the literature is set in a different era? in the country rather than on the street corner? in spring instead of winter? Have students discuss the changes they make.**
- **Let students rename characters, change the sex of characters, change a major personality trait or physical characteristic of a character, and then have them rewrite a section. Character is pivotal in most literature. What happens when one of these characteristics is changed? Why?**

Certainly we as teachers need to be careful with students, whose egos are, necessarily, intimately, tied up with their creative attempts. I offer as an example the following poem, given to me some years ago by one of my high school students. It is a piece whose major merit lies in its effort to express an idea important to the writer and, actually, an idea important to this discussion as well. Gabriella writes:

Trying won't hurt

I have never fallen down so hard
for it to hurt so bad,
But the biggest hurt of all
is when I don't success.

> For if I don't success and try my best
> It won't hurt as much,
> But, if I don't success and
> don't keep trying, then it hurts.

We have to give our Gabriellas opportunities to try. As they articulate and explore in our class, there will be time to talk about verbs and nouns, about the difference between *success* and *succeed,* and we can help them make their poetry and their prose writing not only expressive but more correct. But just because students such as Gabriella do not have all their skills down pat or understand all the ramifications of English language arts, we do not serve any useful purpose by keeping those students away from the creative or the inventive in the name of developing skills through worksheets and drills. We hope they will succeed, but keeping them away from creative forms, keeping them from attempting, reaching, stretching, is probably far more searing than possible failure.

Let them act it out—after they have warmed up first

Creative dramatics can make magic in a classroom, and certainly students can base short skits not only on full-length plays but also on poems, short stories, and pieces of nonfiction. Good drama anthologies are also available: Don Gallo's *Center Stage,* Judith Barlow's *Plays by American Women,* Lowell Swortzell's *All the World's a Stage,* and Michael Schulman and Eva Mekler's *Contemporary Scenes for Student Actors* all offer a variety of short drama. Regardless of what you base your creative dramatics on, do not forget the human being in all of this; just because your students are young does not mean they have no inhibitions. Just telling students to ''get in front of the class and act it out'' is a recipe for disaster. Students need some help; like most people, they need to get ready.

First, students need to be warmed up for such a skit. This can involve breathing exercises, movement exercises, and games (see mirror images, farmyard, and statues, below). Students can then, in groups or pairs, work on brief skits or do impromptus and present them with much less inhibition and fear.

To expect students just to *do it,* to perform on *your* moment's notice, is unfair and something, frankly, you most likely would not want to do either. Let's look at a few ways to warm up students (the following can be done in sequence).

Relaxation   This activity loosens people up and encourages them to stretch and breathe deeply. Have students stand up and move away from each other so that they can extend their arms out and not hit someone else in the face or back. Let students slowly take a number of deep breaths. Have students stretch their arms above their heads, to their sides, and then bend over and ''bounce'' with their arms hanging loosely to the floor. Let students put their hands on their waists and twist their upper torsos to the left and the right. Have them rotate their heads (*gently,* this can be dangerous) on their necks. Finally, let students shake their arms at their sides, then their legs (one at a time, obviously!).

A variation on this stretching exercise is for students to imagine that they are standing at the foot of a tree and trying to pick an apple just out of reach. Ask students to see the tree, see the apple, then stretch first the left and then the right arm so that they can ''pick'' the apple. (Standing on tiptoe is allowed.)

Farmyard   This is a silly, childish exercise that usually makes students laugh; it also requires that deep breaths be taken, which has a tendency to relax people and loosen inhibitions. Farmyard makes a lot of noise; be prepared for someone down the hall to call for quiet or to investigate what's going on.

Students should be standing and positioned so they can see one another and you. I tell students to imagine we are in the country in a farmyard. We are now all chickens and we must make chicken noises. So we all **cluck** a bit for about a minute or so. Then we become a much bigger animal in the farmyard, a pig, and we **snort and snuffle** for a minute. Watching the chickens and the pigs are the family pets. What does that cat say? We **meow** a bit. The cat, of course, is chased away by its natural enemy, and we **bow wow** as a dog for about a half a minute. (Keep these short—students can get tired of all these ridiculous noises.)

Finally, we see the largest animal in the farmyard and the one (I think) that makes the most satisfying noise. We are a cow, and we all **moo** as a finale. (Make sure everyone makes these noises randomly; there should be no orchestration of the sounds.)

Mirrors   Once students have relaxed with the two exercises above, they are ready to pair up for Mirrors. The purpose is to watch the other person and to mimic, without words or extraneous facial expressions, exactly what that person does. One of the pair stands directly in front of the other and starts lifting hands, moving arms, whatever. The other person, for a minute or so, must be that person's mirror image and do the identical actions he or she sees. Then the roles are reversed.

Statues   Statues adds plot to Mirrors and can be done while the class watches a few students or can be done with everyone in the class participating. You need to put students in trios and have them number off 1, 2, and 3. The three will be given roles (reminiscent of a nineteenth-century tableaux), and they must, again wordlessly, indicate their role by body gesture and position.

Imagine that all the students have counted off. Here are a few scenarios they can arrange in about thirty seconds and then hold for ten seconds or so:

- 1 and 2 are angry at 3.
- 2 is cheating, and 1 is telling 3 about it.
- 3 is in love with 1, and 2 approves.
- 2 is in love with 3, and 1 thinks it's a bad situation.
- 2 is jealous of 3; 1 intervenes.

Clearly, this exercise asks more of students than the others and can be expanded into impromptus:

- Students can strike a pose and have the class guess the general situation.
- Students can be given a situation and have to show it.
- Students can experiment with a tableau and then write about it.

Before I do creative dramatics of almost any sort, I go through most or all of the four exercises outlined above. By the time students are through, they are relaxed, inventive, and ready for experimentation. You may think this is a waste of valuable time, but it is my experience that warming up students for creative dramatics is essential. Regardless of what your purpose is in using creative dramatics, your students need some time, as the song says, to get in the mood.

Art and music

As response through creative dramatics can inspire students, so also can the use of art and music. Letting students who like to draw or paint or put together collages interpret or respond to literature through that medium can unlock a world of connection that might otherwise not exist.

Likewise, our students are often fiercely loyal to certain groups or styles of music, and using the lyrics of their favorite songs or asking them to connect reading with what they listen to can also make literature real or illuminating in a way that would not be otherwise possible.

A key to success in using art and music with literature is **allowing students choice** in what they select and in **being specific with expectations**. Asking students to respond to literature with art or using music and not giving them any other boundaries can result in poorly focussed projects. For example, ask students to select a certain number of songs and discuss how the lyrics relate to the literature; give students dimensions or number of elements to be incorporated into art projects.

If they can't—or won't—read it

Who says that reading aloud to students is just for elementary school? The pleasures of *hearing* literature are manifold and, indeed, can help students who are struggling with material too difficult for them to comprehend easily. Hearing a piece read and seeing it simultaneously on the page can double comprehension; it can also give you the opportunity to gloss or define words that you are relatively sure your students would not readily understand. One student of mine recalls her English class:

> Reading aloud should have been a regular feature of high school English. It is capable of inspiring students, involving them, allowing them to enter another world and experience what I think a high school English curriculum should allow a student to experience, a mind-expanding exploration into new territory, new worlds, a chance to see more than what's in front of the student's eyes when he or she usually looks at the world. Being read to helps students to expand a little, giving them a chance to look at something a little differently, or to understand a different viewpoint or perspective. —Lori Shacreaw

I read aloud most of the Edgar Allan Poe short stories my students studied; my cadence and my vocabulary synonyms helped them get through a lot of the difficult, vocabulary-rich nineteenth-century prose. I also read other, less challenging pieces to classes that featured reluctant readers or virtual nonreaders.

I love to read aloud and always apologize to students for my hogging the reading. Occasionally, though, I ask students to take turns reading literature whose syntax and vocabulary would not be a torture for a volunteer. What we want to avoid, however, is the agony one student describes in her English class:

> Having the students to read aloud was another favorite classroom assignment of the teacher, which could make one's heart pound and cause a major sweat. This was not difficult for me, but I can remember many students stumbling, stuttering, and agonizing over each word while everyone else followed along, trying to figure out who the next reader might be.

Reading aloud adds to the drama of the literature and provides, especially with short works, an impact and power that only a single, sustained reading can provide. If your students can't read or if they really struggle over certain kinds of literature, read it to them or have relatively confident volunteers read all or part of it.

Reading aloud is also very important in drama and poetry. I, for one, cannot imagine reading poetry only silently. Reading a poem a number of times is part and parcel of the experience of the genre, and even if students have looked at a piece in preparation for a discussion or for homework, they should hear it again—aloud—before discussing or writing or anything.

Reading aloud can also address another issue: that of students not doing homework or reading outside of class. Certainly for schools that feature high absentee rates, the expectation that students will prepare their reading before class can lead to serious teacher frustration when a small percentage of students—if any—actually come to class having read what was assigned.

In one teaching year, I had about a forty percent absentee rate for three of my five classes; that meant that I could never count on who would be present for any given class on any given day. The continuity of assignments was destroyed ("No, I didn't read it—I was absent" many of my students would tell me), and in this situation, there was little I could do but adapt. Otherwise, I was forced into the situation of not only failing the students because of school-mandated policies about absences but, when the students did come to class, ensuring that they would not be able to participate. I didn't like that option, and, accordingly, I used poetry, short stories, and very short dramas that could be read in class. I then set up some form of activity that we either started or completed within a fifty-minute period. Students, despite their spotty attendance, could complete work within a class and, for some, it not only meant the difference between passing and failing but also gave them a daily sense of accomplishment and completion.

While this accommodation may strike you as caving in to a bad situation—weak student reading skills and excessive student absences—I would defend it as a realistic compromise. Faced with failing them all virtually from the onset or working with the reality of my students and my school, I chose the latter. And I do believe some of my students learned something along the way as they listened.

If you don't like it either

I've read the sentiment before, and I happen to agree with it: if you really don't like a piece of literature—and this is particularly true of poetry—you probably shouldn't teach it. As self-indulgent as that may seem, I think it is good advice and, within some limits, I follow it myself. The point is that enthusiasm is catching. The reverse is also true. To give one example, if "To the Virgins to Make Much of Time" seems impossibly silly to you, skip it and maybe even Robert Herrick altogether. There is surely some other seventeenth-century British poet whom you can present to your students in an effective and enthusiastic manner. On the other hand, don't assume that what one year you absolutely could not bring yourself to teach will remain on your "yuck list" forever: your tastes will change as you teach, and you need to give literature a second look every year or so. You might surprise yourself.

Remember why you're doing this

When you're faced with objectives and those very official-looking textbooks and five classes of thirty students or so each, it is hard to remember just why you are reading literature. Don't forget the joy of it, the possibility that some of your students, not all certainly, but some, will become lifelong readers due in part to what happens in *your* class. Don't forget the laughter and the joy; it's why you are doing this.

For many beginning teachers the curriculum requirements and what it seems the school or the school system expects can become an overwhelming weight; there is the fear, reasonable or not, that you will be judged by how much material you cover or how efficiently you cover it. For some teachers, the scores their students make on large-scale exams are also a concern.

But at some point, although you cannot wave away or minimize these very real issues, you also have to make some choices about what school expects versus your responsibility to your students. To some people, even some teachers in the classroom, a "free" reading day once a week would seem a waste; time spent becoming mirror images and creating skits would appear frivolous. But what you are about is more than pages in the textbook and passing scores on literature tests. As highbrow as it may seem when you contemplate the down and dirty realities of third period, you are in that class to invite reading and thinking, to give students with minds and hearts and psyches windows onto the world we know is in books. You are a guide to something bigger than the competency test, the unit exam, the departmental requirements, or even the SATs and admission to college. While it is not always true that there will be conflict between reading and talking and thinking and what school "expects," there may be. And when that occurs, remember why you are a teacher, why you got into this business in the first place. As one of my students wrote:

> I do empathize with my former teachers' predicament of being caught in the bureaucratic wheel wherein they were required to spit out so many units of grammar, prose and poetry to every high school student. [But] somewhere within all of the guidelines, budgets and politics, the students' personal expression, interests, goals and motivators were forgotten.
>
> —ELLEN SIGLER

Your guiding north star is not the curriculum guide; you need, while trying to be responsible to the demands of your job and the expectations of the system, also to hold true to your vision for yourself and your students. It's a lot to ask; it's also very important.

Without holding true to that vision you may find yourself relatively lost and feeling, as some do, that you are in the classroom "delivering" a package of instruction at someone else's behest. That's not what you want to spend any part of your life doing; while balancing the expectations may be the tightrope act of your life, the stakes are huge, and the effort is worth it.

FOR YOUR JOURNAL

Pick a favorite piece of literature—a play, a poem, a short story, or a novel—that you think you could teach in middle school or high school. How would you prepare students for this piece of literature? Think about three or four activities you could do during or after the reading; write about them. Can you imagine this piece of literature being challenged or censored? For the sake of argument, imagine it is. What reasons would you advance for using it in the classroom?

REFERENCES

Professional sources

Abrahamson, Richard F. and Betty Carter. *Books for You.* 10th ed. Urbana, IL: NCTE, 1988.

———. *Nonfiction Books for Young Adults: From Delight to Wisdom.* New York: Oryx, 1990.

American Library Association. *Hit List. Frequently Challenged Young Adult Titles: References to Defend Them.* Chicago, IL: ALA, 1989.

Anaya, Rudolfo. "The Censorship of Neglect." *English Journal* 81 (September 1992): 18–20.

Burress, Lee and Edward B. Jenkinson. *The Students' Right to Know.* Urbana, IL: NCTE, 1982.

Bushman, John H. and Kay Parks Bushman. *Using Young Adult Literature in the English Classroom.* New York: Macmillan, 1993.

Carlsen, G. Robert. *Books and the Teenage Reader.* 2d ed. New York: Harper & Row, 1980.

Christenbury, Leila. "Becoming an Urban English Teacher." *English Journal* 68 (November 1979): 31–33.

————. *Books for You.* 12th ed. Urbana, IL: NCTE, forthcoming.

————. "Creating Text: Students Connecting with Literature." In *Literature and Life: Making Connections in the Classroom.* Classroom Practices in Teaching English, edited by Patricia Phelan, vol. 25. Urbana, IL: NCTE, 1990.

————. "Marshall, Morrison, and Shange: Voices of the Sisters." *Virginia English Bulletin* 40 (Fall 1990): 106–17.

————. "What Oft Was Thought But Ne'er So Well Expressed: The Use of Quotations in Teaching Shakespeare." In *Teaching Shakespeare Today: Practical Approaches and Productive Strategies,* edited by James E. Davis and Ronald E. Salome. Urbana, IL: NCTE, 1993.

Cline, Ruth and William McBride. *A Guide to Literature for Young Adults.* Glenview, IL: Scott, Foresman, 1983.

Freedman, Samuel G. *Small Victories.* New York: HarperCollins, 1990.

Gilbert, Miriam. "Teaching Shakespeare Through Performance." *Shakespeare Quarterly* 35(5)(1984): 601–8.

Karolides, Nicholas and Lee Burress, eds. *Celebrating Censored Books!* Racine, WI: Wisconsin Council of Teachers of English, 1985.

Kaywell, Joan F., ed. *Adolescent Literature as a Complement to the Classics.* Norwood, MA: Christopher-Gordon, 1993.

McBride, William. *High Interest—Easy Reading.* Urbana, IL: NCTE, 1990.

NCTE. *The Students' Right to Read.* Urbana, IL: NCTE, 1982.

————. *Notes Plus.* Urbana, IL: NCTE, 1990.

Nilsen, Alleen Pace, ed. *Your Reading.* 8th ed. Urbana, IL: NCTE, 1991.

Nilsen, Alleen Pace and Kenneth L. Donelson. *Literature for Today's Young Adults.* 4th ed. New York: HarperCollins, 1993.

The Oxford Dictionary of Quotations. 3d ed. New York: Oxford University Press, 1980.

Reed, Arthea J. S. *Reaching Adolescents: The Young Adult Book and the School.* New York: Holt, Rinehart & Winston, 1985.

Shugert, Diane. *Rationales for Commonly Challenged/Taught Books.* Enfield, CT: Connecticut Council of Teachers of English, 1983.

Tchudi, Stephen N. and Susan J. Tchudi. *The English/Language Arts Handbook.* Portsmouth, NH: Boynton/Cook, 1991.

Tillyard, E. M. W. *The Elizabethan World Picture.* London: Chatto & Windus, 1943.

Whitehead, Alfred North. *The Aims of Education and Other Essays.* New York: Macmillan, 1929.

Wurth, Shirley. *Books for You.* 11th ed. Urbana, IL: NCTE, 1992.

Literature cited

Abdul-Jabbar, Kareem and Mignon McCarthy. *Kareem.* New York: Random, 1991.

Alcott, Louisa May. *Little Women: Meg, Jo, Beth, and Amy. The Story of Their Lives. A Girl's Book.* Boston: Little, Brown, 1968.

Anaya, Rudolfo A. *Bless Me, Ultima.* Berkeley, CA: Tonatiuh-Quinto Sol International, 1972.

Angelou, Maya. *I Know Why the Caged Bird Sings.* New York: Bantam, 1970.

Arrick, Fran. *Chernowitz!* New York: Signet, 1981.

———— . *Tunnel Vision*. New York: Bradbury, 1980.

Baldwin, J., ed. *The Whole Earth Ecolog: The Best of Environmental Tools and Ideas*. New York: Harmony Books, 1991.

Barlow, Judith, ed. *Plays by American Women: The Early Years*. New York: Avon, 1981.

Betancourt, Jeanne. *More than Meets the Eye*. New York: Bantam, 1990.

Blume, Judy. *Tiger Eyes*. New York: Dell Laurel-Leaf, 1981.

Bradstreet, Anne. "Upon the Burning of Our House, July 10th, 1666." In *The Women Poets in English,* edited by Ann Stanford, 52–53. New York: McGraw Hill, 1972.

Bridgers, Sue Ellen. *All Together Now*. New York: Bantam, 1979.

———— . *Permanent Connections*. New York: Harper & Row, 1987.

Brooks, Bruce. *The Moves Make the Man*. New York: Harper & Row, 1984.

Brontë, Charlotte. *Jane Eyre*. Edited by Richard J. Dunn. New York: Norton, 1971.

Carter, Alden. *Sheila's Dying*. New York: G. P. Putnam's Sons, 1986.

Cary, Lorene. *Black Ice*. New York: Alfred A. Knopf, 1991.

Chao, Chang. *Yumengying*. Translated by Lin Yutang. *The Importance of Understanding*. New York: World Publishing, 1960.

Collier, James Lincoln and Christopher Collier. *My Brother Sam Is Dead*. New York: Scholastic, 1974.

Cormier, Robert. *The Chocolate War*. New York: Dell Laurel-Leaf, 1974.

Covington, Dennis. *Lizard*. New York: Delacorte, 1991.

Crutcher, Chris. *Athletic Shorts: 6 Short Stories*. New York: Greenwillow, 1991.

Danziger, Paula. *This Place Has No Atmosphere*. New York: Dell Laurel-Leaf, 1986.

Davis, Jenny. *Sex Education*. New York: Dell Laurel-Leaf, 1988.

Dickens, Charles. *Great Expectations*. New York: Collier, 1969.

Fitzgerald, F. Scott. *The Great Gatsby*. New York: Charles Scribner's Sons, 1925.

Frank, Anne. *Anne Frank: The Diary of a Young Girl*. New York: Modern Library, 1972.

Gaines, Ernest. *The Autobiography of Miss Jane Pittman*. New York: Bantam, 1971.

Gallo, Don, ed. *Center Stage*. New York: HarperCollins, 1990.

———— . *Connections*. New York: Dell Laurel-Leaf, 1989.

———— . *Short Circuits: Thirteen Shocking Stories by Outstanding Writers for Young Adults*. New York: Doubleday, 1992.

———— . *Sixteen*. Dell Laurel-Leaf, 1984.

———— . *Visions*. New York: Delacorte, 1984.

———— . *Within Reach*. New York: HarperCollins, 1993.

George, Jean Craighead. *Julie of the Wolves*. New York: Harper & Row, 1972.

Golding, William. *Lord of the Flies*. New York: Coward-McCann, 1962.

Greene, Bette. *Summer of My German Soldier*. New York: Dial Press, 1973.

Hamanaka, Sheila. *The Journey*. New York: Orchard Books, 1990.

Hamilton, Virginia. *A Little Love*. New York: Philomel, 1984.

Hawthorne, Nathaniel. *House of Seven Gables*. New York: Viking, 1983.

———— . *The Scarlet Letter*. Edited by Brian Harding. New York: Oxford University Press, 1990.

Hentoff, Nat. *The Day They Came to Arrest the Book*. New York: Dell Laurel-Leaf, 1982.

Herrick, Robert. "To the Virgins to Make Much of Time." In *Seventeenth Century Poetry: The Schools of Donne and Jonson,* edited by Hugh Kenner, 304. New York: Holt, Rinehart & Winston, 1964.

Hinton, S. E. *The Outsiders*. New York: Viking, 1967.

Houston, J. W. and J. D. Houston. *Farewell to Manzanar*. New York: Bantam, 1990.

Hurston, Zora Neale. *Their Eyes Were Watching God*. New York: Harper & Row, 1990.

Ibsen, Henrik. *A Doll's House. Four Major Plays*. New York: Oxford University Press, 1981.

Juster, Norton. *The Phantom Tollbooth*. New York: Alfred A. Knopf, 1961.

Katz, William Loren. *Breaking the Chains: African American Slave Resistance*. New York: Atheneum, 1991.

Kerr, M. E. *Gentlehands*. New York: Bantam, 1978.

———— . *Night Kites*. New York: Harper & Row, 1986.

Korman, Gordon. *Don't Care High*. New York: Scholastic, 1985.

Knowles, John. *A Separate Peace*. New York: Macmillan, 1960.

Larson, Gary. *The PreHistory of the Far Side: A 10th Anniversary Exhibit*. Kansas City, MO: Andrews & McMeel, 1991.

Lee, Harper. *To Kill a Mockingbird*. Philadelphia: Lippincott, 1960.

L'Engle, Madeleine. *The Ring of Endless Light*. New York: Dell Laurel-Leaf, 1981.

Lipsyte, Robert. *The Brave*. New York: HarperCollins, 1991.

McKinley, Robin. *Hero and the Crown*. New York: Greenwillow, 1984.

Mahy, Margaret. *Memory*. New York: Margaret K. McElderry, 1987.

Marino, J. *The Day that Elvis Came to Town*. Boston: Little, Brown, 1990.

Marshall, Paule. *Brown Girl, Brownstones*. New York: The Feminist Press, 1959.

———— . *Praisesong for the Widow*. New York: E. P. Dutton, 1984.

Martin, Ann M. *The Baby Sitters Club*. Series. New York: Scholastic, 1986 (and years following).

Mazer, Harry. *The Last Mission*. New York: Dell Laurel-Leaf, 1990.

Miklowitz, Gloria D. *The War Between the Classes*. New York: Dell Laurel-Leaf, 1990.

Milton, John. *Areopagitica*. In *Complete Poetry and Selected Prose of John Milton*. New York: Modern Library, 1950.

Morrison, Toni. *Beloved*. New York: Alfred A. Knopf, 1987.

———— . *Sula*. New York: Alfred A. Knopf, 1973.

Myers, Walter Dean. *Fast Sam, Cool Clyde, and Stuff*. New York: Penguin, 1975.

———— . *Somewhere in the Darkness*. New York: Scholastic, 1992.

Naylor, Gloria. *The Women of Brewster Place*. New York: Penguin, 1982.

O'Dell, Scott. *Carlota*. Boston: Houghton Mifflin, 1977.

Oneal, Zibby. *The Language of Goldfish*. New York: Viking, 1980.

Orwell, George. *1984*. New York: Harcourt Brace Jovanovich, 1949.

Pascal, Francine. *Sweet Valley High*. Series. New York: Bantam, 1983 (and years following).

Paterson, Katherine. *Jacob Have I Loved*. New York: Harper & Row, 1980.

Paulsen, Gary. *Dogsong*. New York: Bradbury, 1985.

———— . *Woodsong*. New York: Bradbury, 1991.

Peck, Richard. *Remembering the Good Times*. New York: Dell Laurel-Leaf, 1985.

Pope, Alexander. *An Essay on Criticism*. In *Alexander Pope: Selected Poetry & Prose*. Edited by William K. Wimsatt, Jr. New York: Holt, Rinehart & Winston, 1961.

Rylant, Cynthia. *A Fine White Dust*. New York: Bradbury Press, 1986.

———— . *Missing May*. New York: Orchard Books, 1992.

Salinger, J. D. *The Catcher in the Rye*. Boston: Little, Brown, 1951.

Schulman, Michael and Eve Mekler, eds. *Contemporary Scenes for Student Actors*. New York: Penguin, 1980.

Sebestyen, Ouida. *Words by Heart*. Boston: Little, Brown, 1979.

Shange, Ntozake. *Betsey Brown*. New York: St. Martin's Press, 1985.

———— . *for colored girls who have considered suicide/when the rainbow is enuf*. New York: Macmillan, 1977.

———— . *Sassafras, Cypress, & Indigo*. New York: St. Martin's Press, 1982.

Shakespeare, William. *The Complete Plays and Poems of William Shakespeare*. Edited by William Allan Neilson and Charles Jarvin Hill. Boston: Riverside Press, 1942.

Siegal, Aranka. *Grace in the Wilderness: After the Liberation, 1945–1948.* New York: New American Library, 1985.

Soto, Gary. *Baseball and Other Stories.* New York: Harcourt Brace Jovanovich, 1990.

Spinelli, Jerry. *Space Station Seventh Grade.* New York: Dell, 1982.

Strasser, Todd. *Angel Dust Blues.* New York: Dell Laurel-Leaf, 1979.

Swortzell, Lowell, ed. *All the World's a Stage.* New York: Delacorte, 1972.

Tarkington, Booth. *Penrod.* New York: Grosset & Dunlap, 1914.

Taylor, Mildred. *Let the Circle Be Unbroken.* New York: Dial, 1981.

——— . *Roll of Thunder, Hear My Cry.* New York: Bantam, 1976.

Thomas, Joyce Carol, ed. *A Gathering of Flowers: Stories About Being Young in America.* New York: HarperCollins, 1990.

Thompson, Julian. *The Grounding of Group Six.* New York: Avon, 1983.

Twain, Mark. *Adventures of Huckleberry Finn.* Berkeley: University of California Press, 1985.

Voigt, Cynthia. *Come a Stranger.* New York: Atheneum, 1986.

——— . *Izzy, Willy-Nilly.* New York: Atheneum, 1986.

Walker, Alice. *The Color Purple.* New York: Harcourt Brace Jovanovich, 1982.

White, E. B. *Charlotte's Web.* New York: Harper, 1952.

——— . *E. B. White: Writings from* The New Yorker *1925–1976.* Edited by Rebecca M. Dale. New York: HarperCollins, 1990.

Woolf, Virginia. *A Room of One's Own.* New York: Harcourt, Brace & World, 1929.

RESOURCES

There is a dizzying array of helpful and practical resources for the teacher of literature; the following, grouped by category, is just a small indication of that wealth.

Helpful periodicals and journals

The ALAN Review. Published by Assembly on Literature for Adolescents, NCTE, 1111 W. Kenyon Road, Urbana, IL 61801-1096. $15 for three issues.

Booklist. Published by American Library Association, 50 E. Huron Street, Chicago, IL 60611. $60 for 22 issues.

English Journal. Published by NCTE, 1111 W. Kenyon Road, Urbana, IL 61801-1096. $40 for 8 issues.

Horn Book Magazine. Published by The Horn Book, Inc., 14 Beacon Street, Boston, MA 02108. $38 for 6 issues.

Journal of Reading. Published by International Reading Association, 800 Barksdale Road, Box 8139, Newark, DE 19714-8139. $38 for 8 issues.

Signal Newsletter. Published by International Reading Association. Editorial Offices: English Department, Radford University, Radford, VA 24142. $10 for 3 issues.

School Library Journal. Published by R. R. Bowker Company, 249 W. Seventeenth Street, New York, NY 10011. $67 for subscriptions, to be sent to P.O. Box 1978, Marion, OH 43305-1978.

Voice of Youth Advocates (VOYA). Published by Scarecrow Press, P.O. Box 4167, Metuchen, NJ 08840. $27 for 6 issues.

Selected YA novels: ten to turn them on

This annotated list was originally published in USA Today, "Volumes of Interest to Adolescents," March 26, 1991, p. 4D, and was compiled by Leila Christenbury.

Fallen Angels. Walter Dean Myers. New York: Scholastic, 1988. Vietnam is tough for any American GI, but maybe even tougher if you're Richie Perry, seventeen, from Harlem.

The Goats. Brock Cole. New York: Farrar, Straus & Giroux, 1987. Camp is supposed to be fun. But what happens when a boy and a girl are the victims of a practical "joke"—stripped of clothes and abandoned on an island? It's not easy, but the "goats" learn—and triumph.

Hatchet. Gary Paulsen. New York: Bradbury, 1987. Brian's parents are divorced, and he is flying to the Canadian wilderness to visit his father. But the plane crashes and the pilot dies, and Brian, with only the hatchet his mother gave him as a parting gift, must engineer his own survival.

Interstellar Pig. William Sleator. New York: Dutton, 1984. The beach is a bore when, first of all, you can't go out in the sun and, second of all, you're with your parents on vacation. Yet what about those glamorous people in the cottage next door who keep playing that weird game called "Interstellar Pig"? And why are they so interested in your playing, too?

Long Live the Queen. Ellen Emerson White. New York: Scholastic, 1989. Meg's mother is the president of the United States, and she gets to live in the White House. It's a great life—until Meg is kidnapped by desperate terrorists who just really may kill her.

The Moves Make the Man. Bruce Brooks. New York: Harper & Row, 1984. Jerome is black; Bix is white. Bix plays baseball; Jerome plays basketball. Bix is troubled; Jerome is pretty well adjusted. Yet, for a time at least, they are friends, and Jerome tries to teach Bix how the moves really do make the man.

Permanent Connections. Sue Ellen Bridgers. New York: Harper & Row, 1987. Rob has had trouble in school and with drugs—so when his uncle in North Carolina breaks his leg and needs help on the farm, Rob's parents ship him from the city to the country for a change of scene, school, and maybe a second chance to grow up.

Remembering the Good Times. Richard Peck. New York: Delacorte, 1985. Friends can lose sight of friends—even the closest of buddies can miss danger signs. Buck, Kate, and Trav make a good trio—until one, the "perfect" one, cracks under the strain.

The Secret of Gumbo Grove. Eleanora E. Tate. New York: Bantam, 1987. Gumbo Grove, South Carolina has a secret, a secret that is in the center of the overgrown and neglected black cemetery. With the help of the elderly church historian and an assortment of crazy friends, Raisin uncovers the mystery—and the importance of heritage.

Stotan! Chris Crutcher. New York: Dell, 1986. Four friends, senior members of the high school swim team, accept the coach's challenge: seven days of gruelling physical and emotional tests. Their goal? To become *stotans,* a powerful combination of both stoics and spartans.

Other selected multicultural literature

The following titles are a just a bare indication of the quantity of fiction, nonfiction, and poetry collections available on multicultural themes.

African American

Black Americans of Achievement. Series. Nathan Irvin Higgin, editor. New York: Chelsea Books, 1991 (and years following). Series includes biographies of seventy-five African Americans.

A Hard Road to Glory: A History of the African American Athlete. 1619–1918. 1919–1945. Since 1946. Arthur Ashe. New York: Amistead Press, 1993. A series of three books giving historical background to noted African American athletes. Written by the late tennis great.

Madam C. J. Walker: Entrepreneur. A'Lelia Bundles. New York: Chelsea Books, 1991. Award-winning biography of the first African American millionaire, who made a fortune creating and marketing haircare products, written by Walker's great-great-granddaughter.

The Road to Memphis. Mildred D. Taylor. New York: Dial, 1990. There is racial tension in the South of the 1940s, but friends make the danger endurable.

Malcolm X: By Any Means Necessary. Walter Dean Myers. New York: Scholastic, 1993. Readable biography of the controversial leader by the award-winning young adult author.

A White Romance. Virginia Hamilton. New York: Putnam & Grossett, 1987. Details an ill-fated match between African American Talley, a track star and "good girl," and David, a Caucasian drug dealer.

Asian American

Child of the Owl. Laurence Yep. New York: Dell, 1977. With her father in the hospital, Casey goes to live with her grandmother in San Francisco's Chinatown.

Children of the River. Linda Crew. New York: Delacorte, 1989. A Cambodian girl escapes the Khmer Rouge to live in Oregon.

Famous Asian Americans. Janet Nomura Morey and Wendy Dunn. New York: Cobblehill Books, 1992. Brief biographies of fourteen famous Asian American writers, artists, athletes, and businessmen.

The Joy Luck Club. Amy Tan. San Francisco: Ivy Books, 1989. Bestselling novel telling the life stories of a group of women who have emigrated from China to America.

No-No Boy. John Okada. Seattle: University of Washington Press, 1980. When Japanese American Ichira returns home to Seattle after two years in prison for refusing to fight in World War II, he faces family problems and racism.

A Thousand Pieces of Gold, Ruthann Lum McCunn. Boston: Beacon, 1981. Biography of a Chinese woman who comes to California when her impoverished parents in China are forced to sell her.

Latino

Animal Dreams. Barbara Kingsolver. New York: HarperCollins, 1990. A novel about two sisters, one in Arizona, one in Nicaragua.

Gaucho. Floria Gonzalez. New York: Dell, 1977. Gaucho wants to return to Puerto Rico and leave El Barrio in New York City behind.

Hispanics of Achievement. Series. Rodolfo Cardona, editor. New York: Chelsea Books, 1991 (and years following). Includes biographies of twenty-nine Hispanics.

The House on Mango Street. Sandra Cisneros. New York: Vintage, 1989. Forty sketches of growing up in poverty.

Living Up the Street. Gary Soto. New York: Dell, 1985. Stories of growing up in the Fresno, California barrio.

Lupita Mañana. Patricia Beatty. New York: Beech Tree Books, 1992. Lupita and her brother must risk the dangerous border crossing to enter the United States from Mexico.

Native American

American Indian Myths and Folktales. Richard Erdoes and Alfonzo Ortiz, editors. New York: Pantheon, 1985. Useful collection of major myths and folktales.

Anapao: An American Indian Odyssey. Jamake Highwater. New York: Lippincott, 1977. Anapao (the Dawn) seeks permission to marry from the House of the Sun in this mythological tale.

The Indian Lawyer. James Welch. New York: Norton, 1990. Sylvester Yellow Calf leaves the reservation to go to Stanford Law School.

The Owl's Song. Janet Campbell Hale. New York: Avon Flare, 1974. When Billy White Hawk leaves the Benewah reservation in Idaho, he faces many challenges.

Trigger Dance. Diane Glancy. Boulder, CO: Fiction Collective Two, 1990. Collection of short stories about Native Americans dealing with mainstream culture.

A Yellow Raft in Blue Water. Michael Dorris. New York: Warner Books, 1988. Rayona, fifteen, leaves the reservation to find herself.

Other countries

Annie John. Jamaica Kincaid. New York: New American Library, 1983. The title character both loves and clashes with her parents and eventually leaves her island home of Antigua. **Caribbean.**

The Bride Price. B. Emecheta. New York: G. Braziller, 1976. Aku-nnu loses her father, and when her uncle adopts her, it is only to sell her for money. **Nigeria.**

Chain of Fire. B. Naidoo. New York: J. B. Lippincott, 1989. Apartheid blights a young woman's life. **South Africa.**

Emma in Love. H. Arnudel. New York: Scholastic, 1971. Emma faces a choice between her boyfriend and her academic career; neither of her parents provides a role model for her decision. **Scotland.**

Frankie's Story. C. Sefton. London: Methuen, 1989. The religious and political war in Belfast makes a young woman doubt she can continue to live in her homeland. **Ireland.**

Kiss the Dust. Elizabeth Laird. New York: Dutton, 1992. Tara and her family must flee their country and hide in refugee camps. **Iraq.**

The Leaving. Budge Wilson. New York: Philomel, 1990. Nine coming-of-age stories tell of life and self-discovery. **Canada.**

Pennington's Seventeenth Summer. K. M. Peyton. London: Thomas Y. Crowell, 1972. A brilliant pianist and a true rebel, working-class Pennington fights with everyone—including himself. **England.**

Shahhat, an Egyptian. Syracuse, NY: Syracuse University Press, 1978. A journalist chronicles the life of a young field worker who wrestles with his culture and his religion, Islam. **Egypt.**

The Silver Crest: My Russian Boyhood. K. Chukovsky. New York: Holt, Rinehart & Winston, 1976. Making one's way can be difficult in a society that offers few resources for an individual without education and money. **Russia.**

A Hand Full of Stars. R. Schami. New York: Dutton, 1990. Opposition to the conservative forces of family and government make a young man take responsibility for his future. **Syria.**

Two Weeks with the Queen. M. Gleitzman. New York: Putnam, 1991. Forced to visit relative in England for a few weeks, a young man learns tolerance and reconsiders his values. **Australia.**

Totto-Chan: The Little Girl in the Window. T. Kuroyanagi. New York: Kodansha International, 1981. Adjusting to a traditional school is difficult for individual thinker Totto-Chan. **Japan.**

Other professional resources

An asterisk indicates that the resource addresses multicultural issues.

ALA. *Intellectual Freedom Manual.* 4th ed. Chicago: ALA, 1992.

*Baker, Houston, ed. *Three American Literatures: Essays in Chicano, Native American, and Asian Literature for Teachers of American Literature.* New York: MLA, 1982.

Beach, Richard and James Marshall. *Teaching Literature in the Secondary School.* New York: Harcourt Brace Jovanovich, 1991.

Beetz, Kirk H. and Suzanne Niemeyer, eds. *Beacham's Guide to Literature for Young Adults.* Vols. 1–3. Washington, D.C.: Beacham, 1990.

*Bell, Roseann P., et al. *Sturdy Black Bridges: Visions of Black Women in Literature.* Garden City, NY: Anchor Books, 1979.

Bland, Joellen. *Stage Plays from the Classics: One-Act Adaptations from Famous Short Stories, Novels, and Plays.* New York: New Plays, 1987.

*Blair, L. "Developing Student Voices with Multicultural Literature." *English Journal* 80 (December 1991): 24–28.

Boynton, Robert W. and Maynard Mack. *Introduction to the Short Story.* 4th ed. Portsmouth, NH: Boynton/Cook, 1992.

*Brooks, Charlotte, ed. *Tapping Potential: English and Language Arts for the Black Learner.* NCTE, 1985.

Bull, Barry L., Royal T. Fruehling, and Virgie Chattergy. *The Ethics of Multicultural and Bilingual Education.* New York: Teachers College Press, 1992.

Capun, Mary Ann and Cynthia Suárez. "Biracial/Biethnic Characters in Young Adult and Children's Books." *MultiCultural Review* 2 (June 1993): 32–37.

*Charles, Jim. "Celebrating the Diversity of American Indian Literature." *The ALAN Review* 18 (Spring 1991): 4–8.

*Christian, Barbara. *Black Feminist Criticism.* New York: Pergamon, 1985.

Ciardi, John and Miller Williams. *How Does a Poem Mean?* 2d ed. Boston: Houghton Mifflin, 1975.

Duke, Charles R. and Sally A. Jacobsen, eds. *Poets' Perspectives*. Portsmouth, NH: Boynton-Cook, 1992.

*Frankson, Marie Stewart. "Chicano Literature for Young Adults: An Annotated Bibliography." *English Journal* 79 (January 1990): 30–35.

Gallo, Donald, ed. *Speaking for Ourselves: Autobiographical Sketches by Notable Authors of Books for Young Adults*. Urbana, IL: NCTE, 1990.

———. *Speaking for Ourselves, Too: More Autobiographical Sketches by Notable Authors of Books for Young Adults*. Urbana, IL: NCTE, 1993.

Grossman, Florence. *Getting from Here to There: Writing and Reading Poetry*. Portsmouth, NH: Boynton/Cook, 1982.

*Hull, Gloria T., Patricia Bell Scott, and Barbara Smith. *But Some of Us Are Brave: Black Women's Studies*. New York: The Feminist Press, 1982.

Kelly, Patricia P. and Warren P. Self, eds. *Teaching Nonfiction*. Virginia English Bulletin 42 (Fall 1992).

Koch, Kenneth. *Wishes, Lies, and Dreams: Teaching Children to Write Poetry*. New York: Chelsea Books, 1970.

*Ling, Amy. *Selected Bibliography of Asian-American Literature: Redefining American Literary History*. New York: MLA, 1990.

*Mitchell, Arlene Harris. "Black Adolescent Novels in the Curriculum." *English Journal* 77 (May 1988): 95–97.

Moffett, James. *Storm in the Mountains: A Case Study of Censorship, Conflict, and Consciousness*. Carbondale, IL: SIU Press, 1988.

Monseau, Virginia R. and Gary M. Salvner, eds. *Reading Their World: The Young Adult Novel in the Classroom*. Portsmouth, NH: Boynton/Cook, 1992.

O'Brien, Peggy, ed. *Shakespeare Set Free: Teaching* Romeo and Juliet, Macbeth, *and* A Midsummer Night's Dream. New York: Washington Square Press, 1993.

Peck, Richard. "The Great Library-Shelf Witch Hunt." *Booklist*. 88 (January 1, 1992): 816–17.

Purves, Alan C. et al. *How Porcupines Make Love II*. New York: Longman, 1990.

Reichman, Henry. *Censorship and Selection: Issues and Answers for Schools*. Urbana, IL: NCTE, 1990.

*Romero, Patricia Ann and Dan Zancanella. "Expanding the Circle: Hispanic Voices in American Literature." *English Journal* 79 (January 1990): 24–29.

Rygiel, Mary Ann. *Shakespeare Among Schoolchildren: Approaches for the Secondary Classroom*. Urbana IL: NCTE, 1992.

*Schon, Isabel. *A Hispanic Heritage, Series II: A Guide to Juvenile Books about Hispanic People and Cultures*. Metuchen, NJ: Scarecrow Press, 1985.

*Smith, Barbara, ed. *Home Girls: A Black Feminist Anthology*. New York: Kitchen Table—Women of Color Press, 1983.

*Stover, Lois. "Exploring and Celebrating Cultural Diversity and Similarity through Young Adult Novels." *The ALAN Review* 18 (Spring 1991): 12–15.

*Trimmer, Joseph and Tilly Warnock, eds. *Understanding Others: Cultural and Cross-Cultural Studies and the Teaching of Literature*. Urbana, IL: NCTE, 1992.

Tsujimoto, Joseph I. *Teaching Poetry Writing to Adolescents*. Urbana, IL: NCTE, 1988.

Twayne's United States Author Series: Young Adult Authors Books. Boston: G. K. Hall, various years.

CHAPTER 6

TEACHING LANGUAGE

Language, be it remember'd, is not an abstract construction of the learn'd, or of dictionary-makers, but is something arising out of the work, needs, ties, joys, affections, tastes, of long generations of humanity, and has its bases broad and low, close to the ground.

—Walt Whitman, *Slang in America*

It Ain't Necessarily So: The English Language Arts Teacher as Language Expert

It may not be right, but it is true: very few of us in English teaching have the sense of language that Walt Whitman celebrates; most of us don't see the linguistic nature of language as central to life or vital to our professional preparation. If on the other hand you have had courses in the history of the English language or in applied linguistics or in comparative grammar, you are in the lucky minority. Most people who are prepared to teach English language arts do not have a strong language background although, clearly, language is at the heart of our business.

Jane Dowrick describes a teacher who was definitely the exception:

My teacher began the year by explaining the importance of knowing what words meant and why they came to mean what they did. *Etymology*, he explained, might be difficult to distinguish from *entomology,* since words, like insects, could wriggle away from close examination. He introduced the idea that all words had roots, many of which were Latin. In all of my public school years, I had never before realized that there was a history to our language, stretching back to the beginning of the spoken word. As I recall his approach, I realize that he was actually teaching us the language of English, almost as if he had been teaching a foreign language. . . . Using etymology as a focal point, the lessons covered a wide range of literature and grammar topics. His delight in teaching us was obvious. My enduring interest in the English language, and my own desire to teach was surely influenced by him.

Very few of us entering teaching are like the teacher Jane Dowrick describes. As readers and appreciators of literature, however, it is most often *assumed* that we know something about language, when actually for most of us, our knowledge is spotty at best. As George Gershwin's song from *Porgy and Bess* proclaims, "It ain't necessarily so." Most of us know little about language or about the science of language; for most people, linguistics is unfamiliar territory.

Prescriptive vs. Descriptive: The World of Linguistics

Linguistics, the study of and the science of language, is a very complex field with a dizzying array of areas. There is, in one branch, **psycholinguistics** (language in relation to mental processes). Psycholinguistics includes **morphology** (the shape of language), **phonology** (the sound of language), **semantics** (the meaning of language), and **syntax** (the structure of language in word and sentence patterns). Another branch of linguistics is **sociolinguistics** (language in relation to culture or behavior) and **stylistics** (the study of literary language). **Historical linguistics** considers the history of language through time, and **anthropological linguistics** looks at language as a social phenomenon, a form of behavior. Linguistics looks at all aspects of language, from how very young children acquire speech to how remote Indian tribes in South America transcribe their language to the history of a verb form. Linguists work as much in laboratories (with actual tapes of people's speech) as in classrooms (with students) and libraries (with research studies); theirs is virtually a universe of study.

In a well-known and widely quoted "occasional paper," "Never Mind the Trees," linguist Suzette Elgin writes that an English teacher needs to know a few basic linguistic principles. Among other concepts, Elgin urges all of us to know about **grammar**, **dialect**, **register**, and a little bit of the **history of our language**. She also notes that we as teachers should have a basic grasp of **"normal" human language development**, **what languages do**, and, crucially, **how to find answers to questions** about language and linguistics.

For the purposes of this chapter, we are going to look at a very small (more restricted even than Elgin cites) and practical portion of language, **applied linguistics**. Please look at the references at the end of this chapter for further resources; this section on language is a quick excursion, not a full tour, and you may want to know much more about a number of other areas of language.

We know that many people, especially those who equate others' pronunciation or vocabulary or usage with their innate human worth, are highly frustrated by the field of linguistics. These individuals are often looking for authoritative, definitive rules of right and wrong when it comes to language use and language choice. They want, essentially, **prescriptive** information from linguistics, rules and regulations, dos and don'ts, shoulds and oughts and musts.

Linguistics, however, is anything but prescriptive. In fact, maddening to many, it does little or nothing about decreeing right and wrong; it assumes no right or wrong except in context. Linguistics tells and defines what *is* and is thus not *prescriptive* but *descriptive*. It looks at *ain't* and *he don't* and *I should of done my homework* as legitimate, recognizable, definable (if variant) forms of language. When you study historical linguistics, in fact, you find that *ain't*, a scorned and generally unacceptable usage, was standard in Dickens's time in England. Indeed, it is considered appropriate today for many upper-class English speakers—Queen Elizabeth and Prince Charles among them—in the United Kingdom. Linguistics would also tell you that the scorn for *ain't* is almost wholly disproportionate:

it communicates and has only lately, historically, become the despised form it is in some contexts today. Similarly, *he don't* is nothing more than the mismatch of a singular pronoun and a plural form of the verb *to do;* linguistics would note that there is no diminution of meaning in *he don't,* while it certainly is what is called a class marker of a negative sort. (Some would assume the utterer of *he don't* is not particularly well educated.) Finally, *I should of done my homework* could be described, if we took purely a descriptive approach, as a transcription of *have* to *of,* an understandable equivalency based on what most people actually hear when they rapidly say *should have, could have,* etc.: the *have* sounds, to many speakers, sound like *of,* and they therefore write *of* for *have.*

In all cases in the study of linguistics, English language arts teachers seeking immutable standards of correctness will not find the ammunition they may be looking for. And linguistics will remind us again and again that what is considered acceptable and what is considered unacceptable shifts over time. It is the very nature of language to change. Linguistics also reminds us that

- **There are no languages or forms of language that are inherently "superior" to others.**
- **There are no languages or forms of language that are inherently easier or harder to learn or even "prettier" to the ear.**
- **The association of certain usage forms with class markers—certain people from certain economic strata will use certain linguistic forms–is not only arbitrary in almost all cases but will also shift over time.**

Two principles: language changes/there is no "bad" language

James Stalker, former chair of the NCTE Commission on Language, lists a few things English teachers should know about language. His list is similar to Elgin's. Stalker tells us

> that all languages, including our own, are in a constant state of flux;
> that all languages are comprised of variants which are used for different purposes and enjoy different levels of acceptability;
> that all languages and varieties of languages serve a multitude of functions;
> that all languages and their varieties are orderly and, therefore, can be described and explained through complex structures, including syntax (sentence structure), but including as well phonology (the system of sounds), morphology (word structure), semantics (meaning), discourse (structures larger than the sentence), and pragmatics (language use in context).(4)

This is a fairly extensive list of what teachers should know, but it is unified by two important principles: first, that language never stays the same—it changes—and, second, that variations in language do not make that language *wrong, bad,* or even *inappropriate.*

These two principles may be odd if we believe that our language is stable and that changes in it—new words, such as *fax* and *VCR;* nouns that are now used as verbs, such as *impact* and *interface;* and other variations, such as *lite* for *light*—are to be resisted. Stalker reminds us that this fear is an old one:

> The belief that unmonitored change will eventually destroy the language arose in the Eighteenth Century, became a belief to be reckoned with in the Nineteenth Century, and has survived lustily in the Twentieth. Those who believe that change is inevitably going to destroy English believe as well that change can be controlled, if not stopped, by prescribing

a set of rules which, if followed, will insure that some changes will be arrested and others will be channeled in appropriate directions.(7)

Using a more homely but perhaps more memorable metaphor, the essayist E. B. White tell us:

> The living language is like a cowpath; it is the creation of the cows themselves, who, having created it, follow it or depart from it according to their whims or their needs. From daily use, the path undergoes change. A cow is under no obligation to stay in the narrow path she helped make, following the contour of the land, but she often profits by staying with it and she would be handicapped if she didn't know where it was and where it led to.(143)

The reason, of course, that this feeling has any relevance to us is that "historical events determined that English teachers were to be the primary transmitters and enforcers of these rules" (Stalker, 7). The misperception by many is that those rules can fix a language, which, by its very nature, shifts and changes and, rather delightfully, makes itself new.

Think for a minute about your knowledge of literature: from Old English to Middle English to modern English, from *Beowulf* to *Hamlet* to Joyce's *Ulysses,* from Edmund Spenser to Gerard Manley Hopkins to Sylvia Plath, from Addison and Steele's *The Tatler* to the *Washington Post* or the *Los Angeles Times*, language changes and the evidence is all around us. And despite the hope of some such as Jonathan Swift, who wanted to "fix . . . our Language for ever" (Bolton, 117), our language continues to shift and change.

For example, think of the word *fun.* Is it a noun or an adjective? Is it both? We say, "I had fun at that party," and it is a noun; we go to a "Fun House" at a carnival or a Halloween celebration, and *fun* in that construction functions as a compound noun. But what do we say about the commonly heard comment, informal though it may be, "It was a fun time"? Clearly *fun* in that circumstance is an adjective modifying *time;* while a speaker in a formal situation would not be likely to use such a construction, is it wrong? Is it not the use of *fun* as an adjective? Clearly, what we are seeing is a developing acceptance of *fun* as both noun *and* adjective, which will mean that in years hence "It was a fun time" or "I had fun" will be widely acceptable usage.

In addition to the concept that language changes is a second concept that language can be *wrong* or *bad.* The latter ignores the fact that certain language forms provide what linguists call **class markers**. Thus, when a student of yours says "He don't know" rather than "He doesn't know," there is an immediate assumption about that student's educational—and social and economic—background. Truth be told, there is little real difference between the two sentences; they both convey that *he does not know.* The subject/verb disagreement of the first, however, is a form that is associated with the uneducated or economically disadvantaged and, regardless of its ability to convey information, is considered unacceptable to many speakers. You can think, I'm sure, of similar constructions that in your community and your context, are equally powerful class markers.

The arguments can get terribly petty, zeroing in on acceptable variations rather than on the big issues of standard and nonstandard practice. I once encountered a woman who was most interested in my work as an English teacher, and inquired intently how I pronounced the word *mauve.* My pronunciation, she said, would tell her a great deal about my education and erudition because, according to her standards, there was only one right way to pronounce the word. Of course, I failed her test: my pronunciation is from my regional heritage, m*æ*v (mawve). Hers was the other variant, m*ō*v (mowve), and she instructed me to change the way I pronounced the word. While most dictionaries cite both pronunciations, this speaker found her choice the only right choice. We were both talking about the light purple color, but, for this person, it became much more than color and intelligibility; the pronunciation of mauve became a crucial issue.

Clearly, I don't like conversations such as those above. I find them unhelpful and unpleasant. One speaker corrects another; someone gets to feel superior; someone gets to feel wrong. It is, of course, one thing to encounter such a dispute with a peer. It is another to encounter it in class. We need to remember that language variants are not just of the egregious sort (*he don't know, teacher*); they can wander into more rarefied territory.

When we discuss "good" English, most of us rely on the language used by the most reputable of speakers. And yet, as Robert C. Pooley in *The Teaching of English Usage* reminds us, the issue is complicated:

> "[G]ood usage is the usage of the best writers and speakers" . . . is probably the expressed or implied standard of good English in almost every American schoolroom today . . . [yet] the chief difficulty lies in the interpretation of the terms "reputable" and "the best writers and speakers." For example, at the same time that these definitions of "correct" English were current, nearly all grammar books listed as undesirable English the use of the split infinitive, the dangling participle or gerund, the use of the possessive case of the noun when naming inanimate objects, the objective case of the noun with the gerund, and the use of *whose* as a neuter relative pronoun, among many others; yet all of these uses may be found in the authors who form the very backbone of English literature and who are "reputable" and "the best writers" in every sense of the words. If the standard makers defy the standards, to whom shall we turn for authority? Moreover, the use of literary models tends to ignore the canon of *present* usage, for by the time an author has come to be generally recognized as standard his usage is no longer "present." And among present speakers, who are best? Any careful listener who has heard a large number of the most prominent platform speakers of the day has still to hear one who does not in some manner violate the rules of the books. Are all great writers and speakers at fault, or is it possible that the rules are inaccurate?
>
> The way out of this perplexity is to shift the search for standards away from "authorities" and traditional rules to the language itself as it is spoken and written today. (11–12)

Thus we turn to what is actually around us in language and from that source make determinations about "correct" and "incorrect."

The Language of Hate

While the previous section details that language naturally changes and that there is actually no "bad" language, what about the language of hate, language used to demean, exclude, shock, or hurt? All of us, some perhaps more frequently than others, have been the target (possibly the originator?) of language that was designed to wound. And schools and classrooms are places where such language can crop up and be an issue both for teachers and their students.

We must acknowledge that language is a two-edged sword and while, in this book, we concentrate on the positive power of words, we would be naive if we did not recognize that language can also be used as a potent weapon. As teachers, one way we can blunt such language is to demystify it and to examine it rationally. It is not inconceivable—not even that shocking or daring—to place the insult of the week or even the obscenity of the month on the board and to bring it directly into our lesson plan. We can briefly discuss origin and meaning and use and, yes, examine with our students why the word or words are so powerful and so repugnant. There may be some snickers and some inappropriate comments at first, but looking directly at the language of hate can defuse it.

We must remind our students that of and by themselves, the words hurled at people of varying races and religions, sexes and ages—words hurled, in short, at anyone who is not of the identical size, shape, sexual orientation, and origin of the insulter—have no power. However, we invest in those words a certain potency that comes from history and context. In addition, in the case of some of English's most taboo obscenities, strength comes from the very sound of the words and the clustering of explosive or hard-to-pronounce consonants. Just think to yourself of the more famous of the "four-letter words" used to curse or condemn, and you will see a remarkable concert of consonants. Many times, just saying those words moves the mouth and the lips in ways that lend the pronunciation power and impetus.

Talking about such language and bringing it into our classroom is one way to deal with it. While we can forbid its use within our classroom walls, forbid it being used against us as teachers or against students by students, we cannot, realistically, wipe the halls or the cafeteria or even our communities of certain words or phrases or language used to demean. Literature is full of instances where insult started animosity, misunderstanding, and even tragedy; where language resulted in conflict, war, and death. Shakespeare's plays are filled with insult, as are the works of the eighteenth-century writers Alexander Pope and Samuel Johnson. Certainly George Orwell's novel *1984* and his essay "Politics and the English Language" are testaments to how words can shape thought and be used not only to wound but to pervert truth. The 1960s American comedian Lenny Bruce was obsessed with the subject, and the movie based on his work, *Lenny,* with Dustin Hoffman in the title role, is a powerful visual testament of how Bruce hurled himself against such language and its power. Taking the power of language—its negative power—into account may be one of the more potent aspects of language we can bring into our classroom.

The Question of Spelling

A much lower level aspect of the issue of "bad" language is the question of spelling and its importance. In fact, however, many people equate most of what we do as English language arts teachers not only with correct grammar but also with correct spelling.

I know of no study that shows a correlation between intelligence and spelling. And yet many people equate misspelled words with ignorance and poor education. Certainly as a teacher you are expected to be almost perfect in your spelling—an expectation that, frankly, is not inappropriate. As the teacher, you have a responsibility to spell consistently and correctly. On the other hand, spelling is really only a small part of English language arts and should not take a disproportionate amount of class time.

It will help you, however, if in their language study, your students learn a little bit about the history of English spelling. Linguist Mario Pei terms the English spelling system "the world's most awesome mess" (310) and for many of our students, that description is accurate. Students need to know that correct spelling was only very recently perceived as an issue. In fact, only very recently (in the last few hundred years) has the spelling of English words been at all regularized, have dictionaries, as repositories of the "correct" way to spell a word, entered wide use. Samuel Johnson published his *Dictionary* in 1755; spelling instruction in this country entered the classroom around that same time. We have only to look at our own nation's original documents—and the correspondence of our not-so-distant forebears—to see that literate people used a dizzying array of forms to spell the very same words. Having students

- **Keep a spelling log with their own frequently misspelled words,**
- **Explore the "spell check" feature of most word processors, and**
- **Research a few words and their variant spellings over the years**

are three avenues by which students can improve their spelling and appreciate its diversity. While not in every assignment, certainly in final draft writing we can expect that students check their spelling and conform to a standard. Of course, many learning-disabled students have more than ordinary difficulty with correct spelling; for those students more patience and more time is necessary. (For a more complete discussion, see the McAlexander et al. book, *Beyond the "SP" Label,* listed in the references section of this chapter.)

One final word: many English teachers trust they are expanding their students' language by giving them a number of vocabulary words to learn, both spelling and definition, every week or so. The words are chosen by the teacher (or the text), given to the students, and tested regularly.

The lasting effect of the above practice is negligible; as a student of mine, Laurie Messer, recalls:

> The vocabulary tests [in English class] were standard tests taken from the teacher's manual, and some last minute cramming was all that was required to learning the spelling and definitions of the words for the multiple choice tests. Some teachers did try to individualize the vocabulary exercises to make them more interesting and to show us how to use the vocabulary words in "real life" . . . But generally no one really ever learned the vocabulary words, and I think the teachers hated the exercises just as much as the students.

The point is that people will expand their store of words, their language, their vocabulary, when they use the words *in context* or when they have a *need* for the words. As language lovers and as teachers we must create vocabulary/spelling lists which have some relevance for our students, lists which come from

- **Reading (words they recently read that they did not know the meaning of).**
- **Life (words that are used frequently by their family or in their neighborhood or on their after-school job that they do not think are as frequently used by those outside those contexts.**
- **Classwork (words that they have encountered in English or other classes that are new to them or that they consistently misspell or stumble over).**

It is not impossible to have students working on individual lists within a class setting; a teacher can keep track of such lists by collecting them on a regular basis, and students, with some prior direction and organization, can demonstrate their mastery of their individual spelling lists by choosing a selected number of words and using them or defining them on a quiz.

At any rate, to present students isolated lists will not help them score higher on the SATs or any other vocabulary or language-based test. It will, however, encourage them to see language as nothing more complicated than the memorization of disconnected lists of words. Letting students participate in their own spelling/vocabulary lists and encouraging them to expand those lists can not only give students more control over this aspect of English language arts but also show them that they, too, live in a world of language. It is not confined to the vocabulary presented in a textbook; it is in their world and all around them.

For Your Journal

Make a list of "class markers" that in your community might signal the status of the speaker. Think of both "stigmatized" forms of words and forms that might signal a highly educated (or affected) person.

Think of words that you feel have entered the language relatively recently (such as *fax*) or are being used in ways that are not traditional (such as *fun time*).

Make a list of words that you have difficulty spelling; write a brief statement of *why* you think you stumble on those words (actually, most spelling mistakes are logical!). Then go to the library and look up the *etymology* (origin and development) of your spelling demons in a resource such as *The Oxford English Dictionary*. What are the origins of the words? What different spellings do they have? What are their different meanings?

The Five Grammars

Most people associate English language arts—and language in particular—with the idea of grammar. "I'd better watch my grammar," they tell you when they find out you are or are planning to be an English teacher; "I liked English, but I hated grammar," they might recall; "What's the grammar rule?" they might ask you. Actually, what people are referring to is not grammar at all but **usage.** You probably already know that, but you might wonder about these different manifestations of what most people call **grammar.** They are not all the same animal, and that is why researchers discuss at least three or sometimes more grammars. What are they?

The five grammars described by Patrick Hartwell are summarized by Mark Lester in *Grammar in the Classroom*:

- **Grammar 1**: Our internal, unconscious rule system. The grammar that we have in our heads.
- **Grammar 2**: The scientific analysis of grammar. The linguist's model of Grammar 1.
- **Grammar 3**: Usage. What people mean when they say that someone doesn't use very good grammar.
- **Grammar 4**: The schoolroom version of traditional grammar. The grammar that is found in secondary textbooks.

- **Grammar 5:** Stylistic grammar. The use of grammar for the purpose of teaching style. Among the approaches included here would be sentence combining. (335)

Grammar 3 and Grammar 4 are what most of us are familiar with; note, however, that they are only part of the picture of grammar. Lester notes:

> The best-known grammar of English is traditional grammar, or more accurately, the conventional schoolroom version of traditional grammar. The latter has been the mainstay of English education in America since the time of the Revolutionary War, and every educated person in the English-speaking world has at least a passing familiarity with its terms and concepts. (187)

Thus, as teachers, our major emphasis is on Grammar 3, which is essentially usage. In order to teach Grammar 3, we may use a handbook or textbook, Grammar 4. When we analyze literature or with sentence combining (see below), we are using Grammar 5.

Don't be confused, then, when people talk about grammar and its importance in your classroom; they are probably referring to usage rules and to the usage texts themselves.

So What Do We Do About Teaching Grammar?

What do we do with grammar? Many teachers and the public believe the teaching of grammar is important because it improves our students' writing and speaking. Unfortunately, however, especially when done through books and worksheets and rule memorization, the teaching of grammar does not result in improved—or even different—speaking and writing. While many assume that when students do not improve after years of grammar study it is either the student's fault (they just didn't get it) or the quality of instruction (the teacher did not teach it enough; the teacher did not teach it clearly enough; the teacher didn't teach it at all), it is the opinion of many researchers who have looked for decades at the results of formal grammar instruction on student language and composition that that is just not the case. The difficulty seems to lie in two areas: how grammar texts are set up and how teachers are encouraged to teach grammar.

Let's consider the issues. We acquire language messily, aurally, by mimicking patterns. The verb *acquire* is deliberate here: we don't really *learn* our native language as we learn most other things. We do, however, *acquire* it by a rather indirect process. The small child does not consciously choose verbs or adverbs or clauses or phrases; he or she produces what he or she hears and by trial and error becomes an accomplished language user. By the time that small child is ready for school, he or she actually has most of the syntax needed to produce relatively complex conversation or discourse.

We often seem to ignore this competence, though. In secondary and middle school, we ask students in traditional "grammar" classes to go back and label with abstract terms and possibly with conceptual representations (such as diagramming) what they are naturally producing. The hope is that understanding the abstract framework of what they are doing will make their language "better." And that transfer just does not occur. As E. B. White writes:

> Children obviously do not depend for communication on a knowledge of grammar; they rely on their ear, mostly, which is sharp and quick. (143)

Think about the abstract pattern that students study: in most classes, it proceeds from rule memorization to worksheet/example practice to actual writing. The problems lie directly in that pattern: the rules are not sufficiently inclusive or clear; the examples for practice are deliberately restricted so that they will fully conform to the rule; and unfortunately the rule and the example often do not bear a relationship to real student speaking or writing. And we expect our students to move from rule and restricted practice to the universe of their own sentences. The transition is most times just not made.

For example, think about the last time you needed to verify a grammatical construction you used in a research paper or an essay. If you went to a standard usage "handbook" (or "grammar"), you probably had a very hard time finding a direct answer to your question. The fact is, however complex they might sound, the rules in most "grammars" are presented in very simplified versions, and the illustrations of those rules are rarely comparable to the highly complex constructions even elementary-school-age children are capable of producing.

So what do we do? In some cases, regardless, we are expected to teach grammar in our classrooms. While no research buttresses the transfer, some persist that knowledge of the rules will indeed improve our students' speech and their final drafts. Some also feel that "grammar" instruction, a familiar and traditional part of language arts, should remain part of the late-twentieth-century English class.

Again, what do we do? If nothing else, if no single other strategy, we need always to remember context. If we teach grammar, we need to teach it not as a separate unit but as it relates to specific issues in our students' writing and in their speech. We need to make sure that the students who study an aspect of grammar have a need for it and can, in fact, use that aspect in their class work. To do otherwise is to teach a skill or a piece of knowledge that has no application at all or has application to only a very few students in our classes. As Lester notes:

> [T]he most important implication of the research on grammar and writing is that teaching grammar in isolation from writing has little effect on students' ability to deal with error. Students will connect grammar with writing only if we explicitly link the two. (366)

Lester suggests teaching grammar in four general areas:

> grammar terminology to provide a shared vocabulary for talking about grammar and writing;
> key grammatical concepts (the sentence, inflection, tense, agreement) that underlie most written error;
> practical techniques for monitoring error in their own writing; and
> sentence combining [more on this later in the chapter] as a unique bridge between grammar and writing. (366)

Similarly, Rei R. Noguchi, in *Grammar and the Teaching of Writing: Limits and Possibilities*, looks at a number of studies of the errors that students most frequently make in their writing and the errors that are most closely associated with nonstandard, "stigmatized" forms. Examples of the latter are *he don't*, *we ain't*, and the other forms I've discussed in this chapter that are considered clear class markers of a negative sort. Again, Noguchi suggests that teachers concentrate on limited segments of grammar instruction: the sentence, the subject, the verb, and the modifier. He writes:

> Although these four . . . may at first seem woefully inadequate to hard-working grammar teachers, I present this "bare bones" set because of their potential utility in identifying and

correcting the more frequent and more highly stigmatized stylistic errors. At the very least, students will need some idea of what constitutes a sentence (in contrast to a nonsentence) in order to correct sentence boundary errors (fragments and run-ons); they will need a notion of what constitutes a subject and a verb, not necessarily to identify sentences or independent clauses (although that will help), but in order to identify and correct subject-verb agreement errors (and other incorrect verb forms); last, they will need a general notion of what a modifier is to identify and correct various (not all) kinds of punctuation errors. (33)

As far as the time spent on these subjects, Nancie Atwell, in *In the Middle,* advocates using "mini-lessons" for such grammar instruction; she devotes no more than ten minutes or so at the beginning of class to go over what a number of students—if not all—need to know or review. Confining instruction in grammar, in usage (the choices speakers make when they talk or write), and in mechanics (surface conventions of spelling, punctuation, capitalization, and so on) can be very helpful to students. Asking students to generate their own rules from their reading—and their own writing—can also be very helpful.

 FOR YOUR
JOURNAL

Find a grammar-and-usage or grammar-and-composition text. You might borrow one from a teaching friend or a high school or middle school student. Leaf through the text and pick one rule of usage or "grammar" and look at the exercises in the book that relate to that rule. Now rewrite the rule in your own words and make up your own examples to help students practice that rule. Put both the rule and your examples on a sheet of paper and then exchange the paper with a friend. Have your friend do your examples. How successful is your grammar sheet? Finally, browse through some of your own recent writing: can you find a sentence you have read that illustrates the rule you have selected? If so, how helpful is your rewritten rule in telling you why what you wrote is correct?

Students' Right to Their Own Language

One of the most controversial—and difficult—issues for English teachers is their responsibility to students who speak what is considered "nonstandard" English, English that violates the usage rules we often mistakenly call "grammar." For traditionalists, the role of the English teacher is that of corrector and keeper of the standards; in this scenario, English teachers need to stop their students from speaking or writing in a nonstandard way. The question involves the definition of dialect and whether it is prestigious or nonprestigious. Linguistics tells us that meaning or intelligibility is rarely the issue; social attitude and cultural norms determine the value and prestige. We know that nonstandard English does not affect the ability to read or think or write and rarely interferes with meaning. It is therefore hard to defend logically the traditional English-teacher-as-corrector role. When we advocate the eradication of nonstandard English in our classroom, we are more in the business of linguistic etiquette than in the business of better communication.

What, though, should a teacher do? People outside and inside the school really expect us, as English language arts teachers, to address the issue of standard and nonstandard language in our classes. After debate and discussion and even some soul searching, the National Council of Teachers of English issued *Students' Right to Their Own Language,* a position statement, which, among other things, maintains:

> The history of language indicates that change is one of its constant conditions and, further-more, that attempts at regulation and the slowing of change have been unsuccessful. . . . Dialect is merely a symptom of change. . . . Diversity of dialects will not degrade language nor hasten deleterious changes. Common sense tells us that if people want to understand one another, they will do so. Experience tells us that we can understand any dialect of English after a reasonably brief exposure to it. And humanity tells us that we should allow . . . [all] the dignity of . . . [their] own way of talking. (18)

What does this mean? It means, practically, that correcting a student's speech can be harmful and, further, futile. When students perceive a need to adopt a different dialect, they will do so—as they do when they leave your class and enter the lunchroom or their cars or their homes. As discussed earlier in this chapter, telling or teaching students that their language is *wrong* or *bad* is not only damaging but *false.* Reminding students, how-ever, that different choices of language are appropriate for different contexts—for exam-ple, that their language may influence whether they get a job or a loan, that their language could be a barrier to some people—may be more accurate. If students perceive the need to change, they will do so. Teachers need to offer students instruction but also to be sen-sitive to the fact that students who do not consistently or firmly conform to standard English or what they perceive as "school talk" may be doing this deliberately. And, I firmly believe, *they have that right.*

On the other hand, we need to be in a position to offer students language choices and options. African American educator Lisa Delpit writes in "The Silenced Dialogue":

> To imply to children or adults . . . that it doesn't matter how you talk or how you write is to ensure their ultimate failure. I prefer to be honest with my students. Tell them that their language and cultural style is unique and wonderful but that there is a political power game that is also being played, and if they want to be in on that game there are certain games that they too must play. . . . [S]tudents must be *taught* the codes needed to participate fully in the mainstream of American life. (96, 100)

We would hope, as linguist and African American Geneva Smitherman-Donaldson has advanced, that every student will know three languages: first, the "standard" dialect of English or what she terms "the language of wider communication" (170); second, a street or home dialect of English; and third, one foreign language. With this "tripartite language policy" (Smitherman-Donaldson, 170), students might be more equipped to thrive in the world. It is not outlandish to give students exercises in which they speak or write in first one and then a second dialect. Certainly the Shakespeare-summary exercise in Chapter 5 asks students to write using different forms of language, and its language-play aspect is a large part of the exercise's appeal to students.

In *Language Exploration and Awareness,* Larry Andrews gives us three points about "good" English that may help summarize this discussion. Andrews notes that language that is successful, or "good," is

> appropriate to the speaker/writer's purpose;
> appropriate to the context;
> comfortable to both speaker and listener. (92)

Students who want to be taken seriously will choose different language from that chosen by people who are trying to make their audience laugh; their **purpose** will guide their language. All students know—and instinctively adjust to—the different demands of **context**, shifting language choices depending upon where they are—school, home, work. Students also know that language choices are often made in response to the listener; for example, there are certain phrases and words they would not use with grandparents that would pass unnoticed by their peers. Knowing when to adjust and how to use language successfully to communicate is a more powerful skill than is any monolithic list of (to steal from a title of a language book) *dos, don'ts,* and *maybes* of usage.

Language Play/Language Games

We also need to remember the wonderful world of language play and language games. As children, all of us had some exposure to—and delight in—games with words, rhymes, riddles, puns, jokes, and stories. How sad it is that in middle and high school we seem to leave all of this richness behind in the name of being more serious and academic. We need to recapture the broad and fine idea of play—experimentation—with language.

There are many resources available that can lead you and your students to working with a number of areas of language study. **Etymology** (the origin and history of words), **semantics** (the meanings of words), **doublespeak** (deliberate deception in language, often used in politics), **dialect** (the wonderful variations of both pronunciation and word choice), are just a few of the fascinating topics you can pursue.

You need to remember that language is literally all around us and that although it may not be immediately apparent to you, your students are adept at language play. What they play with and toy with may be wholly outside the classroom—in the cafeteria or in the parking lot or at the mall—but you can, with some encouragement, have them bring what they know and use into the classroom. The following is a sampler of activities.

Puns and plays on words

Puns and plays on words are used in menus, billboards, advertisements, and other aspects of daily life. A local church billboard reads, for example: "Seven days without God makes one week [weak]." Such puns and slogans are creative uses of language and can be tools not only to encourage students to explore homonyms but to look at how such homonyms are effective. (*Week,* a noun, is the direct object; *weak,* a modifier, is the predicate adjective; *one* is, in the first sense of the sentence, an adjective but a pronoun in the second sense of the sentence.)

Another such pun or slogan is the fairly recently coined insult terming a person "a legend in his own mind," a play on the more familiar phrase, "a legend in his own time." Both words, *mind* and *time,* are nouns used in parallel constructions that not only have a near rhyme, but also convey widely different meanings.

Advertising offers many such puns and plays on words. Some of my students collected a few recently, taken from billboards, signs, and print advertisements:

- YULE LAUGH; YULE CRY (billboard advertisement for a Christmas movie).
- COFFEE BRAKE (sign on outside of convenience store).
- TIPPING IS NOT A CITY IN CHINA (sign on wall of restaurant).
- SOME OF OUR GUESTS LIKE THE IDEA OF A MOUSE IN THE ROOM (advertisement for a motel chain featuring in-room computers).
- FASTER THAN THE SPEED OF FRIGHT (billboard advertisement for a roller-coaster at a local amusement park).

- HO ^{3} (T-shirt slogan for Christmas: Ho Ho Ho).

Puns can also be the basis for jokes, as in the following *Snakey Riddles*:

Question: What does a polite snake say after he bites you?
Answer: Fangs a lot! (Hall and Eisenberg, 18)

Question: What did the snake say when it stopped biting the giraffe's neck?
Answer: It's been nice gnawing you! (Hall and Eisenberg, 26)

Have students recall puns, plays on words, or even jokes they have seen or create new ones that make a statement, promote a product, advance an idea, or provide humor. Then have them:

1. List the possible homonyms or similar sounds for the crucial word or words.
2. Label the part of speech and the sentence function of the word or words.
3. Explain, in prose, how the sentence can be read two—or more—ways.

Relative meanings/semantics

Certainly the women's movement has sensitized all of us to the varying uses of language, especially when describing people's behavior. "He's assertive, she's pushy" language is all around us, and our language provides an array of degrees of intensity, of approval or disapproval, all of which can be conveyed by words. Look at *minimal, average,* and *maximum* as degree distinctions for color (pink, red, scarlet) or weight (slim, thin, emaciated) or any other characteristic you might want to describe. Your students can come up with a number of "families." Use the following headings, and have students make a chart such as the one below:

MINIMAL	AVERAGE	MAXIMUM
creek	stream	river
plump	fat	obese
big	huge	gargantuan
pretty	lovely	gorgeous

Other possible areas for word families include colors, behaviors, size, weather.

First names

Names are important in any culture and often reveal a great deal about the thing named and its importance. Ask your students to consider the following as they list first (not last) names:

1. List as many names for each category as you can.
2. The names should come from your own experience or that of someone in the group.
3. After you have listed the names for each category, try to write a brief statement about what the names seem to have in common or what observations could be made about this group of names. (Look in particular for the number of syllables, incidence of consonants, and incidence of vowel clusters.)

Categories: Names with definite English meaning (Pearl); names with definite meaning in a foreign language (Marguerite is *daisy* in French); names that are considered in this culture "clearly masculine" (Robert) or "clearly feminine" (Angeline); names that are androgynous (Courtney); blended names (Jonalee); foreign equivalents (John, Juan, Jean, Johannes); nicknames (Spike, Cool); names for pets (Spot, Red) (Born, 83).

Where words come from

The origin of words is fascinating; some words are derivations of other words (*present/presentation*), some are abbreviated forms (*ad/advertisement*), some blend two or more familiar words (*smoke-and-fog/smog*), some are acronyms made from the first letters of each word in a phrase (*AIDS*), some come from proper names (*bourbon*). Look at the following list: can you find out where the words come from? Can you add any words to the list?

fan	teflon	rad	radar
UNESCO	cologne	bra	gasahol
scuba	rayon	orient	hamburger

(Parker and Riley, 65–69)

Euphemism

Newspapers and magazines, like most forms of the popular press, often use phrases and words that mean something relatively different from their surface meaning. Politics, too, uses euphemism all the time. A candidate promises to investigate "revenue enhancement," for example, while an ad in a local newspaper touts "friendly service" and a letter to the editor discusses the "human spirit of America." What do these phrases really mean? What is gained by using such phrases? What is lost?

Look at an issue of a magazine or newspaper and find as many "doublespeak" or euphemistic words and phrases as you can. For each:

1. List the phrase or word.
2. Define what you assume, from context, it *really* means.
3. Suggest a more accurate replacement or defend the word or phrase as it stands.

NCTE's *Quarterly Review of Doublespeak* is a great resource and you may want to look at it.

Minidictionaries

Dictionaries can be great fun and can provide not only information but also a look at what is popular, what is in, and what is out. Within a group, have students compile a minidictionary of words or phrases that seem indigenous to their school and its students. Have students:

1. List the words or phrases.
2. Define the words or phrases.
3. Use the words or phrases in a single sentence.

Games such as these can open the world of language for our students; students can also design and enjoy their own language play.

Daffy definitions

In the spirit of puns, students can also make their own lists of unusual definitions of words, using a first and second definition. My students came up with the following double and very daffy definitions, complete with grammatical explanations:

> **dilate:** 1. To grow in size 2. To die late, live too long (*die,* verb, cease to exist + *late,* adverb, after the usual time)
>
> **fast days:** 1. Days of abstinence from food 2. Days you live and eat in a hurry (*fast,* adverb + *days,* noun)
>
> **nitrate:** 1. A salt of nitric acid 2. Night rate as opposed to day rate (*night,* adjective + *rate,* noun).
>
> **shamrock:** 1. A four-leaf clover 2. A fake stone having the appearance of something valuable (*sham,* adjective + *rock,* noun)

Students can compile similar definitions for a specialized dictionary of "punny" words.

Sentence Combining

Sentence combining is an activity that asks students to put together very short sentences into one longer sentence. For example, a student, given the following short sentences:

> 1.1   My friend is furry.
> 1.2   My friend is fuzzy.
> 1.3   My friend is named Dog.

could combine the three into one:

> My friend is furry, fuzzy, and named Dog.

Equally correct would be the following minor variations:

> My friend, Dog, is furry and fuzzy.
> My friend is furry, is fuzzy, and is named Dog;
> My furry, fuzzy friend is named Dog.

As William Strong, a major proponent of sentence combining, writes, the origin of sentence combining comes from linguistic research:

> The transformational model proposed that language is governed by a finite set of rules for sounds, word formation, and syntax, all operating harmoniously. It is these rules, linguists hypothesized, that all neurologically normal children figure out and internalize, without being taught them in the conventional sense. . . . [Transformational grammar asserted] that typical sentences are actually comprised of many constituent kernels, each contributing in a patterned way to overall meaning. (3)

The practical application of sentence combining stems from the observation that older writers have a tendency to produce sentences that are longer, denser, and more **syntactically mature** (Strong, 4, 6, 12). Such writers would never string very short sentences together ("My friend is furry. My friend is fuzzy. My friend is named Dog.") Younger or beginning writers do, however, use such short sentences. Getting beginning writers to "make" more complicated sentences could be speeded up, researchers hypothesized, by practice in combining sentences. Researchers also hoped that practice would enable student writers to generate those more complex structures with ease and **fluency.**

The issue quickly arose, however, as to how long-lived the "gains" are: in other words, if students continue to combine sentences over a period of time, will they, after the exercises are over, maintain those more syntactically mature sentences and write more complex structures? Actually, the research studies are fairly divided, and we are now not very sure that working with combining sentences will, over the long period, permanently change our students' writing and make it more syntactically complex.

On the other hand, sentence combining is a relatively no-risk, no-threat technique to allow students to play with language and along the way to increase their native abilities to make new sentence structures. **Fluency,** the characteristic of writing with relative ease, is also a reason to use sentence combining; the exercises often help students become more comfortable with writing and to spin out sentences with less hesitation. While some of the almost extravagant claims for the benefits of sentence combining have faded, the gains cited above are strong enough to make sentence combining a useful activity in the English language arts classroom.

(If you are interested in looking deeper at the linguistics background of sentence combining, you might check the references section at the end of this chapter and look for the names Kellogg Hunt, Frank O'Hare, John Mellon, and Francis Christensen.)

Let's take a look at some typical sentence combining exercises. They come in two varieties, **open** and **signaled.** With open exercises, students combine the sentences in any order to make a single, longer sentence. The following is an example taken from William Strong's excellent sourcebook, *Creative Approaches to Sentence Combining.* Students make eight sentences from the pairs listed below.

1.1   Carol was working hard on her test.

1.2   Sue slipped her a note.

2.1   Carol unfolded the paper carefully.

2.2   She didn't want her teacher to see.

3.1   The note asked for help on a question.

3.2   The question was important.

4.1   Carol looked down at her paper.

4.2   She thought about the class's honor system.

5.1   Everyone had made a pledge.

5.2   The pledge was not to cheat.

6.1   Carol didn't want to go back on her word.

6.2   Sue was her best friend.

7.1   Time was running out.

7.2   She had to make up her mind.

8.1   Her mouth felt dry.

8.2   Her mouth felt tight. (Strong, 29)

There are truly dozens of ways each pair could be combined, and each combining is, unless it strays significantly from the original sentences, equally correct. While you and your students could come up with eight sentences rather different from the following, here is one version of the combined sentences:

1.   Carol was working hard on her test when Sue slipped her a note.
2.   Carol unfolded the paper carefully; she didn't want her teacher to see.
3.   The note asked for help on an important question.
4.   Carol looked down at her paper, and she thought about the class's honor system.
5.   Everyone had made a pledge not to cheat.
6.   Carol didn't want go go back on her word, but Sue was her best friend.
7.   Time was running out, and she had to make up her mind.
8.   Her mouth felt dry and tight.

The above sentences about a real school issue can also be used by students as the beginning of a writing exercise—what should Carol do?

Signaled exercises, unlike the open exercises above, ask students to do specific things with sentences and to combine the sentences in a directed way. The directional signals are, in this instance, noted at the end of the sentence and are set in all caps. Try to combine using the signals:

1.1   Fifteen years of statistics reveal SOMETHING.
1.2   The pool of new teachers has shrunk. (THAT)
1.3   The shrinking is *steady*. (-LY)
1.4   The shrinking is *dramatic*. (-LY) (Strong, 37)

While the combinations of the first, "open" exercise cited above can be very varied, the final sentence generated by the above four sentences should, according to the signals, read:

Fifteen years of statistics reveal that the pool of new teachers has shrunk steadily and dramatically.

Using these kinds of exercises, either signaled or open, once or twice a week for brief periods can help students "play" with structures. Using the blackboard or an overhead projector, you may want to start by showing students how to do this in a class demonstration. Students can do these exercises at their desks, with a friend, or in a small group. Sharing the different variations is always helpful, and taking a limited amount of time is important. Spending repeated class periods on sentence combining exercises, however, can wear everyone out; in this case, as with much in instruction, less is more.

Once students are comfortable combining sentences in either both open and signaled mode or just the open mode, they can move to what I consider one of the more useful aspects of sentence combining. I have students take open exercises and look at the semantic effects they have created. For example, consider the following short sentences. The two sentences were made ("de"combined) from one original sentence in Richard Wright's *Black Boy* (Memering and O'Hare, 265):

1.1   I went upstairs.
1.2   I felt like a criminal.

We could, without much effort, generate a number of combinations:

> I went upstairs, and I felt like a criminal.
> I went upstairs, feeling like a criminal.
> I went upstairs and felt like a criminal.
> Upstairs I went and felt like a criminal.
> Upstairs, feeling like a criminal, I went.
> Upstairs I went, and I felt like a criminal.
> Feeling like a criminal, upstairs I went.
> Feeling like a criminal, I went upstairs.

If this were a class, I would record these possible combinations on the board or the overhead and ask a number of questions. I would want students to look at the sentences and then to discuss, in turn: which seem to be the most effective sentences? powerful? personal? What are the differences? similarities? Why? Without going into a great deal of explanation, we as readers know that every combination above conveys a slightly different meaning, done through language and placement of that language. Simply put, the meaning—and effect—conveyed by "I went upstairs, and I felt like a criminal" is a bit different from "Upstairs I went, and I felt like a criminal" or "I went upstairs, feeling like a criminal." And, in order to talk about that semantic difference, students have to deal with issues of language; in the sentences cited immediately above, students will, sooner or later, have to mention the place of *upstairs* and why that inverted location makes a difference (as it certainly does). In fact, to talk about *upstairs,* students will have to deal with the concept of its relation to the verb *went* and, possibly, name *upstairs* and its function (adverb) in the sentence. Also, how does the participial phrase *feeling like a criminal* make a different impression than the complete sentence *I felt like a criminal*? Why? What does it convey? Why would we want to use a complete sentence instead of a participial phrase? Voilá! We have not only considered semantics, but we have done some grammar teaching.

This is not, as with other issues in sentence combining, a question of what Richard Wright actually wrote in *Black Boy* (as mentioned the two sentences are formed or decombined from one original sentence) or what, indeed, is the "best" answer. We are looking at choices and options and shades of meaning, and while some combinations may not reflect the intent of the two sentences or make much sense (for example, "I went criminally upstairs" or "Criminally, I went upstairs"), making sense is not the point of this exercise. You need not feel that you, by the way, should know precisely the difference between the many variations cited above. It is enough, rest assured, that you and your students consider those choices and semantic differences. Whether or not you agree or can always precisely define why one sentence is doing something a bit different than another, looking at them and talking about them gives you a forum and an occasion to consider and discuss subtleties and nuances in word order and phrasing. This exercise gives all of us as readers an invitation to talk.

On the other hand, if you are starting this exercise with little or no knowledge of traditional grammar, you will be handicapped in your teaching and discussion. In order to talk with your students and deal with what they combine, you need to know, on sight, the basic terms and structures. These include the parts of speech, phrases, clauses, subjects, and objects. If you are not ready for that now, you will have to stick to more confined exercises and wait to introduce such discussions until your own knowledge of terminology and function is up to speed. (The Kolln book in the resources section of this chapter is a basic text.) You can, of course, start with a few sentences and, on your own, study what your students might come up with. However, you'll need to know your grammar before you launch into using sentence combining to discuss semantics and usage. But you knew that anyway, didn't you?

The Glory of Language

In all cases it is good to remember that while we may want students to know and be able to use "correct" or "standard" English—the language of those who approve loans, give diplomas, and hire employees—we need to remember two things.

First, we need to understand that "standard" language is fairly arbitrary, and second, that "correct" language has changed and will continue to change. We have an obligation to make our students' options broad, to help them—and invite them—to learn "standard" and "correct" English, but we need to place the issue in perspective and to acknowledge that those two terms get placed within quotation marks for a reason. And that reason is that there is just no immutable, definable, *standard* English and no immutable *correct* English.

The English teacher as Language Cop is a sad picture, but you know very well that most people associate your role in the classroom with the primary task of correcting and reshaping speech. Even for many of your students for whom such school experiences were painful—or futile—there is the expectation that you, new English language arts teacher, will do it right, do it effectively, and do it a whole lot.

Knowledge is your armor. Language shifts. Differences in language are not to be condemned or squelched. Mechanics and usage have a place in final draft writing. Without them we would have a difficult time understanding meaning; our students need to be able to present finished prose that is clear. On the other hand, we are about larger things than teaching students to memorize the functions of the semicolon and to fear the split infinitive and, regardless of the circumstances, rarely to use slang or colloquialisms. As difficult as it may be, we need to balance our obligation to teach correctness with an ethical mandate to respect our students and the language they bring to us, and to honor meaning before form.

When students walk into our classroom self-conscious about their speech, worried about how they talk, afraid to express what they know—or don't know—we are in a territory of pain and difficulty. Many of our students don't have an academic vocabulary; some have variations of speech that are unfamiliar even to some of their peers; some use, almost exclusively, a lot of slang and street talk. Your students may seem confident, brash, even display a certain linguistic bravado. But underneath that may be a fair amount of insecurity. It is your job to create a lively, positive, language room: there is a place for all kinds of talk in our classes, just as there is a place for all of our students. To do any less is to silence them; and that is the one thing we simply cannot, in all conscience, do.

FOR YOUR JOURNAL

Choose *one* of the following activities; both of them can be very illuminating about *your own* language background and, of course, they are also appropriate for your students.

Your language acquisition

Elizabeth A. Poe writes that students can answer the questions in Part I; they will need to interview parents for Part II to find out the answers about themselves and their own language acquisition. The following are excerpts from her suggestions.

Part I

1. List the children in your family according to their birth order, age differences (number of months older or younger than you), and sex.
2. What language or languages are spoken in your home?
3. Do you remember anything about learning to talk?

Part II (for parents)

1. What are your first recollections of my speech development?
2. What were my first words?
3. How old was I when I spoke them?
4. Did I have any problems with my ears? If so, what?
5. Did I play with children who were older than I was? Who?
6. What sort of things were done that helped my language development?
7. Who did these with me?
8. Did I talk much once I learned to talk?
9. Do you remember anything I said that you thought was funny? (Poe, 113–14)

Writing a linguistic autobiography

Mark A. Christiansen writes that students need, in order to write linguistic autobiographies, some data about themselves. The following are excerpts of some of the questions he suggests that students consider for their final paper.

Family Background

1. What is your racial or ethnic background?
2. To what extent have members of your immediate family affected your language? (Remember that your mother was probably your first English teacher.)
3. Have any elderly relatives influenced your language growth? How?
4. Does anyone among your relatives speak a foreign language? As a result, have you looked upon the English language differently?
5. What is your father's and/or mother's occupations? Are there specific words associated with their jobs?

Leisure Time Activities

1. What is your favorite hobby/sport? Are there words associated with it that you have learned?

2. How much recreational reading do you do? Has your vocabulary been expanded because of this reading?

3. Have you traveled much? When you have been away from home, have any people ever called attention to certain expressions you use? Have people ever made fun of your dialect? If so, how did their cajoling make you feel?

4. Have your peers had any effect on your pronunciation or vocabulary? Do you use much slang? Are there certain idioms that you use with your friends or in a social group that you do not use with your parents?

5. Do you work after school or during the summer? Has your vocabulary been affected as a result of this employment?

Formal Education

1. What is (are) your favorite subject(s) in school? Have you encountered any new words from studying this subject?

2. Have you studied a foreign language? Do you use any terms from that language?

3. Have you made any attempt to change your grammatical constructions or usage? If so, what specifically have you altered?

4. When you speak, are you conscious of using certain gestures, facial grimaces, and vocal inflections? If so, how do they support what you say?

5. Do you have more difficulty expressing yourself in writing than in speaking? If so, why?

Residence

1. To what extent has the urban, suburban, or rural area in which you live affected your speech?

2. Do you watch much television? Have you adopted certain expressions used by your favorite TV performers?

3. Have you moved from one residence to another? If so, how have the neighborhoods been different? Has the neighborhood in which you now live affected your speech? (Christiansen, 119–21)

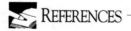 REFERENCES

Andrews, Larry. *Language Exploration and Awareness: A Resource Book for Teachers*. New York: Longman, 1993.

Atwell, Nancie. *In the Middle: Reading, Writing, and Learning with Adolescents*. Portsmouth, NH: Boynton/Cook, 1987.

Beowulf. Rowland L. Collins, ed. Bloomington: Indiana University Press, 1965.

Bernstein, Theodore M. *Dos, Don'ts, and Maybes of English Usage*. New York:

Bolton, W. F. *The English Language: Essays by English and American Men of Letters 1490–1839*. Cambridge, England: Cambridge University Press, 1966.

Born, Bernice. "Studying Personal Names." *Virginia English Bulletin* 37 (Spring l987): 81–88.

Bruce, Lenny. *How to Talk Dirty and Influence People: An Autobiography*. New York: AMS Press, 1991.

Christensen, Francis. *Notes Toward A New Rhetoric.* New York: Harper & Row, 1967.

Christiansen, Mark A. "Writing a Linguistic Autobiography." *Virginia English Bulletin* 37 (Spring 1987): 119–21.

Delpit, Lisa. "The Silenced Dialogue: Power and Pedagogy in Educating Other People's Children." *Harvard Educational Review* 58 (August 1988): 280–98.

Elgin, Suzette Haden. *Never Mind the Trees: What an English Teacher Really Needs to Know About Linguistics.* National Writing Project: Occasional Paper No. 2, 1–15. n.d.

Gershwin, George. "Porgy and Bess." New York: Gershwin Publishing, 1935.

Hall, Katy and Lisa Eisenberg. *Snakey Riddles.* New York: Dial, 1990.

Hartwell, Patrick. "Grammar, Grammars, and the Teaching of Grammar." *College English* 47 (February 1985): 105–27.

Hopkins, Gerard Manley. *The Poetical Works of Gerard Manley Hopkins.* Edited by Norman H. Mackenzie. New York: Oxford University Press, 1990.

Hunt, Kellogg. *Grammatical Structures Written at Three Grade Levels.* NCTE Research Report No. 3. Urbana, IL: NCTE, 1965.

Johnson, Samuel. *Dictionary.* Philadelphia: J. Maxwell, 1819.

Joyce, James. *Ulysses.* Paris: Shakespeare and Company, 1924.

Lester, Mark. *Grammar in the Classroom.* New York: Macmillan, 1990.

McAlexander, Patricia J., Ann B. Dobie, and Noel Gregg. *Beyond the "SP" Label: Improving the Spelling of Learning Disabled and Basic Writers.* Urbana,IL: NCTE, 1992.

Mellon, John. *Transformational Sentence Combining: A Method for Enhancing the Development of Syntactic Fluency in English Composition.* NCTE Research Report No. 10. Urbana, IL: NCTE, 1969.

Memering, Dean and Frank O'Hare. *The Writer's Work.* Englewood Cliffs, NJ: Prentice Hall, 1980.

NCTE. *Quarterly Review of Doublespeak.* Edited by William Lutz. Urbana, IL: NCTE. (various years).

NCTE. *Students' Right to Their Own Language.* Urbana, IL: NCTE, 1974.

Noguchi, Rei R. *Grammar and the Teaching of Writing: Limits and Possibilities.* Urbana, IL: NCTE, 1991.

O'Hare, Frank. *Sentence Combining: Improving Student Writing Without Formal Grammar Instruction.* NCTE Research Report No. 16. Urbana, IL: NCTE, 1973.

Orwell, George. *1984.* London: Secker & Warburg, 1987.

———. "Politics and the English Language." In *Shooting an Elephant and Other Essays.* New York: Harcourt, Brace, 1950.

Oxford English Dictionary. New York: Oxford University Press, 1971.

Parker, Frank and Kathryn Riley. *Exercises in Linguistics.* Boston: Little, Brown, 1990.

Pei, Mario. *The Story of English.* Philadelphia: J. B. Lippincott, 1952.

Plath, Sylvia. *Collected Poems.* Edited by Ted Hughes. Boston: Faber & Faber, 1981.

Poe, Elizabeth Ann. "Teaching High School Students About Language Acquisition." *Virginia English Bulletin* 37 (Spring 1987): 113–18.

Pooley, Robert C. *The Teaching of English Usage.* Urbana, IL: NCTE, 1974.

Shakespeare, William. *Complete Plays and Poems of William Shakespeare.* Edited by William Allan Neilson and Charles Jarvis Hill. Boston: Houghton Mifflin, 1942.

Smitherman-Donaldson, Geneva. "Discriminatory Discourse on African-American Speech." *Discourse and Discrimination.* Edited by Geneva Smitherman-Donaldson and Tuen A. vanDijk. Detroit, MI: Wayne State University Press, 1988.

Spenser, Edmund. *The Complete Poetical Works of Edmund Spenser.* Boston: Houghton Mifflin, 1908.

Stalker, James C. "What Should English Teachers Know About Language?" *Virginia English Bulletin* 37 (Spring 1987): 3–23.

Steele, Sir Richard. *The Tatler.* Edited by Donald F. Bond. Oxford: Clarendon, 1985.

Strong, William. *Creative Approaches to Sentence Combining.* Urbana, IL: NCTE, 1986.

White, E. B. *E. B. White: Writings from* The New Yorker *1925-1976.* Edited by Rebecca M. Dale. New York: HarperCollins, 1990.

Whitman, Walt. "Slang in America." *Walt Whitman Prose Works 1892*. Vol. 2, 573. Edited by Floyd Stovall. New York: New York University Press, 1964.

Wright, Richard. *Black Boy*. New York: Harper & Row, 1945.

RESOURCES

As this chapter has indicated, language and linguistics is a huge and complex field. Below you will find some comprehensive works and some more accessible ones. The Heath book is a fascinating study of two language communities; the Shuy is a readable introduction; the Parker, Kolln, and Weaver are excellent teacher resources, as is the well-known Whole World Catalogue 2, *published by the Teachers and Writers Collaborative. The Willinsky is a fascinating study of Canadian high school students and their language.*

Baldwin, James. "If Black English Isn't a Language, Then Tell Me, What Is?" *New York Times*. July 29, 1979.

Baron, Dennis E. *Grammar and Good Taste: Reforming the American Language*. New Haven, CT: Yale University Press, 1982.

Baugh, Albert C. and Thomas Cable. *A History of the English Language*. 3d ed. Englewood Cliffs, NJ: Prentice-Hall, 1978.

Chomsky, Noam. *Syntactic Structures*. The Hague: Mouton & Company, 1957.

Cleary, Linda Miller and Michael D. Linn. *Linguistics for Teachers*. New York: McGraw Hill, 1993.

Dillard, J. *Black English: Its History and Usage in the United States*. New York: Random House, 1972.

Elgin, Suzette. *What Is Linguistics?* 2d ed. Englewood Cliffs, NJ: Prentice-Hall, 1979.

Hayakawa, S. I. and Alan R. Hayakawa. *Language in Thought and Action*. 5th ed. New York: Harcourt Brace Jovanovich, 1990.

Heath, Shirley Brice. *Ways with Words*. Cambridge, England: Cambridge University Press, l983.

Hodges, Richard E. *Improving Spelling and Vocabulary in the Secondary School*. Urbana, IL: ERIC/ NCTE, 1982.

Hurford, J.R. and B. Heasley. *Semantics: A Coursebook*. Cambridge, England: Cambridge University Press, 1983.

Kolln, Martha. *Understanding English Grammar*. 3d ed. New York: Macmillan, 1990.

Labov, William P. *A Study of the Non-Standard English of Negro and Puerto-Rican Speakers in New York City*. Final Report, U.S. Office of Education. Cooperative Research Project no. 3288. 1968.

Lehmann, Winfred P. *Historical Linguistics*. 3d ed. New York: Routledge, 1993.

Lightfoot, D. *The Language Lottery: Toward a Biology of Grammars*. Cambridge, MA: MIT Press, 1982.

Parker, Frank. *Linguistics for Non-Linguists*. Austin, TX: Pro-Ed, 1986.

Shuy, Roger. *Discovering American Dialects*. Urbana, IL: NCTE, 1967.

Sledd, James. "BiDialectalism: The Linguistics of White Supremacy." *English Journal* 58 (December 1969): 1307–29.

Smitherman-Donaldson, Geneva, ed. *Black English and the Education of Black Children and Youth*. Detroit, MI: Wayne State University Center for Black Studies, 1981.

Smitherman-Donaldson, Geneva and Tuen A. van Dijk. "Introduction: Words That Hurt." *Discourse and Discrimination*. Edited by Geneva Smitherman-Donaldson and Tuen A. Van Dijk. Detroit: Wayne State University Press, 1988.

Teachers and Writers Collaborative. *The Whole Word Catalogue 2*. New York: Teachers & Writers Collaborative, 1977.

Weaver, Constance. *Grammar for Teachers*. Urbana, IL: NCTE, l979.

Willinsky, John. *The Well Tempered Tongue: The Politics of Standard English in the High School*. New York: Teachers College Press, 1988.

CHAPTER 7

TEACHING WRITING

Writing is a lonely act that is never really performed alone.

—**Donald M. Murray,** *Expecting the Unexpected*

Fifth Period, Wednesday Afternoon

It is fifth period, Wednesday afternoon. The English teacher of this tenth-grade class has placed the writing topic of the day on the board: "What Democracy Means to Me." The students walk into class and see the large letters on the board; they groan a bit as they get into their seats. The bell rings. After taking attendance, the teacher begins the class briskly and tells the students, "Class, I would like you to write your response to the topic I've put on the board. It's something that I am sure all of you have an opinion on. You have the entire period. You might start by outlining your thoughts and then writing from that outline. All papers are due at the end of class and will be graded on both content and form. Do try to be careful with your work—remember, neatness counts."

While there are grumblings from the students and some pained looks exchanged between the rows, the class gets down to work. The teacher stands at the podium, grading some quizzes from the earlier periods, and keeps an eye on the students. While occasionally she walks to a desk to answer a question from an individual, the group is generally quiet. Some fidget at first, some make a few notes, and some start to write, stop, and then ball up their paper and start fresh. Most destroyed papers result in a trip to the trashbasket; too many of those trips, and our teacher begins to frown at the offenders.

Quiet reigns for almost fifteen minutes, but after that time, about two-thirds of the class are clearly through. The students shift in their seats, talk a bit; some put their heads down on their desks and retreat. The teacher calls for silence, reminding the class of the importance of the assignment and of not disturbing their neighbors. The students settle down, and those who are still working on their essays work until the final bell. Standing at the door, the teacher collects the finished papers as students file out of the room. Everyone has turned in something, and the students leave, looking largely relieved to be through with this particular fifth-period English class.

That night, our English teacher looks over the essays. She first frowns, then groans. These final drafts, the product of fifty minutes of writing and recopying are, first of all, terribly short: they average a little over a handwritten page in length. Worse, they are largely lifeless, filled with clichés, and seem to repeat endlessly the same stale points about the necessity of democracy punctuated with the same old platitudes about how wonderful it is to live in America. There are precious few original thoughts, not to mention much evidence of care in writing. Nevertheless, our teacher gamely attempts to respond to the pieces and give the students a grade, as promised, on form and content. About three hours later, she dispiritedly calls it a night and goes to bed. Just why can't those students in fifth period write?

What went so wrong for this teacher and her students?

Why is this scene so familiar in schools and why, further, is the outcome so predictable—and so unsatisfactory?

A Traditional Model of Teaching Writing

The above scenario reflects what we might call a traditional model of teaching writing. It is not the model you will find reflected in many of today's composition texts, but it is how most people have been taught—if not how they have actually learned—to write. What are its elements?

In the traditional model, **topics** are wholly teacher determined and are relatively divorced from student experience and knowledge. "What Democracy Means to Me" is an extreme example but not that unbelievable. Many school writing topics tend to be fairly abstract and, for most middle school and high schoolers, of little burning or immediate interest.

There is in this model limited attention to helping students "get in" to a draft of writing. There is little attention to invention strategies or **prewriting**. Students are expected to come up with ideas on their own, and they may be asked to submit an outline of those ideas—which it is assumed is constructed before the writing—with their final paper. As we all know (many of us from experience as students), most students write the outline *after* they have completed their final draft.

Another feature of the traditional model is limited **time** to write; most students are given a class period or a very few days to complete a final draft. Many times this writing is done wholly outside class which means that **collaboration** among students or sharing of drafts is rare and **help** from teachers is infrequent. In the traditional model, students write in isolation, by themselves, and figure out, by themselves, if what they have written can be revised or how it can be revised.

A further characteristic of the traditional model is the type of **response**. First, this response comes only from the teacher, and second, it is a response that is almost wholly **summative**, in that it results in a final grade with limited comments on content and extensive comments on organization and form. The opportunity to **revise** and resubmit the paper for a second look is usually not possible in the traditional model.

The **audience** in the traditional model is always the teacher. Because no students see drafts and the teacher alone reads and grades, the paper is written for him or her; sharing or even publication of work in an outside source or even within the classroom is rare.

Finally, the **structure** of a writing assignment is often given to students in the form of a formula which they are to follow and from which they are not encouraged either to vary or move beyond. The five-paragraph theme and similar structures are part of this formula approach.

Jenni Gallo, looking back on her high school career, describes writing in the traditional model:

> We were . . . alone when we wrote; one set of eyes saw our papers. Our rhetorical situation was narrowly defined; we never would have thought of writing a paper for anyone but our teacher. Our parents might have seen our writing, but their advice was usually editorial; peer input would have been seen as violating the honor code. We essentially wrote in a vacuum; we were not even writing for ourselves. . . . When we wrote, we were supposed to know our ideas already; we found out about organizing note cards and creating an outline, but we never discussed how papers actually got written or about the lack of a "correct" process. We never had the option to revise our mistakes so I viewed my papers and their ideas as immutable.
>
> A clear division existed between creative and academic writing. . . . The rules certainly eliminated the use of "I" in my writing.

What is limited about the traditional model?

There is one central flaw in the traditional model of writing; it ignores much of what we know about how real writers write and thus inadvertently makes the practice and learning of writing pretty difficult. Real writers are folks who work at the newspaper as well as those who create novels and poetry. Real writers are also in offices of varying types; they write letters, contracts, ads, informational brochures, manuals, and procedures. Real writers make their living writing all sorts of things and, sadly, what they experienced in most middle school and high school classes bears little relation to what they actually practice in their jobs.

The experience of writers

I have not been a teacher all my life. In the middle of my career I left teaching; for four years, I wrote and edited full-time, working on press releases, memos, letters, ads, brochures, newsletters, and a magazine. I wrote in an office every day for a variety of audiences and with an end product, publication, in mind. Those four years were not easy ones—I found I missed students and the classroom and did not particularly like the isolation of an office. On the other hand, I learned a lot about real writing, and I think that those four years have helped me put the teaching of writing into clearer perspective.

I found in my four years of writing and editing that I wrote about things I knew about—or wanted to know about—and that in my job, I could take some time coming up with ideas. I never had to produce a finished product in fifty minutes or less.

I also did not write alone; I asked the advice of other writers and readers, read aloud to them, shoved drafts under their noses, and made extensive revisions: changing, adding, deleting, sometimes rewriting entirely. At times what I wrote was not anywhere near what the powers that be wanted; in those cases, I went back to my office and tried again. In short, in the real world I was never "failed" for writing that missed the mark. I was not demoted or fired, and my salary was not cut when whatever immediate piece of writing was not up to standard. I was expected, simply, to go back and do it again.

The traditional model does not take much of the above into account and, further, restricts the writing to one audience—the teacher—a grade-giving, credit-determining audience at that. The traditional model also posits that writing can be done in a limited period of time, by formula (a number of formulas are routinely taught, including the five-paragraph theme), and that that formula will be relatively all-purpose for a writer's needs.

Finally, the traditional model does not allow for rewriting or even starting all over again, as I often did in my job. Again, this is not the experience of real writers.

Listen to a few student voices as they recall their school experiences trying to write:

> We learned how to formulate thesis statements. And to back them up with examples. Of course there is a negative involved here too. There was only one way to write a paper. You had to include your thesis in the first several sentences of the paper, and it had to contain three topics which were to be the subjects of the next three paragraphs, and then you had a conclusion. No variations allowed.
> — Mitra Palmer

> I also found among my memories graded papers which were bleeding red ink with corrections on grammar, but no comment on structure, style, content, or tone. Although I was taught the correct format for a composition paper, I had no recollection of lessons on writing. We were expected to follow the basic format including an introduction, body, and conclusion, which was a great place to start, but after that, we were lost. Our revisions consisted of correcting all grammatical errors and resubmitting the paper to the teacher.
>
> — Melissa Chai

> I never felt secure about writing because we were never really taught how to do it. We were given a format, a subject, and a whole list of don'ts, but we never had the practice or the individual help to develop our skills. It's hard to understand but we spent so much time year after year going over the same grammar rules which none of us ever really kept straight, and yet we never broke down all the different parts of writing to work on. It was just expected periodically throughout the year, graded and handed back and quickly forgotten. I never even asked what a comma splice was even though it was written in red at least five times on every paper.
> — Julie Morrison

> I was not a student who possessed "a gift for writing" and was told that I lacked depth and breadth to my writing. . . . It is difficult to forget those endless "themes" assigned and "cringing with fear" when asked to develop my own paper topic. My inadequacy resulted from the lack of writing skills, and from the inability of teachers to guide students to think for themselves.
> — Brenda Gates

[My teacher] taught us to write. That is, she taught the five-paragraph theme, that crumbling pillar of the high school curriculum. [She] espoused what she termed the Keyhole Approach to organization, illustrated below.

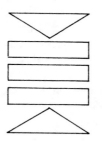

The inverted triangle represented the introduction, which began broadly but which culminated in the specific thesis statement listing the three points. It was always placed at the end of the first paragraph. The three blocks represented the three paragraphs that made up the body of the paper—one paragraph for each point. The first sentence of each paragraph identified the point to discuss, and the last sentence provided some kind of transition into the next point. The final triangle illustrated the conclusion, as it began with a restatement of the thesis and then grew more general. As you can imagine, such a strict form can be confining, and this form spawned such thrillers as "Three Benefits of Reading" (an actual student paper—mine). It produced lifeless, predictable prose, and a safe outline to follow forevermore. But this outline did make me see the need for a clear sense of organization in writing, and made me aware of the moves I was making as a writer. . . . However, for the longest time I didn't realize that the Keyhole Approach *wasn't* the best idea *all* the time. I had decided that, since it always worked for me (those hideously boring essays earned me "A's"), it would work all the time. So, for a while at least, I wrote uninspired papers limited to three main points and one-paragraph introductions and conclusions.

—Connie Chantelau

Many students do learn to write despite experiences like those above, but for others the whole learning-to-write process is an ordeal, especially when it follows closely the characteristics of the traditional model. Some students never learn and have, for their pains, uncommonly uncomfortable memories of what, in English language arts class, it meant to "write." And for teachers, upon whom the determination of what is good writing solely rests, the traditional model can be exhausting and difficult. The teacher in the traditional model controls, determines, and judges all: he or she makes the assignment, sets up the relatively unvarying structure, and is the sole responder to and evaluator of the writer.

When the traditional model demands that writing follow a formula, students can adhere to a cookbook approach only too well, as Debbie Martin, in her student teaching, observed in a writing assignment on satire:

The general pattern for the seniors was to copy *verbatim* the definition of satire for their opening paragraph. Then they added a sentence that stated the three satirical characters they were going to discuss. They wrote a paragraph on each of the three characters which was a listing of the characteristics copied off the study sheet. . . . they then added one original sentence to each of the three paragraphs that explained why these characteristics were other than expected. They closed with an original one-sentence concluding paragraph.

This is not what most writing teachers want.But what can we offer in the traditional model's place?

FOR YOUR JOURNAL

Think about your own writing history in school—how you "learned" to write. How did you get your ideas? What kind of paper and pen did you use? Did you have a special place or time of day to write? Did you share your writing with a parent? a friend? Did you make notes before you wrote? talk to yourself? draw? How was your writing received in school? What help did you get to improve? What happened when you went to college and wrote? Was it different? Why? Why not?

A New Model of Teaching Writing

The traditional model of teaching writing has not been a comfortable way for many students to learn to write—although, admittedly, many have taken the structure and used it and modified it to their advantage. Today, most English language arts teachers use what is termed a "new" or "process" model for teaching writing, a model that is not so much based on an ideal of how writing *should* proceed but on how studies of the behaviors of real writers show that it actually proceeds. A "new" model of teaching writing is more closely based on what we know real writers do. While certainly it owes a great deal to the traditional model and is derived from it, much of the practice of this model emerged from teacher researchers watching student writers, both adept and not so adept, write. Researchers also tried to analyze what professional writers actually produced. The picture that has emerged is far different from what went on in the fifth-period class described at the beginning of this chapter. Much composition teaching today concentrates on the act of writing and rewriting and less on the finished draft; it is oriented more toward process, not product.

In *Learning by Teaching* Donald M. Murray outlines what he calls "teaching writing as a process, not product:"

> What is the process we should teach? It is the process of discovery through language. It is the process of exploration of what we know and what we feel about what we know through language. It is the process of using language to learn about our world, to evaluate what we learn about our world, to communicate what we learn about our world.
>
> Instead of teaching finished writing, we should teach unfinished writing, and glory in its unfinishedness. We work with language in action. We share with our students the continual excitement of choosing one word instead of another, of searching for the one true word. . . . This process of discovery through language we call writing can be introduced to your classroom . . . as soon as you accept the full implications of teaching process, not product. (15)

In this model, the **topic** of writing is one which students help determine and which is related to their interests and knowledge. Students are given an opportunity for and help with **prewriting** to give them ideas and a starting place. The **time** to write is extensive and takes place in *and* outside class. Students show their drafts to each other and to the teacher in a **collaboration**, which gives them response at the draft-writing stage. Peer groups are a major source of feedback to writers during their drafting.

A final draft receives a **response**, and if it needs work in areas, students can **revise** and resubmit the paper. This response is **formative**, in that it helps students change and refocus and possibly improve. The audience for this writing is not just the teacher but also other students. Widening the audience is achieved through collaboration in **peer groups** and also through the publication of student writing through anthologies, class display, and schoolwide posting and distribution. Finally, the **structure** of the writing emerges from the topic; it is not predetermined by the teacher.

The following chart summarizes the two models:

	TRADITIONAL MODEL	NEW MODEL
Topic	teacher determined	teacher-and-student or student determined
Prewriting	limited or none	extensive
Time	limited	extensive
Help/Collaboration	none	extensive
Response	from teacher only	from teacher and peers

Response (cont'd)	summative	formative and summative
Revision	limited	extensive
Audience	teacher only	teacher and others
Structure	provided by teacher	provided by student and nature of topic

A student preparing to enter teaching recalls an especially successful writing assignment; while it does not contain every element of the new model cited above, it worked powerfully because of two factors, topic and prewriting:

> One year our teacher led a class discussion on busing at the time just before it became a reality. Our class was all-white and the discussion did not get very lively, but I still remember coming away from the discussion with very definite opinions—just what I needed to get started on the assigned paper. Though it was a very simple topic, we just had to argue for or against busing, we really had to think to come up with why we felt the way we did and why we took the positions we did.
>
> What made this an effective activity, and one that should have been part of most writing activities in high school English was the fact that it was a current issue, one that was in the news and very controversial. Students knew busing could affect them; it was close to their lives instead of being some vague and unreal topic that would have been hard to get a handle on . . . [it was a] real issue to grapple with. —LORI SHACREAW

A new-model writing class

Nancie Atwell's award-winning *In the Middle* outlines one model for turning a classroom into a writing workshop; her book is practical and specific. One of the surprising things most beginning teachers find is that, as set up by teachers such as Atwell and others, a classroom writing workshop can be carefully monitored and managed. It is not what many teachers fear: a free-for-all where students just come up with ideas, write a little bit, talk a little bit, and then turn in something when they please. It can be orderly, and certainly it can help students produce writing they have a commitment to and that actually says something, writing that is far better than what students usually produce.

Atwell's book will help you see how a real teacher keeps track of her students and their stages of writing, how she organizes her classroom; and how she provides accountability. If you are interested in a step-by-step approach to teaching writing—as well as reading a very interesting book—pick up a copy of *In the Middle*.

A word on "process" writing: uses and abuses

The traditional model for teaching writing emphasized the end result, the final product. As we have pointed out before, the new model, by contrast, puts a great deal of attention on the specifics of getting to the product—on the process. Thus the new model for teaching writing is often called a process model.

What does this mean? Process writing asks us to pay attention to the ways real writers write. Real writers do not write in a straightforward or linear fashion, as below:

STEP ONE: Get an idea
STEP TWO: Outline that idea (Do not go back to step one)
STEP THREE: Write (Do not go back to step two)

STEP FOUR: Revise what is written (Do not go back to step three)
STEP FIVE: Recopy (Do not go back to step four)

Looking at how real writers write, we see that very few writers follow this pattern. And yet this is often what we expect within English language arts classes and how we "organize" our students.

What happens with real writers? We think, watching such writers write and asking them to talk about their writing, that the various "steps" in the process very often occur with amazing simultaneity. A writer might get an idea and start to put something down, which gives her another idea; while adding that idea, perhaps she realizes that something is not right with what she first wrote, and she crosses it out. She has, essentially, gotten an idea, written, gotten another idea, written, revised, even edited, all in a fairly unorderly way and sometimes virtually simultaneously. We call this pattern *recursive*, and it is far from being the step-to-step or *linear* pattern of step one to step two to step three to step four to step five.

We think real writing looks something more like this, with the "steps" going forward and backward and forward:

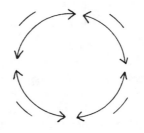

The implications for us as teachers are serious: we cannot spend Monday getting ideas, Tuesday writing, Wednesday revising, and Thursday editing. If we put students on such a schedule, even in the name of process writing, we are not truly letting students explore or use their recursive process.

We need to help students get started and then give them time to use and develop their own patterns for working through drafting to a final (or somewhat final) version. They may be getting ideas on Wednesday and Thursday, writing on Friday and Sunday, and getting more ideas on Monday. If we believe writing is truly recursive, we create a schedule that allows for that recursiveness. This does not mean we abandon our students and give them three days to figure it out for themselves; we need to help them during this time and using a workshop format. In a process model, however, you cannot completely confine writing behaviors to certain blocks of time—because it doesn't work that way. Teachers who try to schedule the process are actually abusing the term—and not really helping their students. Giving students time over a period of days to write and prewrite and revise is more helpful than predetermining which writing "step" a group will be involved in on any given day.

FOR YOUR JOURNAL

Think about the last writing assignment you did for a class. Try to remember how you actually got ready to write, how the writing itself went, how much time it took, and what kind of revision or rewriting you did. Did you show the draft to a friend? Did you read the words aloud to yourself? Was it important that you use a pen, pencil, typewriter, word processor? What, in short, was your *writing process* for this last assignment you did?

Writing Groups: Questions, Answers, and Reasons

Helping students with their writing is part of our task as teachers. I also use writing groups when teaching writing and, while it is strictly not part of the process model, it has been, for me, invaluable. It capitalizes on the collaborative aspect of writing—as Donald Murray notes in this chapter's epigraph—and helps students see their work as broader than just between themselves and the teacher. The importance of this aspect of teaching writing cannot be overstated.

The idea of writing groups scares some teachers. There is of course the fear that students will get out of control in the groups, but an even greater fear is that students not only don't know what to do but will do nothing in their groups but share their own ignorance about writing. It is, after all, the teacher's job, isn't it, to be the determiner of what is good writing?

These fears need not be realities. When students are told what a writing group is for, when the tasks and procedures are outlined, there is little real chance that a writing or response group will either get out of control or get lost. Students need to be introduced to writing groups; they need to model the behavior in a "fishbowl" kind of exercise (see page 188); and they need an accountability structure for what they do in their groups. Some groups will be able to talk about drafts and take notes on their copies productively; other groups will need checklists and worksheets that they turn in with their drafts to encourage them to stay on task. Regardless, writing groups can work very effectively in the middle school and the high school.

Don't writing groups "do" the teacher's job?

But what about the concern that response to writing is the teacher's job and that students in a writing group are doing nothing more but sharing their ignorance?

The utility of the writing group is that it exposes students to the writing of others. Gone is the isolation of one person writing his or her draft and never hearing or seeing what other students are doing. The writing of other students teaches; a draft presented in a writing group may be significantly better or significantly worse than the work of the other members of the group. Nevertheless, in a writing group students get to read and consider a range of writing—one another's drafts. Often I wonder what effect it has on students to read only and see only the polished, analyzed, credentialed work of the great, whom we know can write: Annie Dillard, Lewis Thomas, Henry David Thoreau, Martin Luther King, Jr. Letting students see and work with the writing of those like themselves who are learning to write can be a heartening experience.

Writing groups also tap into the collaborative, *each one teach one*, aspect of learning. If a student gets lost reading another student's draft, if the point just seems to disappear, that student—the reader, not the writer—will need to figure out why and articulate it. By trying to help a peer, the person will have to put a name on the problem area, give some sort of advice about what to do. It makes all students in the group consider and grapple with issues of writing in an immediate way, which is far more active than responding in a large group to whatever the teacher asks students to look for and discuss. Students can become more independent, and there is a double learning that can take place. In order for Ellen to help Mark with his writing, Ellen has to figure out what the issue is; by helping Mark, Ellen is helping herself.

The numbers game: help with the paper load

Finally, we need to think about the sheer impossibility of the teacher's task in the area of writing. It is an overwhelming job: the numbers, ladies and gentlemen, are just not in our favor and will not be in the near future, unless there is a major overhaul of the educational system.

In a famous article in the very first issue of *English Journal* (Vol. 1, No. 1, 1912), Edwin M. Hopkins asked, "Can Good Composition Teaching Be Done Under Present Conditions?" The article lamented the number of students in the average English teacher's class and noted that with the time it took to teach and respond to writing, it seemed an impossible situation. Little has changed between 1912 and today. Most English language arts teachers see a large number of students every day; I have a student teacher who recently, in a burgeoning suburban school, saw 167 students a day. What, practically, does this mean?

Let's look at the numbers. Let's imagine that you give *one class a week* a writing assignment. They are taking their writing seriously, and you want to give them a response to their drafts before they do a final version. You are not using writing groups; you want to make all the comments and suggestions yourself.

Let's say you spend a moderate amount of time—*ten minutes per draft*—for this one class of twenty-five to thirty students. That's anywhere from 250 to 300 minutes—between four and five hours—just to give students an intermediate response to a draft. When you receive final versions, of course, you will spend another ten minutes or so per paper—and that's another four to five hours. This is for *one class* to do a single piece of writing to which you respond and then evaluate and grade; it has worked out to about eight to ten hours of your time outside of teaching and preparation.

This eight to ten hours is, by the way, in addition to work for your other three or four classes and outside whatever else you are having this same writing class do. Is it any wonder English language arts teachers avoid giving writing assignments and, if they do, only work with final drafts?

The writing group can help a teacher handle some of the paper load. He or she can circulate among the groups and feel confident that with proper preparation, students can share what they are working on and get feedback from other readers, not just the teacher. It's a practical solution that not only has a sound pedagogical basis, but that also may help to save a committed writing teacher's sanity.

Procedures for implementing a writing group

The composition of a writing group can be heterogenous or homogenous; in other words, you can either mix writing ability or keep writers of the same ability in a single group. I have had most success with a heterogeneous group of three or four members; I also always mix males and females and members of majority and minority racial or ethnic groups. I think diversity works well and prefer to use it in my classes.

I always ask my students for an ungraded writing sample a few days before we get into writing groups. We do some prewriting together, and I have students write about a personality characteristic of theirs or something that they are good at outside of school. It's an assignment that allows students to talk about something they know about and are interested in—themselves. I read these writing samples, looking at them with an overall general eye; it is holistic grading. While I respond to what students have written, I do not give the papers a letter grade. Students get credit, of course, for having done the writing, and for my own purposes, I place the papers in stacks; one stack for the strong writers (1s); one stack for the middling writers (2s); and one stack for the writers who, at this point at least and within the context of this group, look like they will need work and help (3s). Whereas one writing sample is no sure indicator of writing ability, and this sort of 1 to 3 holistic scoring has limitations, the procedure gives me a handle on where the student might be at that moment in my class.

Using this quick diagnosis, I then construct the writing groups, mixing the 1s, 2s, and 3s as well as the males, females, and ethnic groups. So, for example, a single writing group of four might have, in ability, one 1, one 3, two 2s; in gender, two females, two males; in racial mix, three Caucasians, one African American. I do not, by the way, share the numerical designations of their writing sample with students until the end of the course. It is initial diagnosis, based on a single piece of writing, and its function is only to allow me to create intermediate groupings.

I talk with my students about why writing groups are important, giving them much the same argument I have outlined above. I assure them I will be circulating among the groups as they work. I then give them the following handout, and we go over it:

WRITING/REVISION GROUPS

In groups of three or four, you will have a class session to share one another's papers, suggest changes, and reinforce what you feel are the strongest parts of the shared papers. Every member of the group must participate in the revision and should, while being respectful of the others' writing, make a conscientious effort to help the others improve their drafts.

TIME
Group of three, 15 minutes apiece
Group of four, 10–12 minutes apiece

PROCEDURE
1. **One person should give copies of his or her rough draft to the members of the group.**
2. **The person should then read the draft aloud to the group—there should also be no preliminary apologies or explanations, just the reading.**
3. **The person should then pause for a few minutes to allow the group to consider, look over the draft, make marks, make notes.**
4. **The discussion of the draft should then start and include both negative and positive remarks. In all instances, the group should try to be specific about the paper. Comments such as "I don't like this paragraph" are not helpful; comments such as, "In this sentence, this**

word seems too strong" or "This section seems out of place—could you move it more to the beginning of the paper?" are more useful and will help an author in changing and revising a draft.

5. While the writer of the draft would do well to listen to suggestions and comments, the paper belongs to the writer, not the group. It is conceivable that the writer will listen to suggestions and hints and decide to accept only some of them in revision.

QUESTIONS TO CONSIDER*

- Ideas and Content: To what extent is the draft clear? interesting? convincing? Are details used well? Are main and secondary ideas balanced?
- Organization: Can a reader follow where the draft is going? Are there helpful transitions? Where can points be made clearer?
- Voice: Does this draft read as if it were written by a real person? Can you "hear" the voice of the writer? Is there flavor, honesty, humor here?
- Word Choice: Are the words used fresh? striking? appropriate for the content?
- Sentence Fluency: To what extent does the writing move the reader along? Are the sentences varied or do they all sound the same?
- Conventions: Are there areas where the writer needs to check spelling? punctuation? paragraphing? capitalization? Do any of these errors interfere with the meaning of the draft?

Then, using a duplicated copy of an anonymous student draft, I ask students to enact a "fishbowl" writing group and role play.

Four student volunteers sit at the front or in the center of the room and pretend they are the group discussing this draft; one student volunteers to be the author, and the others are members of the writing group. The group follows the procedures outlined in the handout. The "author" begins by reading the draft aloud. The discussion then proceeds. The rest of us watch in silence, noting not so much what is said about the draft but what kinds of remarks are made and by whom: who talks, who doesn't, how it goes. After about ten minutes of observation, we stop the role play, and we talk about what we saw.

Then I have four different student volunteers do the fishbowl again. Not surprisingly, the second group is always different from the first; they not only have the benefit of having watched the first fishbowl, but they usually have different ideas of their own and different ways of interacting. Again, we discuss how the group went.

It is only after taking a writing sample, grouping students, explaining the purpose and intent of a writing group, giving students some written instructions, and doing a number of fishbowl exercises that my students are comfortable beginning work in a writing group. Even then checklists can be necessary to keep students on task—checklists that I discuss and briefly review—as well as teacher circulation among the groups. Groups can take a bit of time to bond, and they may have questions that need to be answered. To have students just "get in groups and talk about one another's drafts" is not possible for most; if we care about the process, we need, as outlined above, to:

---

*These questions are adapted from *Creating Writers* by Vicki Spandel and Richard Stiggins.

1. **Model the process, step by step.**
2. **Reinforce the process.**
3. **Monitor the process.**

When students are asked to take on roles they do not understand and for which they are not prepared, chaos and upset can ensue.

How often groups are re-formed is a context issue; I prefer groups that last for a semester at least, but you may want to change your groups more frequently. Personality conflicts between students, discipline issues, students whose writing skill changes so drastically that they would benefit from other peers, groups that for whatever reason are not productive or harmonious, are additional reasons to reconfigure writing groups. As you sit in on the groups you will be able to sense who is working well and who is not; use your judgment to determine when and if a writing group needs change.

Conferencing with Students

Besides groups, another activity that is helpful to students is the brief conference. It may seem impossible to talk about a draft individually with each student in a class of thirty, but you can do it if the conferences are kept brief and are conducted while other writing/reading activities are going on. Let's imagine that students are working on their writing and you are available, at your desk, for five-minute conferences with people who want to talk. You could, conceivably, confer with seven or eight students and still have some time to circulate among the class or do some large-group instruction. Many students want the privacy—and the reassurance—of a conference. In *Learning by Teaching*, Donald M. Murray, discussing writing conferences, notes they should be short and frequent and limited to one concern at a time. He also offers conference guidelines for teachers:

- **The student responds to the text or to the experience of producing it.**
- **The teacher listens to the student's response to the text and watches how it is presented.**
- **The teacher reads or listens to the text from the student's perspective.**
- **The teacher responds to the student's response.** (163–64)

Practically, what does this mean? It might mean that a conference would start with questions that ask the writer how he or she views the draft (text). Murray offers the following typical questions a teacher might use in a writing conference:

- **What did you learn from this piece of writing?**
- **What do you intend to do in the next draft?**
- **What surprised you in the draft?**
- **Where is the piece of writing taking you?**
- **What do you like best in the piece of writing?**
- **What questions do you have of me?** (159)

Other questions I use include:

- **What do you think of what you have written?**
- **How difficult was it to get this far?**
- **How easy was it to write about this subject?**
- **What do you want to work on?**
- **Where are the draft's strengths? weaknesses?**
- **What can I help you with?**

Notice that all of the questions above, and the whole tenor of the conference itself, is focused not on the teacher's making the draft better—or correcting it or improving it or criticizing it—but on making the writer look at his or her own work and selecting what he or she sees—or doesn't see—as an issue. This kind of indirection may make you worry that you are not doing your teacherly job; after all, aren't we supposed to mark up and evaluate and determine what is good writing and not good writing? What Murray and many others believe, however, is that students will learn, will work on, what they, not we, perceive as important in their drafts. A conference that allows students to focus on selected aspects of their writing will ultimately produce more *learning* than a list of "corrections" we might hand a student in a conference setting.

The Place of Correctness

When some teachers think of the process model of writing, they get uncomfortable because that model of writing does not, as the traditional model did, value the final product as the most important focus of the writing. Indeed, writing teachers who emphasize a writing process and writing groups are often accused of not valuing the final product at all and of not valuing correctness.

Whatever model of writing you use, correctness is important. The key, though, is where; correctness, I feel, is important—in a final draft. We need to school ourselves as teachers not to expect students—and not to ask students—to be concerned about spelling or grammar or surface issues while they are, as Dan Kirby and his co-authors write in *Inside Out,* "getting it down" (39 ff.). Getting it down is first. Getting it right is second. If we ask students to do both simultaneously we can cripple them and their writing. They need to draft and cross out and struggle first, then they need to go back and consider correctness. Asking students to do it all at the same time is asking for something that real writers don't practice at all; correctness has a place, but that place is firmly at the end of the writing process.

When I work with student drafts, if it is near the end of the process I will note that students should look up certain words or check for punctuation or rework certain constructions that are either not standard or not conveying clearly what the writer means. Sometimes I will place a mark by every line of a draft where something needs to be reconsidered; students can ask one another, their group members, or they can consult their usage handbooks or dictionaries. They can, of course, also ask me, but I try to get them to pursue other sources—and thus learn to be more independent of me—as much as possible.

The point, of course, is not that correctness should be valued in and of itself but that our students need to see that correctness serves meaning. When surface errors interfere with reading, they are serious impediments. As preservice teacher Julie Morrison writes in her journal:

If teachers can make their students actually see how grammatical mistakes rob their papers of the meaning intended, then they will see the importance of "correctness," not for a good grade or just to appease the teacher, but because they deserve to be taken seriously. Their ideas warrant the reader's attention, not the grammatical errors. So if students realize that their misspelled words, or subject-verb disagreement trips the reader and distracts his attention, then maybe they will see worth in writing correctly.

Correctness is important, but *what* students say is paramount. Too many people associate writing only with spelling, English language arts class only with using "correct" grammar. We read that the public worries about declining standards in language, but most of those worries seem to refer only to the most surface of surface errors! Would that the public criticize recent graduates of high school because they are writing lifeless stuff, not because that lifeless stuff is misspelled. We need, as with literature, to remember why we are in the classroom: it is not to point out errors; it is to get students, in their writing, to grapple with ideas and then, only then, to present those ideas in a correct form.

But What About Grammar?

You can teach a definition of a part of speech and test it. You can have students label participles in sentences and mark if the choices are right or wrong. It's testable, gradable, and can be put in fill-in-the-blank or multiple-choice format. It's harder, on the other hand, to gauge whether an opening to an essay is "effective" or not; it gets difficult putting into words why one description says more, is more evocative, than another.

Many teachers feel that grammar definitions and examples are fairly cut and dried and, further, that they bear direct relation to the quality of people's writing.

While the first statement is true, it is the second that is problematic. As we discussed in Chapter 6 on language, the transfer effect of the identification of the parts of speech, the carryover from labeling gerunds to writing them, has just not been verified by studies of students and their writing. The way grammar is presented in school— separate from writing as something to be memorized or tested in isolation—makes its relation to the production of good writing very tenuous. While grammar can be truly fun to study for its own sake (yes, it can!) and the nomenclature of grammar often indispensable to analysis of literature and to some revision activities, the amount of time spent on isolated grammar study in most classrooms is probably wasted.

What we need to do is integrate the terms, the description of the language, with the actual production of language in writing. Grammar study *before* writing will not improve writing; no studies confirm that cause-and-effect relationship, although most people assume it has just got to exist. Grammar study *with* writing or with revision can, I think, be useful.

Imagine you have a student who keeps writing the same sentence patterns, subject/verb, subject/verb, subject/verb: "He drove down the lane. He saw it. He had been looking for it." You want the student to break out, vary what he is writing. Now would be the time to look at sentence patterns, at inverted verbs, introductory participial phrases, adverb clauses, periodic sentences. Maybe the student does not need to look at all of the above; maybe the student doesn't need all of the nomenclature to know that you can start a sentence off with something describing something, and then complete the sentence as usual ("Driving down the lane, he saw what he was looking for"; "What he was looking for was down the lane"; and so on). Work with sentence combining could certainly help such a student.

As cited in Chapter 6, Nancie Atwell in *In the Middle* makes a convincing case for "mini-lessons" in grammar that take about ten minutes at the beginning of class and that relate, are directly tied to, her students' writing (77). Such an arrangement can make grammar instruction effective and possibly helpful. Memorizing the usage handbook's definitions, making lists, identifying items on tests, rewriting or identifying someone else's usage mistakes, are not, I think, worth our time and just do not do what we want, which is to improve student writing.

Now They've Written It—What Do You Do With It?

Whether you are looking at individual papers or a group of papers in a portfolio, there are a number of activities you can perform with the final versions of student writing. In general, the major activities are **response, evaluation,** and **grading,** all of which are different and which will be addressed in the next section. Before we turn to them, however, a few points are important.

First, we need to return to the idea of correctness. We probably do not want to emulate the following conscientious but I do think ultimately misguided teacher. For whatever reasons, she felt called to look at her students' writing in a way that more than likely took her a huge amount of time and more than likely was not as productive as other activities. Sheryl Miller recalls:

> [My eleventh grade teacher] once explained to us her procedures in evaluating our work. First, she would read it through for content to see if it "hit" her. She would then read it a second time for accuracy in facts and whether it was correct in form and content. She would then read it a third and final time for spelling, but not in the usual way. She read it *backwards* word-by-word to make sure that she did not miss anything. . . . Every two red marks counted as a point off the grade for the paper. . . . She may have been extremely critical of our papers, but she made absolutely sure that we were very careful about what we submitted for a grade.

While there is a place for correctness, and while students *do* need to exercise care with what they submit for a grade, a teacher who reads with such exhaustive thoroughness may not find his or her efforts yielding a commensurate student improvement.

Second, there are a few practical points to be made about what a teacher can and should do with student writing. Every teacher develops a certain set of procedures; these are some of mine.

Before I look at student papers I review the assignment. And, by the way, that assignment should be written out in an assignment or topic sheet given to students; I usually reread that sheet myself and also mentally rehearse what the general topic called for. I try to imagine the different ways students could approach such an assignment and, possibly, how my wording of the assignment could have led a student astray.

I then read all of the student papers in as close to one sitting as I can handle; reading in one sitting keeps me fresh and, I think, more consistent. When papers are read at one time, it is easier for me to have a feel for them as a group. As I read, I put the papers in stacks of what I feel are "like" papers as far as quality. One stack is for excellent papers, one for good papers, one for papers that seem less successful. During my reading, and at the end, too, I will move papers from one stack to another depending upon second—and even third—thoughts about the writing. Only at the very end do I take the papers in their stacks and, after a final look, give each paper a grade. I also write comments to students on a separate sheet; I started this habit while teaching high school because many of my students had so much difficulty writing, and when I wrote on—marked—their papers it felt less like help to them than a violation. So I changed my old pattern of writing *on* papers, and I now keep my writing separate from theirs. You can certainly write on papers if you wish; you might, however, try to be sensitive to how your students react to your marks on their final work. You might try using pencil over pen, purple ink rather than red. If, whatever format you use, writing on a student's work becomes an issue, writing on a sheet that can be attached to a final draft is a sensible alternative.

Reviewing the assignment, reading in one sitting, placing papers in tentative grade "stacks," and writing comments on separate sheets are all part of what I do with student papers. But to get back to those three activities we need to distinguish among: **responding, evaluating,** and **grading**.

Responding/Evaluating/Grading

The three activities are not necessarily mutually exclusive, but each differs somewhat from the others. When we **respond** to students, we make an effort to talk to them, writer to writer, reader to writer; the issues of quality, good/better/best, are not of primary importance. When I respond to a student paper, I try to do three things:

1. **I link something the student has written to me personally.** Yes: I had a similar experience; that would anger me, too. That happened to a friend of mine.

2. **I tell the student what I like about what he or she has written.** I pick one or two things the student does well and I ask the student to think about it. Your introduction really grabs me—do you have any idea why that opening image is so powerful?. You are using parallel construction effectively here—do you see how?

3. **I ask the student questions about the draft.** Look at your title—is that what this paper is really about? If not, what is it about? Can you find where you could break this long section into two paragraphs? What effect do you think this word has on what you are trying to say in this paragraph?

When I **evaluate** a paper, I put more emphasis on how well I think the paper is doing what it does, on how close the paper seems to come to what it is trying to do. That may mean more emphasis on number 2 above and more direction on number 3 (I am lost in this section; what is it about? Your paragraphs are so long you are combining a number of points; can you break the section on p. 2 into two—or three—paragraphs?)

To **grade** a paper requires a letter or numerical designation *and* some sort of final evaluative comment. I use single letter grades and have never found the "split" grade of one letter for content and one for form to be successful. While many teachers like the split grade, as it seems to make a distinction between content and mechanics (surface errors), I have a hard time accepting that distinction anymore. If surface errors diminish meaning—and they can—then content is really intertwined with form. How can we separate them? Is it really possible, if form is so related to content, that a paper receives a B in content but a D in form? For me, one grade seems more logical.

Using student portfolios is also very helpful in grading and evaluating. With a portfolio, students can select from a group of papers what they feel is their best work. No writer shines on every effort, and with a portfolio, students not only have some control over what is evaluated but also they can select the pieces they feel are representative of their talents. Self-evaluation of pieces from a portfolio can also be helpful to get a sense of how a student sees his or her work.

Much like artists have done for years, students present their portfolio of work, which can demonstrate not only their range of writing but also their growth across a given space of time. The Yancey book listed in the references section at the end of this chapter can give you some specific pointers about using portfolio grading in your writing classroom.

Also, one of the best books on evaluating writing is Vicki Spandel and Richard Stiggins's *Creating Writers: Linking Assessment and Writing Instruction,* listed in the references section. Using student examples, it gives a thorough introduction to **analytical** and **holistic** ways of evaluating writing, and the specificity of the book may be helpful to you as you consider how to evaluate student writing.

Finally, we need to be aware that however we react to student writing—response, evaluation, grading, or any combination of the three; using a portfolio or simply looking at individual papers; using analytic or holistic methods—we wield a certain power and influence. Julie Morrison, a student who is planning to teach English, writes how my feelings about her writing even affected her choice of which piece would be printed in our class anthology. I try not to let all of my prejudices show, but I didn't fool Julie one bit:

> To be perfectly honest, I chose the paper that I thought you liked better, the childhood myth. I trust your opinion, much more than my own, and I rely on your experience as a writer to show me what's strong, what works . . . etc. This makes me think about my own responsibility as a responder, when I teach. It's a lot of pressure, I guess, because the teacher's response really affects the students' own appraisal of the writing. I know we've discussed this many times in class, and it's really a scary issue for us since we don't have a whole lot of experience with something that [matters] *so much.*

Without letting this influence overwhelm us, we need to remember that we carry a weight—and thus a responsibility—when we look at student writing.

We also need to remember that we, the teachers, are not the only ones to respond, evaluate, or even suggest grades. Students can also participate in this process, and their shared negotiation can, as Tom Romano points out in *Clearing the Way,* "induce the student to write again" (109). Romano reminds us that a student's "writing future" (109) is what is at stake, and certainly the processes of evaluation and grading should not imperil that future.

For Your Journal

Ask a friend who is in a secondary or middle school to lend you a copy of a student's draft (with the student's permission and with his or her name removed) or get a draft from a peer. Imagine you are the teacher and need to *respond* to the draft. Write a paragraph that you feel gives the student feedback and that offers formative comments. Then write a paragraph that *evaluates* the paper with summative remarks. Finally, place a *grade* on the paper as if it were a final draft. Look over what you have done: how helpful do you think your response and evaluation is? Write a paragraph about how you felt doing this exercise.

The Wonderful and Varied Journal

If we believe that people learn to write by writing, that practice helps with fluency—we are right. How, nevertheless, does even a highly conscientious teacher deal with a lot of writing in four or five classes? The answer for me is the journal, a great tool that can be used in a variety of ways.

I like to start classes with ten minutes of writing; in a **class or learning log journal,** the topic relates to the class discussion, the readings we have done for homework, the activity we just finished. Typical topics might be: in last night's reading, what two things did you notice? What surprised you? List five questions you have.

Another journal is the **personal journal**, which allows students to keep more private and introspective thoughts. It gives students an outlet for their ideas and emotions, and it capitalizes on a powerful subject, themselves. While there are always issues of confidentiality (students may want to write in this journal but not share with you or with others every page), this type of writing can be very effective. Typical topics might be: what is the best thing that happened to you this week? Imagine you are going on a long trip and can take only one personal item with you—what would it be?

A **writer's journal** can be a place where a student keeps notes, records dreams, writes out phrases and story fragments, preserves other prose or poetry he or she has read, all with the idea of using the journal as a basis for future or current writing. Many artists, inventors, and scientists keep notebooks of this sort—writers need them, too. Typical topics might include lists of interesting words, opening lines, snatches of dialogue that could be used in any piece of writing.

Dialogue journals are written on one side of the page with space for someone else—another writer, the teacher, other students—to write back and respond; the subject of a dialogue journal can be quite varied, but its strength lies in the fact that one writer writes to another, and there is an immediacy that this format captures. Typical topics might be: what two things does this class really need? What did you think of the last assembly? What is one question you've always wanted to ask an adult?

Whatever their type, journals need to be written consistently, taken up on a regular schedule, and responded to in a nonthreatening manner. Surface correctness and even neatness are nonissues in journals—although the writing should be legible so that it can be read. Letter grades that absolutely judge quality are more than likely inappropriate for journals; some teachers assess journals on completion or on number of pages written. I usually put a check at the top of each page read or skimmed and write a comment at the end responding to what the student has written. Another response format I enjoy these days is to tape comments that I make as I read through the journal. I can say more to the students on tape, and it is more fun for me to talk to my students than to write to them for this kind of assignment. The students provide the tapes, and their reaction is that an audible response is more personal and more extensive.

Journals are a direct answer to the paper-load issue. If students write regularly in their journal, they are working on their writing, and their sheer writing fluency can be very positively affected. It is hard to stay afraid of writing—to have what is known as **writing apprehension**—when you have to write regularly. Students also learn a few other things through using a journal: they can "work out" intellectual and personal issues through their own writing; not all writing needs to be perfect; not all writing needs to be graded. The wonderful and varied journal can be a powerful part of your classroom.

The Research Paper

It is, as student Beth Hagy notes, "the research paper, commonly known as going to the encyclopedia and expanding" that strikes fear in the hearts of both teachers and students. Most students hate this assignment; most teachers dread not just the difficulty of getting students through the process but the lifeless results of what seem to be hours of preparation. Further, plagiarism is a serious issue in the research paper, and my very brief advice is to give students an opportunity to write about something in which they are interested.

Ken Macrorie talks about the "I-Search" paper, letting students pursue in their research something they want to search out. Certainly we need to remember that primary and secondary research can be done on an amazing range of subjects. It is not just the Romantic Movement in England in the early 1800s or the use of fire imagery in a novel that should be the sole subject of student investigation. Certainly there are students in your English language arts class who may want to research Bret Harte's short stories or Toni Morrison's metaphors. But there are those who can also do excellent jobs researching the history of their neighborhood, the latest innovations in four-wheel-drive technology, the newest theories on the planets, or the influence of the Industrial Revolution on just about everything.

I know this is *English* class. But I also know that when we talk about research, we need to broaden what that definition is and not insist that our students mimic what we necessarily did in our college Victorian Poetry class or American Novel course. Getting students to read and write and ferret out information is the purpose, I think, of a research paper. The subject does not necessarily have to be literary.

One assignment I have had a great deal of happiness with is asking students to research the day of their birth. Students have to read the newspapers—one national, one from the community in which they were born—for the events of the day. They have to interview family members, in particular their parents, about recollections of the momentous date and use personal material such as their own baby book. Students can then concentrate on any aspect of the day: the international scene, the movies playing, the cost of any goods or items, the weather, the sports scores, the car ads. How they weave this together is an individual choice, and I give them guidance on writing this personal yet scholarly account of a day in history.

This assignment gives students a sense of history; it gives them a sense of themselves within and as a part of history. It makes them turn to primary not just secondary sources; it gives them an opportunity not only to interview but to use and interpret those interviews; it asks students to choose what is most important to them; it capitalizes, again, upon that undeniable interest all of us have in that ever-fascinating subject, ourselves. I have never had, I might add, a student plagiarize this assignment or fail to turn it in. There are few activities I can say this about, but "The Day I Was Born" is a relatively sure-fire assignment.

After struggling for a semester in student teaching with the research paper, Debbie Martin wrote her vision of a research paper:

I like the idea of setting up a mini library in my room so that I could talk to *all* the students about how to use the books. The class would have to work on 1-3 different topics as a group but once finished they'd know how to utilize research material. In fact, a collaborative paper—in small groups of three or four—would be a much better idea. We could choose an author and spend one nine-week session reading his/her works, with the second nine weeks spent on critical observations.

While what Debbie writes is only a partial outline, there is, in her comments, an effort to expand the isolation and restricted nature of the traditional research paper.

What We Are About as Teachers of Writing

I have worked with classroom teachers every summer for eight years in my local site of the National Writing Project. The National Writing Project has many sites across the country; it insists primarily, paramountly, that teachers of writing need to write themselves. This principle is the major point of the almost twenty-year-old program, and it has done a great deal to change what is practiced in the classroom. Every summer teachers of all subject matters and all grade levels meet to consider issues of writing. The core of the program is an opportunity to research and share ideas about writing, but it is also about giving teachers an opportunity to write themselves.

Teachers of writing should write. Yes, that is you, too. Whether you keep a journal at home, prewrite with your students in class, contribute an article to your local education or language arts newsletter, dash off a poem or so every month, you need to write. I suspect that one reason English language arts teachers often do such silly stuff in class with writing is that they are not writing themselves and have forgotten what it took, what they needed as writers.

I write with my students. It's not that I do every assignment with them from beginning to end; I take a low-level approach, and it is workable for me.

Let me explain: my students and I do our journals together for ten minutes at the beginning of every class: they share theirs aloud, and I share mine, too. I also, though less frequently, freewrite drafts on the board or the overhead while they write at their desks; and during the year I occasionally show them the revision agonies I go through to produce my own final draft writing for publication. All of it seems to cheer them up immensely: my journal entries are not always profound; they often ramble, and sometimes I can't read my own handwriting. Students whisper and chuckle a bit over the drafting I do in front of them, and once they get to know me, they do ask, looking at my revisions, why I don't get it right the first time when it's clear (hey, it's right here in this section) that the whole point was in that fifth paragraph of the second draft. After all, I'm the teacher. But then, again, maybe all writers are like that, huh?

Yes. And that's the point, and I think you can do that, too. The power of writing with your students makes you a writer with them, not a gamemaster giving them another assignment from which you are completely removed. While not completely devastating, the picture Connie Chantelau sketches below does not, I think, describe how we can help our students become confident writers:

I don't remember ever using peer groups or having individual conferences about my writing; I recall no encouragement to experiment with writing beyond the standard forms; I recall no personal engagement with literature encouraged in writing. I learned how to edit, not revise. I learned to view writing as a product to be written in fifty minutes and graded based on content and grammar. I had no notion of audience other than the teacher and some faceless college examination board. I was trained, however inadvertently, to stay well within the confines of certain forms and language when I wrote, and I never learned how to handle criticism constructively. In high school I wrote safe, well-organized and entirely correct essays with so spunk, no pizzazz, no chutzpa. I was afraid to expand, to try anything different, and none of my English teachers encouraged me to. I never saw my English teachers write; I never heard them read anything they had written. While we wrote, they sat behind their desks, watching, reading, and grading.

What do we want in our classes when we teach writing, when we have our students write? It may be the vision that Julie Morrison describes:

> Students need to write for the sake of writing and not to show that they've read a book or mastered the basic punctuation skills. I want my students to be challenged with their writing and value it as much as they do their own speaking voice. This will take time and lots of practice. We'll need to work together, and learn together. And when my students learn to value what they can say on paper, they will value how they say it, and mechanics will find its place and finally be of some use.

I can't say it any better.

FOR YOUR JOURNAL

Think about the more successful writing experiences you have had in school. What one paper or papers was the most satisfying to you? Why? Was it the grade? the topic? the process of getting the words down? the feeling after you had turned it in? Try to analyze *why* that writing assignment stands as one of your favorite. Finally, what about that experience can you bring into your English language arts classroom? Are there elements you can use with your students? How? Be specific.

REFERENCES

Atwell, Nancie. *In the Middle: Writing, Reading, and Learning with Adolescents.* Portsmouth, NH: Boynton/Cook, 1987.

Christenbury, Leila. "No Ivory Towers: An Open Letter to Karen Jost." *English Journal* 79 (September 1990): 30–31.

Hopkins, Edwin M. "Can Good Composition Teaching Be Done Under Present Conditions?" *English Journal* 1 (January 1912): 1–8.

Kirby, Dan and Tom Liner with Ruth Vinz. *Inside Out: Developmental Strategies for Teaching Writing.* 2d ed. Portsmouth, NH: Boynton/Cook, 1988.

Macrorie, Ken. *The I-Search Paper.* 2d ed. Portsmouth, NH: Boynton/Cook, 1988.

Murray, Donald M. *Expecting the Unexpected: Teaching Myself—and Others—to Read and Write.* Portsmouth, NH: Boynton/Cook, 1989.

———. *Learning by Teaching: Selected Articles on Writing and Teaching.* Portsmouth, NH: Boynton/Cook, 1982.

Romano, Tom. *Clearing the Way: Working with Teenage Writers.* Portsmouth, NH: Heinemann, 1987.

Spandel, Vicki and Richard J. Stiggins. *Creating Writers: Linking Assessment and Writing Instruction.* New York: Longman, 1988.

Yancey, Kathleen Blake. *Portfolios in the Writing Classroom: An Introduction.* Urbana, IL: NCTE, 1992.

RESOURCES

The number of good resources on the teaching of writing is truly astounding; the major theorists have many books to their credit, and you will want to familiarize yourself with many of the authors listed below.

Applebee, Arthur N. *Writing in the Secondary School.* Urbana, IL: NCTE, 1981.

Belanoff, Pat and Marcia Dickson, eds. *Portfolios: Process and Product.* Portsmouth,NH: Boynton/ Cook, 1991.

Belanoff, Pat, Betsy Rorschach, and Mia Oberlink. *The Right Handbook: Grammar and Usage in Context.* 2d ed. Portsmouth, NH: Boynton/Cook, 1992.

Berthoff, Ann E. *The Making of Meaning.* Portsmouth, NH: Boynton/Cook, 1981.

Bizzell, Patricia and Bruce Herzberg. *The Bedford Bibliography for Teachers of Writing.* 3d ed. New York: St. Martin's Press, 1991.

Britton, James, T. Burgess, Nancy Martin, A. McLeod, and H. Rosen. *The Development of Writing Abilities: 11–18.* London: Macmillan Education, 1975.

Bruffee, Kenneth. *A Short Course in Writing.* 3d ed. Boston: Little, Brown, 1985.

Calkins, Lucy McCormick. *Lessons from a Child.* Portsmouth, NH: Heinemann, 1983.

Calkins, Lucy McCormick with Shelley Harwayne. *Living Between the Lines.* Portsmouth, NH: Heinemann, 1990.

Elbow, Peter. *Writing Without Teachers.* New York: Oxford University Press, 1973.

Emig, Janet. *The Web of Meaning.* Portsmouth, NH: Boynton/Cook, 1983.

Flower, Linda. *Problem Solving Strategies for Writing.* New York: Harcourt, Brace, Jovanovich, 1985.

Foster, David. *A Primer for Writing Teachers: Theories, Theorists, Issues, Problems.* Portsmouth, NH: Boynton/Cook, 1983.

Freedman, Sarah Warshauer. *Response to Student Writing.* Urbana, IL: NCTE, 1987.

Fulwiler, Toby. *The Journal Book.* Portsmouth,NH: Boynton/Cook, 1987.

Gere, Anne Ruggles, ed. *Roots in the Sawdust: Writing to Learn Across the Disciplines.* Urbana, IL: NCTE, 1985.

Graves, Donald H. *Writing: Teachers and Children at Work.* Portsmouth, NH: Heinemann, 1983.

Graves, Richard L. *Rhetoric and Composition: A Sourcebook for Teachers and Writers.* 3d ed. Portsmouth, NH: Heinemann, 1990.

Hillocks, George, Jr. *Research on Written Composition: New Directions for Teaching.* Urbana, IL: NCTE, 1986.

Langer, Judith A. and Arthur N. Applebee. *How Writing Shapes Thinking.* Urbana, IL: NCTE, 1987.

Lindemann, Erika. *A Rhetoric for Writing Teachers.* New York: Oxford University Press, 1982.

Macrorie, Ken. *Telling Writing.* Portsmouth, NH: Boynton/Cook, 1985.

Rodrigues, Dawn and Raymond J. Rodrigues. *Teaching Writing with a Word Processor, Grades 7–13.* Urbana, IL: NCTE, 1986.

Selfe, Cynthia L., Dawn Rodrigues, William R. Oates, eds. *Computers in English and the Language Arts.* Urbana, IL: NCTE, 1989.

Shaughnessy, Mina P. *Errors and Expectations: A Guide for the Teacher of Basic Writing.* New York: Oxford University Press, 1977.

Williams, James D. *Preparing to Teach Writing.* Belmont, CA: Wadsworth, 1989.

CHAPTER 8

QUESTIONING

*How do I know what I think until I hear what I say?**

The Power of Talk

The power of talk is one of the English teacher's great resources. Our classrooms can be arenas of conversation where students argue, question, challenge, comment, and observe. And in frequent instances, we and our students can find out what we think or believe through our own conversation—discovering, as the chapter epigraph describes, "what we know" when we have the opportunity to talk and "hear what we say." Certainly, even though some of us would like for students to practice that art of discussion a bit more courteously or calmly or maturely, what we do in class is largely talk.

You as the teacher will mostly initiate and, yes, somewhat control that talk, and one of the most frequent activities in the English language arts classroom is the asking and answering of questions. It can be a highly adaptable, malleable activity when it comes to the consideration of language, literature, and our students' writing. In fact, most teachers are not aware of just how much they do use questions in their classrooms: one research study done by Robert J. Nash and David A. Shiman revealed that teachers who thought they were asking only a moderate number of questions—12 to 20—in any given class were actually asking four to eight times that amount—45 to 150 questions (44).

Talking and answering and asking questions can help clarify our own ideas, not only to others but to ourselves. In its proper context, the asking and answering of questions can be the heart of a lively and learning class.

When I think about the many discussions I have had with classes and students, I remember how awkward it was for me in the beginning of my teaching career to initiate and maintain a discussion. But I did have some successes, and I recall one class in particular, a class with which I never felt I had much rapport, and I remember the day that that class, more than any other, showed me what a discussion could actually achieve.

We had been talking about a poem and the speaker's choices and how—or if— those choices could relate to our own lives.

---

*This quotation is variously attributed and variously written; while
some give the twentieth-century British novelist E. M. Forster credit,
others do not. But it's a great quotation whoever said it.

Learning to question, to talk with these students, I had had a hard time creating an environment where anyone *wanted* to talk. I had taken some advice and tried to slow down, tried to open up spaces in the conversation, tried not to follow my "list" of questions so precisely. My new mode, and I had instituted it for only a week or so, was a bit more comfortable to me. There was for the first time some silence in the classroom, silence that I thought was positive in that it gave students some space to think and to consider. I had, I felt, finally allowed for breathing room.

It only happened once quite this way with this class, but in the space of forty minutes we moved from the poem and its relation to any real person's choices into an area of great interest to my students: drugs. In that conversation, we moved beyond the platitudes about buying and selling and doing drugs and into the realities of the issue. Cassandra, as I recall, got teary in this class talking about how difficult it was for her to curb her own interest in drugs when her stepfather used *and* dealt. James insisted she should be stronger, said he would be in a similar situation; Maurice chimed in with a companion story and a happier ending. Towanda snorted her disapproval of the entire issue and told everyone they were fools. That made Michael laugh, but then he gave his opinion, too.

This was not in my lesson plan and, frankly, some of the details of some of this class conversation alarmed me. In a way, we were all learning names and specifics and incidents and there were, of course, ethical ramifications to what was being revealed, however tentatively, in this class. But the students wanted to talk about this, wanted actually to talk to *one another* about this, and the poem and my classroom structure had seemed to provide the space to do so.

When the bell rang and the students left (and we had, by the way, agreed not to share this conversation with others outside the class), I was both unsettled by what had happened and profoundly satisfied. My class's environment had changed; the students had talked, for the first time in my presence, about something that was truly important to them, about something that was not purely *school*. They had, further, connected that real thing to what we were reading. What had happened was spontaneous and appropriate; while I would not expect or demand students to reveal so much about their personal lives, to talk, as in this case, of their own experiences with drugs, in this class the sharing was student initiated and treated confidentially. It was, despite the disturbing nature of the subject, a glimpse of teacher heaven.

I think most of us want such solid and worthwhile experiences when we ask and answer questions in our classrooms. Indeed, we ask questions not only to prompt personal sharing from our students about their relationship to literature but for a number of other reasons. Asking questions can:

- **Provide students with an opportunity to find out what they think by hearing what they say.** In responding to questions about literature or ideas, students often discover their opinions or reactions. In responding to questions about writing, students discover their ideas in prewriting or clarify their ideas in revision.
- **Allow students to explore topics and argue points of view.** Through questioning, students can pursue an aspect of a topic that appeals to them or can logically defend a theory or belief that they hold, sharpening not only oral but thinking skills.
- **Let students function as experts.** Through questioning, students as well as teachers can probe, explore, and move a discussion into a number of areas.

- **Present students with the opportunity to interact among themselves.** Given the proper setting and environment, students can—and will—argue and debate with one another. Student talk is very important, and it can not only be a stimulus for learning but also lead students to explore topics further or to pursue new topics.

- **Gives the teacher immediate information about student comprehension and learning.** Through questioning, particularly through paying attention to answers, teachers can check for comprehension and mastery. Questioning can serve as a diagnostic tool.

Questions That Teachers Ask

The issue of questioning hierarchies

Confronted with something—anything—to talk about in a classroom, most beginning teachers make an effort to write out the questions they think might be useful and put them in a lesson plan. Certainly for the class described above, I had questions prepared on the poem we were going to discuss. Many times, especially with literature, teachers will use questioning **hierarchies**, scales of importance or categories of schemata that classify question types. Within these schemata or hierarchies, the assumption is that certain kinds of knowledge—and the answers to certain kinds of questions—are considered superior to, more sophisticated than, or requiring higher cognitive skills than certain others.

Following this belief, most creators of questioning hierarchies suggest that teachers ask questions at the lowest level of the scale and then move up, spending the majority of questioning time in the upper reaches of the questioning hierarchy. The logical assumption is that spending all questioning time on "lower-level" or purely factual questions (What was the main character's name? Who wrote this and when? Who is the protagonist's enemy?) is not as productive as spending time on "higher-level" or more sophisticated questions (To what extent is this novel realistic? How does this incident relate to the opening of the short story? What do you think you would do if a similar incident happened to you?). Further, we know that students in so-called remedial or lower-tracked classes are often asked *nothing* but factual or recall questions and are never or rarely asked to consider *why, how,* or *what if.*

A number of sequential (ordered and hierarchical) and nonsequential (nonordered and nonhierarchical) questioning schemata are depicted on the top of the next page.

Each of the schemata represents a type of question or conceptual activity. The sequential schemata imply that certain questions require higher thinking skills than others and probably should be attempted in a set order. Look, for instance, at the Sanders: **memory** is lower on the scale, literally and figuratively, than **analysis**, and **memory** should, according to the schema, precede **analysis**. Some of the schemata, however, simply name different activities without giving them a value or order. Look at the Hyman schema where there is no valuative difference between **definitional** and **evaluative** and no assumption that one should precede or follow the other.

If the workings of the human mind were as orderly as some of the questioning schemata suggest, there would be no problem using such hierarchies when we plan for questioning in our classroom. We know, however, that the studies of real classrooms do not confirm such clean divisions regarding what actually happens when people talk

Sequential Questioning Schemata*

$$
\text{Benjamin Bloom} \left\{
\begin{array}{l}
\qquad\qquad\qquad\text{To evaluate} \\
\qquad\qquad\text{To synthesize} \\
\qquad\qquad\text{To analyze} \\
\qquad\text{To apply} \\
\text{To comprehend} \\
\text{To know}
\end{array}
\right.
$$

Benjamin Bloom
- To evaluate
- To synthesize
- To analyze
- To apply
- To comprehend
- To know

Norris M. Sanders
- Evaluation
- Synthesis
- Analysis
- Application
- Interpretation
- Translation
- Memory

Hilda Taba
- Apply concept
- Interpret concept
- Form concept

Harold L. Herber
- Applied comprehension
- Interpretive comprehension
- Literal comprehension

Nonsequential Questioning Schemata*

Arthur Kaiser: Open ———— Closed ———— Suggestive ———— Rhetorical
Richard Smith: Convergent ————————————————— Divergent
Ronald T. Hyman: Empirical —— Definitional —— Evaluative —— Metaphysical

and when they ask and answer questions. While questioning hierarchies can be a useful starting point, they are not true descriptions of human conversation—and that includes conversation in school. Researchers recording classrooms and classroom talk confirm that schemata are not that accurate a picture and that their use does not always yield what we think it might. For instance, we know:

- Few people—students and teachers—actually approach knowledge in an orderly, paced way, moving smoothly, as the sequential hierarchies would imply, up from one level to another;
- The categories of most questioning hierarchies are not only arbitrary but often overlap, leading to difficulty in actually constructing questions (for example, a question in the Bloom schema that features *analysis* as opposed to *evaluation*)
- The categories of most questioning hierarchies also imply that more superior cognitive sophistication is required for certain operations than for

*Adapted from Christenbury and Kelly, 4.

others (for example, the act of *synthesis,* in the Sanders schema, is superior to *application*).

In addition, the absolute, consistent benefit of asking "higher order" questions is also debatable. We know, for instance, that:

- **Most research studies are unsuccessful in classifying higher-level questioning in actual classroom discussions.**
- **Research studies are similarly mixed regarding higher-level questions resulting in greater student achievement.**
- **Not all students prefer or are comfortable with answering higher-level questions, especially if those questions are not matched by corresponding higher-level questions on tests.**

While some order of questioning is necessary and while a mixture of question types, however defined, is essential, it seems that discussion and questioning in the language arts classroom need not be so rigidly organized as some theorists and practitioners would imply. And while many of the creators of questioning schemata would be the first to caution against using them inflexibly, many lists similar to those above have been abused. They have become prescriptions rather than suggestions or guidelines, and further, they have given an unrealistic picture of human discussion.

A story

I learned about that unrealistic picture in my first year of teaching. My eighth graders, spurred on by one of my more memorable students, Walter O'Brien, taught me.

I had assigned a short story from the literature anthology and, for my afternoon eighth-grade class, had to the best of my fledgling abilities prepared a lesson plan for a large-group discussion. I had questions written out and notes in the margin of my copy of the story; I was ready to start; my materials were arranged on my desk, and on the board behind me were written the date, the title of the story, and the notation "Discussion." I was organized and ready. But I really hadn't counted on my students, specifically on Walter: what I was organized for was not what happened.

The bell rang, and I moved into the hall to await my lively eighth graders. They had some three minutes to change books and classes, and they came toward me, as was customary, laughing, shoving, talking, arguing, bringing all that energy and craziness and bright-eyedness into the classroom. They were energetic and even silly and boisterous at times (the class was right after lunch), but I was coming to like this group caught somewhere between the hilarity of late childhood and the seriousness of teenhood.

Depending on their mood and personality, they entered the class, threw their books on the desk, catcalled across the room, made faces at each other, flirted, hurled insults, yawned, told jokes, smiled shyly, twirled around, stretched, pushed each other, checked hair or makeup in mirrors, and, after their fashion, got ready for the beginning of class.

The second or late bell was ready to ring, and I moved to the center of the class to begin. And then, in the midst of the din and the hubbub, Walter, who with his glasses and careful clothes looked even at thirteen like a young physician or lawyer in training, called out, "Mrs. C., Mrs. C, just tell me, *why did he do that to her?*"

Why did he do that to her? We all knew that Walter's question was about the reading, and I knew that his question was, essentially, the heart of the short story. But I was disconcerted: *I* had not called roll and started the class; *I* was not ready to begin the discussion I had planned; further, the issue of *why he had done that,* that question and the answer to it, was way down on my lesson plan for this class discussion.

But it was, I found, what the class was going to start with. People started talking to Walter, started talking to me, started answering and arguing and looking around to see others' reaction to their answers. In the space of my confusion and Walter's loud voice, the late bell rang, the students got into their seats and, virtually without me, continued arguing with one another as to just *why he had done that.* And we were off.

I think, to this day, my students thought I had somehow planned all this. They were a generous group of people and seemed to always give me the benefit of the doubt, believing implicitly that most good things that happened in the classroom were somehow my doing. But I hadn't planned this at all. I did, however, have the good sense to follow their lead, to seize the moment, to start calling on people and refereeing the discussion, to allow the chemistry to work.

Sure enough, by the end of the class, we had "covered" all the introductory questions I had in my lesson plan. We had also come to some consensus on the overall meaning of the story. We had not started where I had planned; we had not begun as I had envisioned; we had, however, started not only where the students wanted to start but with the most important question. In the middle of the discussion some students had asked about factual details—we dealt with those facts then returned to *why he had done that.* It was wholly out of "order": it also was very effective.

I chewed over that particular class again and again in my mind. While I don't recall that that exact level of excitement ever occurred again—or even in a similar pattern—I knew then that Walter O'Brien and his classmates had taught me something about questioning. In hindsight, I think they taught me to:

- **Follow your students' lead—if they want to talk about something that is not in your order or on your list, let them.**
- **Be flexible with your questions: let a discussion have its own evolution. You don't necessarily have to start with the basic, the recall, questions.**
- **Don't always play it safe: students can lead a class into exciting territory, and giving them that opportunity can be one of the more valuable instructional decisions you make.**

Your classes, like most classes, will be filled with such opportunities. Your job is to get your teacher antenna tuned and when it is appropriate, seize the moment.

The Questioning Circle

Some years ago my friend and colleague Pat Kelly and I wrote a book on questioning. We had a good time writing and talking together, but the most exciting part of our joint writing venture was our talk about questioning hierarchies and how we felt they did not serve us or our students well. On the other hand, we knew beginning teachers needed a place to start when they constructed questions to ask in the classroom: what could we offer them?

We cooked up an alternative questioning schema, which we called "the questioning circle." We felt that this schema, nonsequential and nonhierarchical, offered a logical yet flexible format for questioning and could guide teachers in constructing questions. In the ten years since we wrote *Questioning: A Path to Critical Thinking,* we have heard from teachers all over the country who have used the schema in English language arts, in social studies, and in elementary classrooms.

The schema is made of three areas or circles: the **matter, personal reality,** and **external reality.** The first area, the **matter,** represents the subject of discussion or of the questioning. The second area, **personal reality,** represents the individual's experiences, values, and ideas. The third circle, **external reality** is actually "the world": the experience, history, and concepts of other peoples and cultures.

These areas overlap—as does knowledge—and are not ordered (see the shaded areas in the diagram). In addition, there is one place where *all* the circles or areas intersect—the union of the subject, the personal experience of the individual, and the experience of others. This **dense** area (the black area in the diagram) contains the most significant questions, those that others might term "higher ordered," but it is absolutely open as to how and when anyone arrives at the answers that reflect the intersection of the **matter, personal reality,** and **external reality.**

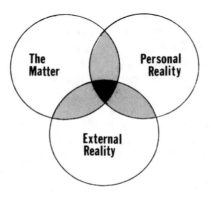

How would a teacher use the questioning circle?

I think that any discussion should contain questions not only from the three separate circles (the matter, personal reality, external reality) but also from the areas any two circles intersect (the three shaded areas) and from the area where the three circles intersect (the black area).

Let's look at the questioning circle as applied to a piece of literature. "Cold Snap" by American poet James Hearst is a brief, image-filled piece about love and loss. My students have little problem picking up on the cold and winter imagery, and they use the outline of the poem as a springboard for discussion: who of us, by thirteen or so, has not experienced a difficult personal relationship, romantic or otherwise?

Cold Snap

The winter night in your face
darkened, and sparkling stars of frost
enameled your eyes. My words
caught on a splinter of ice
and bled to death. As their last heartbeat
sang to the music of the band

my ears felt empty and now
I can't dance with anyone else
with my blood frozen by your white hands.
James Hearst
A Single Focus

Preparing to teach the poem using the questioning circle, and considering a relationship of imagery to reality, a teacher could generate the following:

White questions

Matter: What central image reveals how the speaker's words are received?

Personal Reality: How would *you* define a difficult personal relationship?

External Reality: What part does lack of communication play in relationships?

Shaded questions

Matter and Personal Reality: In what ways are the poem's images appropriate for describing a broken relationship?

Personal Reality and External Reality: Are your experiences with difficult personal relationships similar to or different from those of your friends? How?

Matter and External Reality: How are the poem's images describing a specific incident applicable to a variety of personal relationships?

Dense question

Matter, Personal Reality, External Reality: Which image in this poem do you think best expresses the complexity of difficult personal relationships?

Developing questions for other works of literature is not difficult. While you may choose to write questions for each area--white, shaded, and dense—and thus draw ideas together, the dense question, the intersection of all three, is the focal point of the discussion. In fact, asking the dense question early in the discussion allows students to respond from a variety of perspectives: the text, their personal experience as a reader, and the external reality of the world and other literature. Even if it is entirely personal, students have a basis for responding, and the discussion can build on a variety of perspectives.

Using a dense question early in a discussion can also circumvent the usual, lower-order-to-higher-order movement of a hierarchial questioning schema. The central point, the focal or dense question, need not come toward the end of a conversation at all; it can enter it early and return as the conversation extends and moves and shifts.

◆ FOR YOUR JOURNAL

Select a piece of literature with which you are familiar and choose one part of it— a scene or chapter or similarly defined section. Think of what is *important* to you about that section and write a dense question from the questioning circle that might reflect the three components: the matter, personal reality, and external reality. Using that dense question as a touchstone, work back into the shaded and white questions. Review what you have. How broad a discussion do you think such a "set" of questions might generate? If you can get an opportunity to try out your questions with a group of students, write about how the class went.

Beyond Hierarchies: Questions You Don't Want to Ask

Whether you use the questioning circle or another questioning schema, there are a few general principles to keep in mind when you construct questions. You need to be aware of some questions that because of the way they are phrased will not encourage students to answer fully or even clearly.

Questions you *do not* want to ask include:

- **Yes/no questions:** Questions that can be answered by one word are often not interesting to answer. Further, if the answer is that "easily" delivered, maybe the question itself is rather one-dimensional. **Yes/no** questions also require follow-up questions that can, possibly, make your classroom seem like an interrogation, not a discussion. Consider changing a question such as:

   Is this characterization effective?

   to something more subtle, more complex, and, actually, more worth answering:

   To what extent is this characterization effective?

   Use phrases that enrich and expand the question (**why, how, to what extent**) and keep out of the territory of **yes** or **no**.

- **Fill-in-the-blank-questions:** I have heard myself ask these, and I always wince. In the heat of a discussion, trying to get students to see one thing or one idea, you can find yourself saying,

   The way to describe this passage is _____ ?

   and pausing at the end of the question while you wait for students to come up with the answer. I have also been known to generate this lovely version:

   The way to describe this passage is what?

   Regardless, both versions are really asking for a single word, as if students were to literally **fill in the blank** of your question. What you are asking students to do is to come up with *one word* (your word, by the way) to fill in that blank. Not only are questions such as these difficult to understand, they also require that the students find that one exact word or phrase. That is not what we are about with questioning and discussing, and you want to change such a question to a more straightforward interrogative:

   What do you think is a way to describe this passage?

   You have a better chance of getting a multiplicity of answers--and, yes, perhaps not the answer you were looking for. The latter possibility, by the way, can be very exciting in a classroom.

- **Double questions:** It is hard enough to answer one question, much less two in the same sentence. It's confusing, there is too much to consider at one time, and students often don't know—or, confronted with such a question, don't care—how to answer two questions at one time. Don't let yourself ask a question such as:

> *What are the reasons Anna did not wish Julio to speak, and why did Julio*
> *fail to take her advice?*

Separating those two good and useful questions will be helpful to you and your
students and less confusing. You would ask:

> *What are the reasons why Anna did not wish Julio to speak?*

and then you would proceed to ask:

> *Why did Julio fail to take her advice?*

Further, it may well be that the answer your students come up with to Anna's
motivation do not lead into the question about Julio. By not "stacking and
storing" your questions, you will, perhaps, be more open to adjusting to what
you and your students discuss.

- **Vague Questions:** We all ask them, and in your first years of teaching, regardless of your care and planning, you will ask some truly unfocused questions. It
happens, but it is also something to work on. Don't let yourself ask your class:

> *What did Hester Prynne do?*

The context is just not clear, and you need to give students guidance about
what the question is addressing. Give enough pointers to lead your students
into the possibility of answering and discussing. Ask **when, where, at this
juncture**, anything that will open the specifics. Change the question to:

> *At this point in the novel, what did Hester Prynne do?*

With such a specific, students have a better chance of answering your question.

- **Loaded questions:** English language arts teachers are famous for these, and I
would surmise that you, like me, hated them as a student. They are questions
that tell students that their answers, their discussion, is really not necessary
because there is a set path to follow. **Loaded** questions include gems such as:

> *Why is suspense necessary in fiction?*
>
> *Why do you think Arthur Miller is such a famous playwright?*
>
> *Is this book average or a classic?*

While you may really believe all the above—that suspense is necessary in all
fiction, that Miller is indeed famous and justly so, that the book you are discussing deserves to be a classic—those are *your* assumptions, not your students'. By asking questions like this, you rob your classes of the opportunity to
argue, dispute, explore. You have set what they are to discuss, and in a way you
have also set how they are to discuss it. In addition, be aware that either/or
questions, such as *Is this book average or a classic?* are biased toward the last
choice. It would be a rare student who would chose **average** when the question
is phrased in that manner.

Surprise can rarely operate in a classroom conversation that features
questions like those above. Change such questions to:

> *What do you think is the function of suspense in fiction?*

Arthur Miller is a famous playwright; to what extent you think he deserves that fame?

What is your—or others'—definition of a classic? By that definition, how closely does this book fit that category?

FOR YOUR JOURNAL

For fun, let's take a Bad Questions Quiz. Look at the following awful questions and match them with the characteristics they exemplify:

Bad Questions Quiz

Directions: Read the following awful questions and decide what is wrong with them. Place the letter of the characteristic you choose in the blank to the left of the question.

a. yes/no question   c. double question   e. loaded question
b. fill in the blank question   d. vague question

_____ 1. Does the short story we have just read have a climax?

_____ 2. How is foreshadowing used effectively in *Oedipus Rex*?

_____ 3. Why is the study of dialect important?

_____ 4. The purpose of figurative language is _____ .

_____ 5. How does this image work?

_____ 6. Can you tell me his name?

_____ 7. What is happening in this paragraph and why do you think it is occurring *now?*

_____ 8. Is the main character murderous?

_____ 9. What are the central issues and how do they relate to the piece as a whole?

_____ 10. The best word to describe this section is what?

Answer Key

1.a.	6. a.
2.e.	7. c.
3.e.	8. a.
4.b.	9. c.
5.d. or e.	10. b.

Scoring:

If you scored 80 to 100 percent, you are ready to question effectively. Go to the head of the class!

If you scored 50 to 70 percent, you need to get back to work. Study and try again!

If you scored below 50 percent, review this section before you talk with your students!!

Questioning Behaviors

While control is an important issue in the classroom, it is often the death of questioning. When the asking and answering of questions becomes an inquisition, a challenge, a discipline measure, or just a terrifying event where one is asked to speak aloud, it is virtually impossible to move into real, productive conversation. If you have students who, for whatever reasons, cannot or do not wish to participate in a discussion, don't plan for one until they are ready. You would be setting up both yourself and them for failure. Try intermediate steps, such as having students work in pairs or in small groups until you think they would be comfortable in an all-class discussion.

If, however, you do think your students could benefit from discussion, there are some behaviors and some classroom structures of which you need to be aware.

Arrange your class so that students can see each other   If your students sit in rows so that they cannot see other students' faces, it will be difficult to maintain a large-group discussion. Rearrange your room so that the discussion, the conversation, allows the speakers to see one another's faces, not just the teacher's face. If the desks are moveable, you can place them in a square, rectangle, or circle or even in facing rows.

Learn about wait time and practice it   Wait time refers to the length of time between the asking of a question and an answer or the time between the asking of a first and then a second question. What most of you as beginning teachers fear—what you probably have in the back of your mind when you think of the difficulties of questioning—is the silence after you ask a question. Because even experienced teachers can fear that silence, the tendency is to ask, ask, ask. Remember the statistic cited in the beginning of this chapter about the number of questions teachers *thought* they asked compared with what they *actually* asked? Teachers in that study, who assumed they asked as few as 12 questions in a class asked as many as 150. Imagine, if you can, a fifty-minute period and 150 questions: it works out to about three questions a minute, a question every twenty seconds. It is a pattern that might not be unbearable for part of a period but that could certainly be tiring if continued for almost an hour. Questioning researcher J. T. Dillon says it well:

> Certain studies report undesirable effects [to teacher questioning]. For example, high rates of questioning may yield negative affective outcomes, encourage student passivity and dependence and make the class appear as if it were an inquisition rather than a reasonable conversation. (217)

Give students time with their own answers   Rushing students with their answers (Yes? And then what?), either by adding too many encouraging comments or by conveying that the class and the discussion need to move on, can inhibit a conversation. Conveying calmness and establishing an unpressured environment gives students an opportunity to think and answer and encourages successful questioning. While some students come from backgrounds in which rapidity of speech and response is a sure sign of a successful conversation, not all students share that experience, and too much overlapping talk too quickly can silence them.

Give students your attention when they answer   Maintaining a certain level of eye contact with students lets them know that they have the attention of their listener.

(Extensive, unbroken eye contact can be seen by some students as hostile and challenging, so you will need to adjust the degree of eye contact according to the cultural dictates of your school community.) Head nods and smiles encourage response, while head shakes and frowns generally do not. Turning away from students—even to write their response on the board or overhead—can break the flow of words. Turning toward students and keeping the upper body free of crossed arms (which can be seen as a defensive or negative gesture) can encourage a student to keep talking.

Have students talk to each other, not just to you   One way to let students know that their answers are not solely directed to the teacher is to remind students they are telling the entire class, not just you. That reminder, which should be made in a friendly manner, can be reinforced by alternating eye contact from the student speaker to the class as a whole. The speaker will usually begin, especially if he or she can see other students' faces, to talk to the whole group, not just you, the teacher. In addition, you can move to the side or back of the classroom, taking the visual focus off you and putting it on the students. You are still the teacher, but you are not in front of the classroom. If the class is discussing something—such as a list or a chart—that is on the chalkboard or an overhead, it is *doubly* sensible for you to move to the side of the room. Students can then consider the material and talk without your being between them and the material.

Exhibit a pleasant facial expression and attentive body posture   As mentioned above, frowns, crossed arms, virtually no eye contact, and a turned back will usually make even the most determined student abbreviate his or her answer or perhaps not answert at all. Be pleasant and encouraging with your face and posture.

Be aware of the consequences of praise   Praise that is too strong can, oddly enough, be inhibiting. Most students, when told their observations are brilliant, will rarely attempt a second one; they stop while they are ahead. In addition, as odd as it may seem, continued praise from you the teacher can makes a conversation a game to get teacher points. You can respond positively to comments without resorting to effusive praise.

Use student answers to extend or focus the discussion   As a section in this chapter will reinforce, using student answers in a conversation is the most powerful demonstration of the value you place on student answers. Asking a student how he or she responds to or relates to a peer's observation tells the students that their comments are valued, are important, and can focus a discussion. When students disagree, encouraging them to explore their alternative views and inviting other students to comment on each others' observations can be helpful and interesting.

Let students repeat their own answers   Related to the above is the issue of repeating comments that get lost in the occasional noise of a discussion. When a teacher repeats those comments, he or she takes them over. If a student wants a comment repeated, let the maker of the comment do the repetition. The more student voices—and the fewer teacher comments—are heard in a classroom discussion, the more student thinking and engagement is present.

Watch student body language and behavior   Some of the keys to getting students to respond to one another is tuning in to their reaction during a discussion. Body language is an important key, and head nods, shakes, smiles, frowns, and shifts of position can all indicate agreement or disagreement. Using that body language to invite students to respond can be nonthreatening and also very accurate: asking Marjorie if that frown meant she had something to say, observing to Ricardo that he just nodded, did he want to comment, can work wonders in a discussion.

Make it a goal to call on *every* student in the class   It is only too easy to let the verbally aggressive students respond to most or all of the questions asked in a classroom. Either use your class roll or keep it in your head, but, in a large-group discussion, make it a general goal to have asked *every* student to respond in some way. You may be surprised by what you "get" back; even if students decline to respond or talk, they know that you are interested in their participation and are not willing to let them coast through or hide in a discussion.

FOR YOUR JOURNAL

> Sit in the back of a class where a large-group discussion is going on and watch for behaviors such as those cited above. How many students (keep track and count them) in the class participate? How many comments (count them) are in response to teacher questions? in response to other students' comments? How long (use the class clock or count slowly in your head to measure the seconds) are student answers? How consistent (note this after each question asked) is the teacher's wait time? In general, how would you characterize the teacher's body language and facial expression? Finally, looking at your data and assessing the discussion more generally, write about whether this is a class you would have liked to participate in; why or why not?

When Questions Don't Work

Do remember that questioning is not always the best tool to use in a classroom. Some groups of students may need practice and help before they can function in a relatively orderly manner asking and answering questions. In addition, questions are not appropriate when students:

- **Do not have sufficient background or information to respond or to respond well.**
- **Are not comfortable talking out loud in a large group or even arguing a point in a group.**
- **Are not at ease in your class or with each other.**

Questioning can actually be threatening to students, and you need to remember your classroom context as an important determiner of the appropriateness of asking questions.

If, however, you judge that questioning *is* appropriate with a specific class and that your questioning behavior is also appropriate, there are some strategies you might use.

When students can't/don't/won't answer questions

When students *cannot* answer a question, it may be because what you asked is just not clear or because what you asked is too advanced. First, do think about making your questions as answerable as you can for your students. Second, be sensitive to students' preparation for the level of your question. In general, unless there is a negative chemistry working in a classroom or individual problems with a class, students' inability to answer a question usually lies in the question or the level of the question.

When students *do not* answer questions, it is possible they did not hear the question. It is also possible they did not understand it. Using your wait time, you may want to rephrase a question as well as make sure you are audible. If you are not allowing appropriate wait time, students may not be answering questions because they are not given time to do so. Pay particular attention to the rhythm of your questioning if students are not answering.

When students *will not* answer questions, it may be that their silence is directed toward the subject or, again, toward the act of answering questions. When questioning is not an opportunity to explore but an occasion of tension and anxiety for your students, you should change your approach and avoid direct questioning. When students are more comfortable talking in the class, they will answer questions.

When students give short answers or wrong answers to questions

Short answers are relatively easy to deal with. First of all, make sure you are not asking questions that call for one-word answers; if you are asking for a single piece of information, you are likely to get just that information. On the other hand, questions that ask for extensive information usually get extensive answers. If you are asking questions that should elicit more than one word but students are still giving short answers, address follow-up questions (to the same student) such as:

- **Why do you think that?**
- **How is that true?**
- **Give us an example that illustrates that.**
- **How would you compare your answer with John's (or Felicia's or any other student's)?**

And, again, make sure that your questioning behavior encourages extensive answers. You may unconsciously be hurrying students along or even cutting them off by your own behavior.

Wrong answers are, frankly, tough to deal with. When students try to discuss and attempt an answer, we as teachers are often very distressed to tell students that their answer is incorrect. An obvious solution is not to ask questions that have right or wrong answers. That solution, however, is not foolproof, since even opinion and judgment involve fact and detail. We can, however, make a more concerted effort to ask students to explore options and weigh opinions rather than to determine right and wrong.

When students are incorrect in their answers, honesty is the best policy. If you give the outward impression that every student answer is right in varying degrees, you are not being fair. "No, I don't think so" or "I'm not sure" are gentle ways of telling students they are in error. Also, when a student response is misguided or mistaken, there is often alternative evidence available. If, for example, a student feels that a minor character is actually the hero of the play, it is better to point out a specific passage challenging the contention and ask the student how the passage relates to his or her point than to tell the student, "No, you're wrong."

And finally, moving without comment from a student's wrong answer to another student who you think will supply a correct answer can create problems. Such an abrupt shift may make the first student feel ignored and may in essence place the student providing the "correct" answer in an awkward position. You may want to ask someone else the same question a student has answered incorrectly, but you owe the first student a response and an acknowledgment.

Questions That Students Ask

If the teacher is the only one to ask questions, the process of questioning can be seen as a measure of teacher dominance, inhibiting any student-centered learning environment and encouraging student passivity. The teacher as the only questioner then becomes the arbiter of all answers and classroom concerns, a role that is not only tiring but that does not foster student learning.

Many teachers would like students to generate questions, but teachers need to help the process along. Consider the following techniques:

- **Asking students to write questions for discussion and then using those questions can help students take charge of their learning.**
- **Asking students to write questions for study, for quizzes, or for tests and then using those questions can also help students take charge of their learning.**
- **Turning student comments into questions for other students can be a powerful indicator that you, the teacher, consider student questions important. It also makes the student question the focus.**
- **Encouraging students to question by making an absurd or contradictory statement can also stimulate student questions.**
- **Using questioning games such as *Solve the Situation*, *What's the Question*, *Picture Perfect*, *Twenty Questions*, or *Breaking the Code* can help stimulate student questions (see Christenbury and Kelly, 28–33).**

When students start asking questions in your classroom, it is powerful and useful; breaking their silence and encouraging them to ask questions is one of the more valuable things we can do in the classroom.

Virginia Woolf's novel *To the Lighthouse* contains an image I think of when talking with a class. It is the dining room scene (125ff.) in which the intelligent and sensitive Mrs. Ramsey, unobtrusively presiding over the table, watches and orchestrates and brings out all the disparate members gathered in her house, some of whom are her children and relatives, some of whom are her guests. There is some tension and conflict in the room; the group is not a homogeneous or even harmonious one. Mrs. Ramsey knows, as the dinner begins, that some individuals feel ignored or patronized or unimportant. But with a glance here, a question there, an encouraging smile when appropriate, Mrs. Ramsey watches over the group, gradually getting them to talk with one another and respond to one another, allowing each his or her turn. Using voice and eyes and words, somewhat as we do as teachers, she creates the ground for conversation, "the whole of the effort of merging and flowing and creating rested on her" (126). And as we do as teachers, Mrs. Ramsey asks the questions, gets others to answer, notices, encourages, bides her time. We are, both male and female, Mrs. Ramsey; we watch over the dining room table of our classrooms. And the talk that we encourage there can be the stuff of life.

FOR YOUR JOURNAL

Think about your school history and the asking and answering of questions. Can you describe any questions you wanted to ask in class but didn't? couldn't? Why did you hesitate? Can you describe times when you asked a question that surprised even you? In your classroom as an English language arts teacher, what will your policy be on the asking and answering of questions? How orderly do you want the process to be? how unorderly? Why? What are the kinds of behaviors or remarks that would tend to make you want to terminate a large group discussion? Why? What behaviors or remarks would tend to make you think the large group discussion is successful? Why?

REFERENCES

Christenbury, Leila and Patricia P. Kelly. *Questioning: A Path to Critical Thinking*. Urbana, IL: NCTE, 1983.

Dillon, J. T. "Alternatives to Questioning." *High School Journal* 62 (February 1979): 217–22.

Hearst, James. "Cold Snap." *A Single Focus,* 56. Prairie du Chien, WI: The Prairie Press, 1967.

Nash, Robert J. and David A. Shiman. "The English Teacher as Questioner." *English Journal* 63 (December 1974): 38–44.

Woolf, Virginia. *To the Lighthouse*. New York: Harcourt, Brace & World, 1927.

RESOURCES

Dillon and Wilen are major researchers in the questioning field, and some of their works are listed below; books on critical thinking also often feature sections on questioning.

Dillon, J. T., ed. *Questioning Exchange: A Multidisciplinary Review*. Journal. London: Taylor & Francis, 1987 (and years following).

———— . *Questioning and Teaching: A Manual of Practice*. New York: Teachers College Press, 1988.

Hynds, Susan and Donald L. Rubin, eds. *Perspectives on Talk and Learning*. Urbana, IL: NCTE, 1990.

Schaffer, Jane C. "Improving Discussion Questions: Is Anyone Out There Listening?" *English Journal* 78 (April 1989): 40–42.

Strother, Deborah Burnett. "Developing Thinking Skills Through Questioning." *Phi Delta Kappan* 71 (December 1989): 324–27.

Tiedt, Iris McClellan, Jo Ellen Carlson, Bert D. Howard, Kathleen S. Oda Watanabe. *Teaching Thinking in K–12 Classrooms*. Lexington, MA: Allyn & Bacon, 1989.

Wieland, Sharon. "Leading Classroom Discussions." *CSSEDS Quarterly* 12 (December 1990): 1–4.

Wilen, William W. *Questions, Questioning Techniques, and Effective Teaching*. Washington, DC: National Education Association, 1987.

CHAPTER 9

TEACHING TODAY

Plus ça change, plus c'est la même chose.
(The more things change, the more things stay the same.)

—**French Proverb**

Things Have Changed/Things Have Stayed the Same

It is a truism of the age that times have "changed," that little of what we experience as adults today would be familiar to previous generations because society has been utterly transformed by modern life. Changes are undeniable, advances in science and technology are startling, and what most of us take for granted in communication, medical care, transportation, and standard of life was hardly imaginable fifty years ago.

In education, however, change is not quite so clear-cut: we can turn to the French proverb with which this chapter begins and agree that things have changed but things have also stayed the same. In our schools, while the specifics vary, the broad outline of teaching today is not vastly different from what it was decades ago. For some, this fact is comforting, giving school a familiarity and dependability that is occasionally lacking in other parts of our society. For others, however, the fact that school has not changed so very much is an indictment, a demonstration of the institution's inability to respond effectively to societal change.

The future and predictions of change in the future are not, as one wag noted, what they used to be. It seems that many of the predictions for sweeping revolution in school have just not come to pass. As an institution, school appears to be remarkably resilient to being reformed and transformed, however frequent the calls for restructure and however long the reports that outline that restructure.

To illustrate, a recent study published in the *Phi Delta Kappan* by Donna E. Muncey and Patrick J. McQuillan looks at a broad-based program for school change and concludes that after five years very little had actually changed in the eight targeted schools. The plan for change was clearly outlined; the teachers involved were committed and supported in a network of similar schools. Yet, little really happened over the five years to "reform" the schools. Some of the reasons include the fundamental fact that many faculty members could not agree on what a school's philosophy should be or what were the "best ways to educate students" (487). Another involved the scope of the change; individual teachers seemed to work well with reform efforts, but those efforts did not often move out into the wider school community (488). More telling, however, is the report's observation that "in most of the schools there was not a consensus that fundamental changes in school structure or teaching practices needed to occur" (487), a belief, however misguided, that what we are doing in our school is just fine, thank you.

What does this mean to you? It means that while in your career you may see aspects of school change, you need to know that that change will probably not be overnight or even all that obvious to the outside observer. And if you are coming into teaching with the sure belief that schools as we know them will be transformed in the next few years and really reflect these calls for reform, you will need to adjust your expectations.

School has changed. School has stayed the same.

In high schools and middle schools all over the country, as in years before, classes meet, bells ring, lockers slam, buses arrive and leave. Sounds of band practice float through the halls; announcements are made over the loudspeakers for club meetings and sports and dances. There are cheerleaders, football players, brains, geeks, jocks, freaks, heads, and all the other attendant groups. Some students study; some never take home a book.

But there have been changes: the library is the media center, and the typewriters have been replaced by word processors. The school nurse tends to more serious complaints than headaches, and the guidance counselors deal with problems far beyond deciding which college to attend. Guns are occasionally found in backpacks and lockers, deadly violence periodically erupts in the parking lot, and students by the score use drugs and alcohol. In the American middle and high schools languages other than English can be heard in the majority of cafeterias, and the student body is a mix of races and ethnic backgrounds.

There are still proms and field trips and romances and tests and pep rallies and bake sales; there also are security guards in the halls, classes for new mothers, police sweeps of student lockers, and information on AIDS and date rape.

It's school; it's stayed the same in outline, but it has also changed as our society has changed. And it may be frustrating or it may be heartening, but there are virtually no arguments or issues or controversies in education that have not surfaced in some form in previous years and been discussed and debated in previous years. While the issues are of course never identical, perennial concerns abound in education. Let's look at five such issues that today and in the future will shape—and challenge—your professional life.

Five Contemporary Challenges

Testing and accountability

Since the widespread administration of the Standardized Aptitude Test (the SAT), American high schools have been rated largely in terms of how students perform on that measure. While the SAT is supposed to predict success in college, most people outside—and many inside—schools use SAT scores to judge the effectiveness of the high school and the achievement of students. Although the controversy continues unabated as to what the SAT and other similar tests measure and how they measure it, not to mention the value of measuring at all, standardized testing appears to be here to stay. It is, further, often directly linked to teaching and learning, and many feel that standardized test scores offer the only true "accountability" of the public schools to the public.

Testing, of course, is a complicated subject, as is the occasional controversy that can arise about grading scales of school divisions as well as individual teachers. C. Fred Bateman's "Goldy's Coffee," a brief article in the *Phi Delta Kappan*, is one of the most succinct and most cogent discussions of the varying ways students can be evaluated in testing, and you might want to look at it.

Testing, however, seems perennial and immutable regardless of the approaches taken to it. And while many think that standardized tests are narrow and unrepresentative, and they despise the emphasis on them, it appears that the influence of standardized tests will do little but expand in the near future. Unless schools agree to adopt a more comprehensive—and more time-consuming and expensive—method of testing, paper-and-pencil standardized tests will continue to dominate testing modes. What Theodore R. Sizer recommended some years ago in *Horace's Compromise* is a year-end "exhibition of mastery" (215) by each student. Such a demonstration is individual, specific, and fair, and it is based on more than the ability to determine the one correct answer to a multiple-choice question. Such exhibitions are also unlikely to be widely adopted in public schools, since they require a heavy investment in teacher and student time and would have to be evaluated by methods other than electronic scan sheets. Sizer notes:

> The requirement for *exhibitions of mastery* forces both students and teachers to focus on the substance of schooling. It gives the state, the parents, prospective employers, and the adolescents themselves a real reading of what a student can do. It is the only sensible basis for accountability.
>
> [But] effective exhibitions will be complicated to construct and time-consuming to administer. To be fair, they need to be flexible: not all students show themselves off well in the same way. They cannot, then, merely be standardized, machine-graded, paper-and-pencil tests. (215)

The issue for you the English language arts teacher is that much of what you do in class will not really relate to the standardized test, which traditionally relies upon multiple choice questions with single answers. In addition, the standardized test is largely based on knowledge retention, not judgment or speculation or argument. It is a mismatch and lack of fit between teaching and testing that may not be resolved in the space of your career.

For the present and near future, issues of testing and accountability will continue, at least for the thinking teacher, to be a source of tension and contradiction. The balance between authentic teaching of English language arts and the test will continue to be uneasy.

Technology in the classroom

It started with making the traditional black chalkboards more modern green ones; the change in color was felt to be more soothing to the eyes. Then overhead projectors appeared in classrooms, and libraries started stocking film projectors and portable tape recorders. More affluent districts or those that received special grants were equipped with televisions in each classroom, and some courses and lectures were provided on those televisions via electronic networks. Now the issues of technology have escalated; it may be wildly uneven across school districts and states but, depending particularly upon financing, technology is advancing in the schools, especially in the library/media center. The increasing use of electronic catalogs, laser disks, and CDs for information retrieval, the presence of camcorders and VCRs, is a reality in many high school media centers. Extensive electronic educational networks and a variety of databases for computers and satellite dishes for television reception can link even the most remote schools to a much wider world.

For the language arts teacher, the likely presence of word processors in the classroom or in a writing/computer lab is an additional reality. Some word processing programs help students prewrite; spell checkers and grammar checkers can change the way student writing is composed and evaluated. Clearly, the use of word processing makes issues of legibility and neatness obsolete and makes drafting and revision a far different operation from when all writing was done by hand.

What effect this technology will have on your classroom is not completely clear. A report on information literacy from the American Library Association Presidential Committee envisions a school that would be

> more interactive, because students, pursuing questions of personal interest, would be interacting with other students, with teachers, with a vast array of information resources, and the community at large to a far greater degree than they presently do today. . . . Students' quests would involve . . . searching print, electronic, and video data . . . [and using] the classroom computer, with its access to the libraries and databases of the world. (Ambach et al., 8)

This is heady stuff, and using the technology intelligently, integrating it into the classroom, not just adding it as some sort of glitzy educational video game, will be a challenge for you. If, of course, you are unfamiliar with the technology, you will probably have a more difficult time introducing it to your students. The key, in this case, is not only learning the technology yourself and using your students' technological knowledge, but also being judicious about its application.

The caution about being "judicious" may seem silly to you, but it is true that a number of teachers and schools have simply "added on" computers and word processing without considering their integration and use in the curriculum. There is, certainly, the "new toy" aspect of technology, but students can soon weary of sitting in front of computer screens if they are not given instruction, reasons, and help. A computer and its marvelous software does not automatically help a student find ideas for writing or revising. Access to numerous databases does not frame a research question. A library of videos will not automatically solve a problem. Do look at the resources section for some useful books on computers and their use—and misuse—in the classroom. Using rather than being used by technology, is a real issue in the classroom of today.

For the present and the near future, technology will have an increasing impact on the school and the English classroom; your task will be learning how to use it effectively, not just adding it on as an instructional gimmick.

Teaching critical thinking

Getting students to think has always been a goal of education, at least in theory. Cynics would argue that schools have never been interested in teaching students to think, because if schools really did, their students would revolt and both education and society would be truly transformed. Regardless, the current critical-thinking movement is somewhat different from the past in that it is driven by the concern that what students face today requires not so much knowledge and retention of facts but the ability to define and then solve a problem. Because of the wide availability of facts and information, especially through electronic sources, selection and definition are more important than ever.

On the other hand, as I've already indicated, most standardized tests as they are currently designed have little in them that involves true critical thinking. And in the school curriculum, this connection between testing and instruction is crucial: the bald fact is that if tests do not require critical thinking, critical thinking will not be widely taught in the classroom.

There are a number of books on the market, a few of which are listed in the resources at the end of this chapter, that can give an English language arts teacher help in this area. Certainly when we ask students to make a decision about a piece of literature or a crucial turn of phrase or their own writing, we are asking them to exercise critical-thinking skills. On the other hand, we need to be aware that what some educators call "critical thinking"—and what some books label "critical thinking"—is little more than the old-fashioned memorization or identification of types of arguments and logical tricks and turns, many of which go back to the classical rhetoric of centuries before. Teaching true critical thinking not only takes time but is, frankly, rather messy. Students who are encouraged to look for alternatives and attempt to solve complex problems will not come up with "right" or often even testable answers.

As a teacher confronted with a demand to teach—and possibly test—critical thinking, it will be your responsibility to approach critical thinking in a broad sense. Despite how others may want to simplify the issue, it is not possible to deliver critical thinking as an instructional package in a semester or so.

A national curriculum and national teacher certification

The ideas of instituting a national curriculum and a national teacher certification program in the American public school have been around for a very long time. In the name of national unity, in the name of curricular efficiency, in the name of quality control, both classroom curriculum and teacher certification on a uniform, national scale have been advanced over the years. While it may not be immediately obvious, the presence of both a national curriculum and a national teacher certification would most likely require national testing for teachers and students.

The idea that every student in this country would receive appropriate training regardless of where he or she went to high school—Arizona or Alaska, Mississippi or Montana—can be an appealing one. Likewise, the assurance that every teacher submit to the same standards can be argued as meritorious. Looking at the argument from another perspective, however, the fear is that in the name of a standard, a mindless uniformity would result, robbing schools of their unique, community-based character and teachers of their individuality. Finally, the prospect of additional widely administered standardized tests is appalling to some educators and members of the public.

Regardless of the arguments for and against, national curriculum and national certification are movements you may face in your career. If a national curriculum is indeed instituted and enforced in public schools, you may teach under it and, also, you may have to take a national test—probably something like the current National Teachers Examinations (NTE)—to be certified. While the debate is still a debate, you may want to add your voice to the discussion, particularly through your national and local language arts associations.

You may soon be faced with a national curriculum and national certification and the accompanying tests and implications. It is important that you assess both and take an informed stand.

Multiculturalism

As emphasized throughout this book, the public schools are for the public, and that public comes in different colors and from different ethnic and religious and cultural backgrounds. The presence of *multi*cultures in school is surely not new. But what is new, what you will face more squarely in your career than many of your predecessors in the classroom did, is the proportion of students from many cultures and backgrounds. As of this writing, the Latino population in the United States is rapidly increasing and will, in some school districts, very soon outstrip the Anglo population. Immigrants from the Pacific Rim and Asian countries are also growing in influence and number.

The result is an increased awareness in the schools, if not in the nation, of differing populations that require, appropriately, representation in the curriculum and in school staff and school culture. Like every one of the issues cited in this section, this is not a passing fad but an issue that is here to stay and that you will face in the classroom.

As the English language arts teacher, your responsibility is to be aware of the variety of your students and, if the material from which you teach is not representative of that variety, to amend or supplement it. (You might want to look again at Chapter 5 for multicultural materials and discussion.) As Latino writer Rudolfo Anaya demanded in a speech at an NCTE conference, later reprinted in the *English Journal*:

> Our community stretches from California to Texas, and into the Northwest and the Midwest. But not one iota of our social reality, much less our aesthetic reality, is represented in the literature read in the schools. . . . If you are teaching in a Mexican American community, it is your social responsibility to refuse to use the textbook which doesn't contain stories by Mexican American authors. If you teach Asian American children, refuse the textbook which doesn't portray their history and social reality. . . . But you don't have to be teaching in a Mexican American barrio to insist that the stories and social reality of that group be represented in your textbook. You shortchange your students and you misrepresent the true nature of their country if you don't introduce them to all the communities who have composed the history of this country. To deny your students a view into these different worlds is to deny them tools for the future. (19–20)

Multiculturalism has serious implications for our classroom, our materials, and our interactions with our students.

In the near future the literal complexion of school will change, and you, as a new teacher, need to be aware of, receptive to, and prepared for students from varying walks of life. You will also need to ensure that your classroom materials are balanced and inclusive.

For Your Journal

The five issues cited above may be very different from the ones you assume will be the unresolved tensions/perennial problems you will face in your first years as a teacher. If so, what other issues do you think you will have to confront and solve? How will you deal with them? If, on the other hand, the five issues discussed above approximately cover what you expect to confront in the classroom, choose *one* and discuss what you feel is an approach to that dilemma, if not a total solution to it. What can a classroom teacher do with this issue?

The Popular Culture and Media Literacy: TV, MTV, and the Movies

When you think back on your own years in middle school and high school, you may remember that you were acutely aware of what was in and what was out in a variety of fields: music, dress, movies, television shows. While you may have been less involved in these areas than some of your classmates, you were probably as aware then as you have ever been of what is termed the "popular" culture.

Your students will also be fairly involved in popular culture and are more likely to share common visual experiences than a common novel or short story or poem.

While all of us could lament that our students do not read as much as we would like them to and perhaps spend more time than we are comfortable with sitting in front of a television set or at the movies, the fact is that such visual stimuli are a part of our students' lives, and any negative opinion we might have is not going to change their behavior. Further, visual literacy is an important skill that all our students—and we as well—need to acquire and practice. In most English language arts classes, the visual is used largely as a way to bring pieces of literature to the screen. A recent *English Journal* article suggests novels and nonfiction texts as pairs to recent movies, among them *The Last Emperor, Glory, Roxanne, Mississippi Burning, A Passage to India,* and *My Left Foot.* (See "Books, Films, and Culture" in the references section as well as the Burmester and the Fowler and Pesante articles for more recent lists of videos.) William V. Constanzo's *Reading the Movies* also offers activities with famous films.

But to do nothing with film but always pair it with literature is a bit shortsighted; while such movies can enhance—and encourage—reading and are a legitimate area of study, we need to remember that there is an entire world of the visual that is largely unrelated to published, approved literature. We can ignore this media, or we can use it; clearly, I think the latter is our best avenue.

I suggest that we use the popular culture, bringing it into the classroom rather than constantly pushing it out as if it were something beneath us and our students. Don't forget, however, that visual (or nonprint) materials are as open to censorship questions and challenges as books and magazines are. (NCTE's *Guidelines for Dealing with Censorship of Nonprint Materials* offers advice and resources.)

The following activities can be helpful for our students:

- **TV: Pick a television series (sitcom, soap opera, drama) that you particularly like and watch it over a series of three to five weeks. For each viewing, chronicle, in writing, the plot of the show (including what occurs during each segment or section), the characters, the dialogue, the set(s), and the theme or "point."** Then, using your notes, analyze this show:

    Why it is a good or very good television show?

    To whom do you think this show appeals? (Be specific.)

    If you were asked, what changes would you suggest in the cast, characters, plots, sets, or themes? (Be specific.)

- MTV (or VH–1): MTV is fairly new on the video scene, and you may be familiar with the controversy when it was introduced. When it first appeared on television, people who enjoyed certain singers and groups were upset because they felt that any visual interpretation of a favorite song would destroy the song for them. While that feeling has probably faded, still, for many, the MTV version of a song can be wildly different from what one expects.

  Choose a rock or pop vocalist you like a great deal and pick two or three of his or her songs. Reproduce the lyrics of the song, and also write a page on each detailing what the song is about, why you like the arrangement or instrumentation, why you think the song is one of the best of this artist's performances. Then view the MTV or VH–1 version of the song and discuss how the visual version enhances or detracts from the song, what you found surprising or not surprising at all about the video version, and what you would have added or taken away from the video version (camera angles, dance steps, sets, supporting characters, and so on).

- Movies: Go to a movie that is popular with your friends and watch it carefully, looking for character development (and how that may relate to the actors cast in the roles), camera angles, plot development, background music, theme. After you've seen the movie, write a review (you might want to look at a newspaper for an example) detailing two things you think were very successful and two things you would have changed if you had been the director. Justify all four observations. Finally, write a paragraph telling why you think this movie has been/is so popular with your peers: what about it appeals to them? What does or does not appeal to you?

For Your Journal

Pick one of the three activities above and do it yourself. What did you find? At this point, how close do you think your taste is to that of a middle schooler? high schooler? (Don't chuckle—depending upon your age and background, what you like may not be that different!) On the other hand, if you think doing this according to your own taste is unhelpful, ask a student in middle school or high school to recommend a TV series, a pop recording artist, or a movie. Do the activity and then also ask yourself, Why does this show/film/artist appeal to *students*?

Staying in the Classroom

The strain of teaching is well documented in the popular and educational press. "Burnout," the accumulation of stress to a critical breaking point, is frequently cited as a reason experienced teachers leave the classroom temporarily or even permanently. As exciting as teaching can be, as rewarding as students are, teaching is a high-intensity profession. It is marked by consistent, almost unyielding expectations from a large number of people, students, parents, and administrators alike. In addition, life in a classroom always entails a certain amount of isolation from other professionals; teachers can spend most of their day without any sustained contact with other adults. The pressure, the isolation, and the frequent feeling of being overwhelmed by the demands of the classroom can seem insurmountable after even a few years teaching in school.

The personal nature of professional organizations

Some years ago, on the occasion of the seventy-fifth anniversary of my state English-teaching organization, I wrote about how that association helped save my fledgling and troubled teaching career. In "Growing Up in VATE," I named names and told stories; without the organization and its members, other teachers, I doubt I would be here today, still in the classroom. For me, VATE (the Virginia Association of Teachers of English) and NCTE (the National Council of Teachers of English) have been professional homes, providing me conferences and workshops, books and journals, and more important, teacher friends who continue to stimulate, challenge, and inspire me.

Starting as a member of my local affiliate and then moving through different levels of the organization, I have spent almost twenty years in VATE. I have spent as much time in NCTE. Through those two organizations, I have had opportunities to read and talk and learn; I also have met other teachers who have strongly influenced what goes on in my classroom.

I recommend that if you plan to stay in teaching, you join your local *and* national English-teaching organization. This is, in my opinion, not a luxury but a necessity: those organizations will give you access to thoughtful and tested teaching ideas and provide conferences and workshops where you can share with other teachers. Those people are your colleagues and may, in time, even become your friends—there is, in fact, a highly personal aspect to professional organizations. Regardless, they will influence your own teaching and also give you important companionship in this journey.

Your own reading

Under the pressure of writing papers and reports and preparing for class, it may be very tempting to begin—and to continue--to dispense with time for your own reading. Certainly many conscientious teachers take that route, taking time only to glance quickly at the daily newspaper or to skim professional magazines and articles. With their long hours and very time-consuming work, gone are any and all afternoons engrossed in a novel or Sunday evenings with the latest best-seller.

If you wish to stay in the classroom, I strongly recommend that you not neglect your own reading—whatever that reading may be. Whether it be poetry or science fiction, history or romance, gardening or sailing, accounts of Inuit tribes or Italian countesses or hunting in the African veldt, fine literature or popular schlock, I encourage you to keep reading. It's one of the reasons that you got into this business; it feeds you mentally and emotionally. Without time for your own reading interests, your life can become devoid of the special joy that reading gives us.

Unfortunately, there are many English language arts teachers who have stopped reading; most all of them regret it, and most all of them, citing time pressures, can justify it. If you suspend your own reading, however, I think it will show in your teaching, and it may contribute to some professional unhappiness. On the other hand, if you continue to read you will find that your tastes change and grow, deepening unexpectedly in an area or perhaps shifting into new areas. You will be able to share with your students what *you* are reading; you will be doing something for *you*; and your own reading will reinforce, once again, the power and magic of this business of reading and learning.

Becoming a teacher/researcher

You do not have to be taking a graduate course to do research in your own classroom. As a teacher you may have questions about how or why something did not or did "work" in your classroom. You may want to try out a new technique of instruction or evaluation or organization. Doing your own research with your own students can keep you interested in what is before your eyes and can revitalize your teaching. While it may seem intimidating or terribly complicated, setting up research in your classroom is not impossible and actually not that difficult; the books cited at the end of this chapter, especially the Mohr and MacLean, can be a real help to your work and are written by classroom teachers for classroom teachers. Being a student of your own teaching can be illuminating and rewarding.

The End of the Lifetime Teacher?

It may seem odd that at the end of this section about *staying* in the classroom, I raise the issue of the end of the lifetime teacher. I'm not sure all would agree with me, but it is my feeling, given both the pressures of the classroom and the fairly recent phenomenon of multiple careers within a lifetime, that the person who stays in the classroom teaching for twenty or thirty years will be an increasing rarity. Certainly those who do will have survival skills of the highest order, but some will opt for a second—or even a third—career. Some will leave teaching, of course, only to return, as I did after my four years of writing and editing.

On the other hand, I am not sure that going into the classroom and doing a good or even fantastic job for five or ten years is all that harmful both to the individual teacher and to his or her students. Years and years of experience are valuable, no doubt, but I am not sure that either the students or the system completely benefit from a teaching staff that has unbroken decades in the classroom. Perhaps what I am suggesting is that while you may want to adopt some of the strategies listed above to make sure you stay in teaching and stay there happily, you might reconsider just how long any person can—or should--remain in the classroom.

FOR YOUR JOURNAL

For a minute, imagine that you *do* plan to be a lifetime teacher and stay in the classroom until you are ready to retire. Imagine further that you are entering your fifth year of teaching with many more years ahead of you and with a mild case of burnout. What, for you, do you think are *two* problems you are confronting, two sources of burnout? How do you think you will handle those two problems and renew yourself? Be practical; be specific.

A Question of Ethics: Issues for the Classroom Teacher

The consideration of questions of right and wrong is not confined to churches and mosques and synagogues; it exists outside religious frameworks, too, notably in the schools and in teaching. "The implications for education have had to do with . . . the resolution of moral dilemmas" (119) writes educational theorist Maxine Greene, and those issues of ethics and morals relate to us as teachers. Historian Joel Spring notes:

> Whose moral and social values will permeate the American school? [Nineteenth-century American educator] Horace Mann argued that there were certain moral values that all religious groups could agree upon and that these shared values would become the backbone of the moral teachings of the school. A variety of religious groups have disagreed with this idea from the time of Mann up to the present. (13)

Yet, despite the tensions in the American public school about whose ethics, whose morals, will be directly taught or even discussed, the issue remains. Certainly the act of teaching itself is an ethical act. Educator Gary D. Fenstermacher observes in a book on teaching and ethics:

> What makes teaching a moral endeavor is that it is, quite centrally, human action undertaken in regard to other human beings. Thus, matters of what is fair, right, just, and virtuous are always present. Whenever a teacher asks a student to share something with another student, decides between combatants in a . . . dispute, sets procedures for who will go first, second, third, and so on, or discusses the welfare of a student with another teacher, moral considerations are present. The teacher's conduct, at all times and in all ways, is a moral matter. For that reason alone, teaching is a profoundly moral activity. (133)

We must, as teachers, be fair in our dealings with students and have classrooms where, literally, justice prevails. Further, much of what we do in language and literature and writing also touches upon issues of morality and ethics, and our classrooms should be places not only where individuals demonstrate fair behavior but where issues of right and wrong can be discussed.

English class as ethics arena?

Is English class an ethics arena? It seems impossible in a pluralistic society where, first, not everyone agrees on what is right and what is wrong, and where, second, the schools are secular and public in nature. Disagreement among our students and the nonreligious nature of the public school are not, however, reasons for us to avoid moral and ethical questions. While we need to be aware of prevailing community standards, we would be shortsighted as English teachers to sidestep the important issues that permeate language arts.

Thus, Dimmesdale's behavior in Nathaniel Hawthorne's *The Scarlet Letter,* Celie's actions in Alice Walker's *The Color Purple,* Brutus's choices in Shakespeare's *Julius Caesar,* the attitude of Annie John in Jamaica Kincaid's novel of the same name are all issues of ethics and morals. What were the choices, what were the decisions, what do you think was right, was wrong, and why? For sure, you and your students will not always agree, but it seems a waste of all of our time and of the literature itself not to consider, discuss, and weigh.

I have talked in this book of the power of language both to distort and to illumine; this is a moral and ethical issue. In addition, our students will choose to write of things that are not correct in their lives, in the school, in society, and they will at times want to take stands on ethical issues. To ignore or avoid the world of choices—which is the world of morality and ethics—is to disembowel the English class and to make what we do rather bloodless.

The following subsections may seem preachy to you, and if so, I apologize. I want, however, to call your attention to some topics, rarely discussed in books about teaching, that will affect—and posssibly tempt—you as a teacher. We have great power to do good in the classroom. We can also do harm. Student privacy, fairness to all students, and sexual ethics are three issues we need to consider.

Student privacy/student rights

Beyond what we discuss in class is the way we deal with our students and what they choose to share with us and with the class. As English teachers we are often in a position to hear revelations of sorts from our students, stories, embellished and true, of choices, decisions, triumphs, disasters. In journals, in narratives, in classroom discussions, and in role plays, students often reveal large chunks of their lives. Some of those stories involve fairly intimate details and the public revelation of such would be a personal invasion of privacy. Some of those stories further involve legal issues that have bearing outside the classroom.

Because laws differ from state to state as do school practices, you need to inform yourself about your obligations regarding certain student revelations. Issues involving threats of suicide, drug use or sale, physical or sexual abuse, may come to your attention in your students' writing or conversation. When and how to inform the guidance staff, a building administrator, the school nurse or school social worker of behavior that may be life threatening or illegal is something you need to investigate. Ignorance of the law is not an excuse; ask what your school policies are and act accordingly.

As teachers, we also need to remember that students have a right not only to our respect but also to privacy. Beyond the very serious revelations cited above, students may reveal other details of their lives and those of their family and friends. Tempting as it may be, we should not carry their revelations outside the school sessions for our friends or relatives' edification or amusement. What we may consider atypical or informative or even entertaining stuff is our students' lives, and we need to honor the fact that often— and often with implicit confidence in our discretion—they share those lives with us.

Being fair to all students

None of us find all of our students equally likeable, and we are kidding ourselves if we think we will be completely compatible with every one who comes to class. We have an obligation, however, not only to teach but to evaluate fairly everyone with whom we come into contact. We should not use assignments or grades—it is *wrong* to use assignments or grades—to punish or keep in line whomever we do not like or with whom we have a personality clash. That sort of punitive power is one of students' deepest fears— being failed or downgraded because of the teacher's personal tastes—and we should do nothing to further that fear. While we often cannot change our feelings about students, we are *not allowed* to act on them. It may not be comfortable for us as teachers, but it is part of our obligation to our students to treat all fairly and to rise above petty behavior.

For this reason, you once again need to be aware that you come from a culture and a background that espouses certain values. Further, you have a definite personality which expresses itself in certain traits. To ignore that background and your own personality, to assume that either you have no particular values or tastes or that those values and tastes are generally universal, is misleading. You will occasionally teach students with whom you have little in common, and ignorance of that fact is naive.

You cannot, of course, adopt all of the values and background and personality traits of all of your students, nor should you jettison your own values. You do need, though, to acknowledge that you will occasionally react both negatively and positively to students on the basis of their class and race and sex and individual characteristics. You will also have students with whom you share unresolvable tensions and some of those tensions may be related to personality issues. Fair or unfair, your job as a teacher is to be just, to be professional, and to look at the student as student untinged by personal antipathy.

You are human, and you are certainly allowed to have negative feelings. You are, on the other hand, not only human but a human teacher, and the problem, the ethical dilemma, emerges when your feelings actively influence your evaluation and your interactions with students. Do not indulge yourself in making favorites or making enemies. You are in the classroom to teach all and to teach all fairly. It may be hard, and it may take some conscious consideration on your part, but you must, as an ethical responsibility, deal evenhandedly with all those who share the classroom.

Sexual ethics and your students

When you walk down the halls of your middle school or high school as a beginning teacher and you see relatively immature, even awkward young people, some clearly with one foot still in childhood, you may wonder if I have lost my mind to even suggest that you, a teacher, could ever think of having a personal relationship with one of your students. Even when you consider the more socially sophisticated, physically mature students you deal with, it may, early in your career, seem a sheer impossibility that you would ever think of any of them in a romantic or sexual fashion.

You may never fall in love with one of your students, but experience teaches that many of the ingredients for strong mutual attraction exist in the school. Working closely with students over a period of time, getting to know and like and trust them—and they you—your feelings about their availability and their attractiveness may undergo a marked shift.

In a culture that deifies—and sexualizes—the young, it may become hard to remember that the attractive and often appealing students you teach are not your peers and are not available for socializing and/or romance. When you spend the bulk of your time interacting with young people, you may well find yourself in a position, mutual or not, of being strongly attracted to one of your students. This happens to male and female teachers of almost all ages, to those married and unmarried, and it is a serious ethical issue in our field.

The heart has a mind of its own, and at some point in your career you may convince yourself that a relationship with one of your students is eminently justifiable. You may find yourself in a vulnerable time of your own life; the student in question may be troubled or confused or lonely or just really infatuated with you. There are numerous cases of students and teachers falling in love, having sexual relations, and even marrying. Some of these cases result in scandal and ruined careers and even criminal charges; some of them go on to happier and even permanently happy endings. I doubt there is a school system in this country where teacher/student relationships have not occurred.

The entire issue, nevertheless, is poisoned by the sheer inequality of the players. A student is never in an equal power relationship with a teacher, the latter of whom holds authority, standing, and the weight of the grade. Further, in high school and middle school, students are almost always younger than their teachers, even their young teachers, and regardless of the number of years between the two groups, teachers are generally viewed as parental or older sibling figures.

Using your power as a teacher, consciously or not, to further a sexual or romantic relationship with a student is wrong. It preys on students' vulnerability and trust; it makes school just another place where a young person can be used or exploited. Further—and very practically—most states have laws prohibiting sexual relations with minors, and almost all your students will fall into that legal category. In most states, the legal penalties can be severe; in most states, teaching contracts and even certification can be terminated for such behavior, generally lumped under the rubric "moral turpitude."

On the other hand, this is not a plea for a return to some sort of puritanical past. All of us as human beings are endowed with a sexual identity. It is unrealistic to insist that you not appreciate the attractiveness of your students, that you be immune, as another human being, to their appealing natures. Our students are working on their sexual identities and practicing their personal charm, often in our classrooms and with us and their peers. We would be less than human if we did not respond, if we failed to appreciate in a very real sense their emergence as accomplished young men and women. But beyond that appreciation we must not go. Young people need to find romantic and sexual partners outside the teaching staff, and you as a teacher need to draw a line over which no one crosses. You are in a trusted position as a teacher and violating that trust while the student is in your charge is serious and regrettable. Admiration from a certain distance is the more honorable path.

For Your Journal

Ethics is a broad field, and the topics listed in this section probably touch on only some of the issues. Identify an ethical issue that you think affects the English classroom and that is not discussed here. What is the issue? Why, in your opinion, is it important to teachers and students? What do you feel are possible guidelines for teacher/student behavior with regard to this issue?

Making the Journey

Most teachers know that of all the figurative language we "explain" to our students, metaphor actually comes easiest. Almost all of us use metaphor regularly in everyday language and, possibly, many of us think in terms of metaphors. In literature, in fairy stories, legends, myths, epics, folktales, not to mention poetry, novels, and plays, metaphor is a central element. The metaphors that seem to linger in our minds, the ones that appear and reappear in varying sources, are more likely than not the more central, the more elemental, the more archetypal. And for me, there is a metaphor in life and literature that at least partially represents what I feel this business of teaching is all about.

The metaphor is that of making the journey, a concept so prevalent in literature, in religion, in philosophy, in music, in everyday speech and aphorism that it requires virtually no elaboration. Some describe human existence as a journey from birth to death, and certainly our literature, from across the world and the centuries, is replete with heroes, both male and female, who journey out to discover, rediscover, and confirm. First steps, length, destination, and merit are all part of the lore of the journey metaphor.

The epic heroes Ulysses, Theseus, Psyche, Oedipus, Beowulf, Gawaine, Arjuna, to name just a few, go on long and arduous journeys; the more humble travel not so far but with as great an effect. From classic literature to the more contemporary, the metaphor of the journey is widely used.

From Christian, John Bunyan's central character in *The Pilgrim's Progress,* to Gulliver, in Johnathan Swift's *Gulliver's Travels,* from Milkman in Toni Morrison's *Song of Solomon* to the rabbits in Richard Adams's *Watership Down,* from the questing Miyax in Jean Craighead George's *Julie of the Wolves* to Russel in Gary Paulsen's *Dogsong,* characters in classic, contemporary, and young adult literature make the journey. The American poet Robert Frost wrote of a journey and a road not taken, and, in an even more famous poem, of a journey and the need to go miles and miles before rest. In Virginia Woolf's first novel, Rachel makes a portentous journey in *The Voyage Out;* the journey from Appalachia to Detroit changes Gertie forever in Harriette Arnow's *The Dollmaker.* The "beat" writer Jack Kerouac went *On the Road* literally, as did William Least Heat Moon in *Blue Highways;* they were making their own internal journeys as well.

Who we are when we begin the journey is not, of course, who we are when we end. The journey, of and by itself, shapes and forms us, and often we arrive at a destination a bit differently from the way we had anticipated. And that is the stuff of literature and, of course, of life. The Native Americans who started the Trail of Tears, the African Americans who endured the Middle Passage, the surviving pioneers in the Donner party, the hopeful immigrants who came to Ellis Island, were all different at the end of their journey. Across the Atlantic and Pacific oceans, the borders of Mexico and Canada, immigrants have made the journey into this country, and that journey has shaped them.

As a teacher, you too make a journey, and you too will change. Your reading, your life in the classroom, and inevitably, the lives of those people with whom you will have such extensive and consistent contact, your students, will alter if not transform you.

What I hope for you as you make your journey is what I hope for myself: that we remain open as teachers not only to the wonder of the literature and the language but also to our students' minds and hearts. On my journey, which continues as my teaching life continues, the twists and turns of the path challenge and provoke and inform me and, I hope, help make me a better teacher and a better human being. I hope the same for you.

I have written in this book of the tough times of teaching, and I do not think I have exaggerated. But there is also magic and passion and joy in the classroom; I hope I have written convincingly of that, too. You, also, will see many sides of the teaching life as you make your journey and continue to be and become a teacher of English language arts.

For me—and that is a large part of the authority I claim in this business, my own experience—what is contained in English language arts has shaped my life. The characters in books, the lines from poems, the language I use, the conversations I have, the writing I do, have all formed me as a person. Teaching is, for me, also central: I sometimes think that I am never more myself than when I am in the classroom.

Tomorrow I will teach again. I will bring into the classroom all of me, all of what I know, what I feel, and I will, once again, learn something from the experience and from the students. My journey continues. While I don't make anyone's blood run quicker in every class, every day, I try, and what I teach, the great and glorious English language arts, makes it easier. And the students, for their part, are all the reason to keep trying.

Are all the reason to make the journey.

FOR YOUR JOURNAL

The metaphor of the journey is just one possible description for teaching. I have changed my own personal metaphor for teaching numerous times—and expect to change it again and again. If at this point in your career you were to pick a metaphor for what you think your teaching life will be or currently is, what would it be? Draw the metaphor or describe it (or both); choose a central image that means something to you and that illustrates your current thinking about the profession of teaching.

REFERENCES

Adams, Richard. *Watership Down*. New York: Macmillan, 1972.

Ambach, Gordon M. et al. *American Library Association Presidential Committee on Information Literacy*. Washington, DC: ALA, 1989.

Anaya, Rudolfo. "The Censorship of Neglect." *English Journal* 81 (September 1992): 18–20.

Arnow, Harriette. *The Dollmaker*. New York: Avon, 1954.

Bateman, C. Fred. "Goldy's Coffee." *Phi Delta Kappan* 70 (November 1988): 252–54.

"Books, Films, and Culture: Reading in the Classroom." *English Journal* 80 (January 1991): 82–87.

Bunyan, John. *The Pilgrim's Progress*. 2d ed. Edited by James Blanton Wharey. Oxford, UK: Clarendon Press, 1967.

Burmester, David. "Short Films Revisited." *English Journal* 73 (January 1984): 66–72.

Christenbury, Leila. "Growing Up in VATE." *Virginia English Bulletin* 32 (Fall 1989): 77–80.

Constanzo, William V. *Reading the Movies: Twelve Great Films on Video and How to Teach Them*. Urbana, IL: NCTE, 1992.

Fenstermacher, Gary D. "Some Moral Considerations on Teaching as a Profession." In *The Moral Dimensions of Teaching*, edited by John I. Goodlad, Roger Soder, and Kenneth A. Sirontnik. San Francisco: Jossey-Bass, 1990.

Fowler, Lois Josephs and Linda Hutz Pesante. "Engaging Students with Gaps: The Whale and the Cigar." *English Journal* 78 (December 1989): 28–34.

Frost, Robert. *Collected Poems*. Garden City, NY: Halcyon House, 1942.

George, Jean Craighead. *Julie of the Wolves*. New York: Harper & Row, 1972.

Greene, Maxine. *The Dialectic of Freedom*. New York: Teachers College Press, 1988.

Hawthorne, Nathaniel. *The Scarlet Letter*. Edited by Brian Harding. New York: Oxford University Press, 1990.

Heat Moon, William Least. *Blue Highways: A Journey into America*. New York: Fawcett Crest, 1984.

Kerouac, Jack. *On the Road*. New York: Bucaneer Books, 1957.

Kincaid, Jamaica. *Annie John*. New York: NAL Penguin, 1985.

Mohr, Marian M. and Marion S. MacLean. *Working Together: A Guide for Teacher-Researchers*. Urbana, IL: NCTE, 1987.

Morrison, Toni. *Song of Solomon*. New York: Alfred A. Knopf, 1977.

Muncey, Donna E. and Patrick J. McQuillan. "Preliminary Findings from a Five-year Study of the Coalition of Essential Schools." *Phi Delta Kappan* 74 (February 1993): 486–89.

NCTE. *Guidelines for Dealing with Censorship of Nonprint Materials*. Urbana, IL: NCTE, n.d.

Paulsen, Gary. *Dogsong*. New York: Bradbury, 1985.

Shakespeare, William. *Complete Plays and Poems of William Shakespeare*. Edited by William Allan Neilson and Charles Jarvis Hill. Boston: Houghton Mifflin, 1942.

Sizer, Theodore R. *Horace's Compromise: The Dilemma of the American High School*. Boston: Houghton Mifflin, 1984.

Spring, Joel. *American Education: An Introduction to Social and Political Aspects.* 3d ed. New York: Longman, 1985.

Swift, Johnathan. *Gulliver's Travels.* Edited by Paul Turner. New York: Oxford University Press, 1986.

Walker, Alice. *The Color Purple.* New York: Harcourt Brace Jovanovich, 1982.

Woolf, Virginia. *The Voyage Out.* New York: Harcourt Brace & World, 1920.

RESOURCES

Works on film, television, computers, the popular culture, teacher research, ethical issues, and critical thinking are listed below; the more recent works are, naturally, the more up-to-date and more reflective of today's classrooms. For additional multicultural texts, please see the annotated literature and the books in the resources section of Chapter 5 that have been identified with an asterisk.

Borwell, David and Kristin Thompson. *Film Art.* New York: Alfred A. Knopf, 1986.

Costa, Arthur L., ed. *Developing Minds: A Resource Book for Teaching Thinking.* Alexandria, VA: ASCD, 1985.

Crawford, Leslie W. *Language and Literacy Learning in Multicultural Classrooms.* Lexington, MA: Allyn and Bacon, 1993.

Daiker, Donald A. and Max Morenberg, eds. *The Writing Teacher as Researcher: Essays in the Theory and Practice of Class-Based Research.* Portsmouth, NH: Boynton/Cook, 1990.

Fehlman, Richard. "Quoting Films in the English Class." *English Journal* 76 (September 1987): 84–87.

Fiske, John. *Television Culture.* New York: Routledge, 1989.

Golub, Jeff. *Activities to Promote Critical Thinking.* Urbana, IL: NCTE, 1986.

Holbrook, Hilary Taylor. "Popular Culture and English." *English Journal* 76 (January 1987): 32–34.

Hurlbert, C. Mark and Samuel Totten, eds. *Social Issues in the English Classroom.* Urbana, IL: NCTE, 1992.

Johnson, Ron and Jan Bone. *Understanding the Film.* Lincolnwood, IL: National Textbook Company, 1986.

Jones, Beau Fly, Margaret B. Tinzmann, Lawrence B. Friedman, and Beverly Butler Walker. *Teaching Thinking Skills: English Language Arts.* Washington, DC: NEA, 1987.

Kirby, Dan and Carol Kuykendall. *Mind Matters: Teaching for Thinking.* Portsmouth, NH: Boynton/Cook, 1991.

——— . *Thinking Through Language.* Urbana, IL: NCTE, 1985.

Marzano, Robert J. *Cultivating Thinking in English and the Language Arts.* Urbana, IL: NCTE, 1991.

Meyers, Chet. *Teaching Students to Think Critically.* San Francisco: Jossey-Bass, 1986.

Newcomb, Horace. *Television: The Critical View.* New York: Oxford University Press, 1987.

Price, Hugh B. "Multiculturalism: Myths and Realities." *Phi Delta Kappan* 74 (November 1992): 208–13.

Rodrigues, Dawn and Raymond J. Rodrigues. *Teaching Writing with a Word Processor, Grades 7–13.* Urbana, IL: NCTE, 1986.

Ross, Harris. *Film as Literature, Literature as Film.* Westport, CT: Greenwood Press, 1987.

Saettler, L. Paul. *A History of Instructional Technology.* New York: McGraw-Hill, 1968.

Selfe, Cynthia. *Evolving Perspectives on Computer and Composition Studies: Questions of the 1990s.* Edited by Gail E. Hawisher. Urbana, IL: NCTE, 1991.

Selfe, Cynthia L., Dawn Rodrigues, and William R. Oates, eds. *Computers in English and the Language Arts.* Urbana, IL: NCTE, 1989.

Strike, Kenneth A. and Jonas F. Soltis. *The Ethics of Teaching.* 2d ed. New York: Teachers College Press, 1992.

Strother, Deborah Burnett. "Developing Thinking Skills Through Questioning." *Phi Delta Kappan* 71 (December 1989): 324–27.

Tiedt, Iris McClellan, Jo Ellen Carlson, Bert D. Howard, and Kathleen S. Oda Watanabe. *Teaching Thinking in K-12 Classrooms.* Lexington, MA: Allyn and Bacon, 1989.

Trimmer, Joseph and Tilly Warnock, eds. *Understanding Others: Cultural and Cross-Cultural Studies and the Teaching of Literature.* Urbana, IL: NCTE, 1992.

Wresch, William, ed. *The English Classroom in the Computer Age: Thirty Lesson Plans.* Urbana, IL: NCTE, 1991.

To receive information about NCTE membership, conferences, special interest groups (such as on Appalachian, American, and adolescent literature), and lists of English-teaching affiliates across the United States and in other countries, write NATIONAL COUNCIL OF TEACHERS OF ENGLISH, 1111 W. Kenyon Road, Urbana, IL 61801–1096 or call 1–800–369–NCTE.